DEATH BY FIRE

DEATH BY FIRE

Sati, Dowry Death, and Female Infanticide in Modern India

MALA SEN

Rutgers University Press

NEW BRUNSWICK, NEW JERSEY

First published in the United States 2002
by Rutgers University Press, New Brunswick, New Jersey

First published in Great Britain 2001
by Weidenfeld & Nicolson, Ltd.,
London

Library of Congress Cataloging-in-Publication Data and British Library
Cataloguing-in Publication Data are available upon request.

ISBN 0-8135-3081-4

Printed in the United States of America

Learning Resources
Centre

In memory of Marilyn 'Madhvi' Sardesai, close friend and confidante, who helped Selvi when I could not, despite her own emotional pain and ill health. I will always remember her strength and generosity.

And also to all the women of India, who continue to struggle for social change and justice despite the odds ranged against them.

Acknowledgements

In the course of writing this book, I encountered many women whose courage and determination in the face of harsh realities were truly inspirational. Some I have mentioned in the course of this narrative, and they speak for themselves. Their love and generosity kept me going and is something I shall always remember.

Many other friends and members of my family have helped me through this journey and I would like to mention some of them by name. They gave me endless support and encouragement – even at moments when my own despair with the subject matter drove me to excessive forms of behaviour that, understandably, got on their nerves from time to time.

In Bombay, I think of my mother who has been extremely supportive, despite her anxiety about my overall way of living; my sister Kum, without whose support I could not have functioned; Adil and Veronik Jussawalla, Darryl and Zarine D'Monte, Cyrus and Jill Mistry, who gave of their time and energy, sending me relevant information in the form of contemporary press clippings throughout this time.

In Delhi, my aunt Ashoka 'Mintoo' Gupta, who has tolerated much *tamasha* over my comings and goings at short notice disrupting, I know, her tranquil way of life. Other friends in Delhi are part of this book so need not be named here.

In London, my editor, Maggie McKernan, who has shown endless patience and understanding over broken deadlines, giving me sound advice at almost every step of the way; Christine

Slenczka, who copy-edited the manuscript with painstaking care, giving much attention to detail; Sonia Bailey and Liz Obi, who also gave of their time and energy, spending hours on the phone discussing ideas despite the ups and downs in their own lives; Hubert Nazareth, who helped me through endless technical and financial crises, remaining calm at all times; Farrukh Dhondy and Terence Fitzpatrick, who helped in the same way; Ash Kotak, who supported the idea and encouraged me to write at times when I doubted my own ability to tell a tale of any relevance.

In that sense, this book is the result of a collective effort and shared ideas, although I do not hold anyone responsible for my mistakes, errors of judgement or conclusions. The people I mention supported the idea, contributed their energy and gave me spiritual strength.

I am deeply indebted to the Indian press; to the work of several journalists I have quoted in the course of telling these stories and to the following publications in which their stories appeared: *Rashtradoot* (Jaipur), the *Indian Express*, the Press Trust of India, *Manushi* (magazine), the *Indian Post*, the *Times of India*, the *Illustrated Weekly of India*, the *Telegraph* (Calcutta), *Outlook* (magazine), *India Today* (magazine), the *Pioneer* (Delhi) and *Mid-Day* (Bombay).

And in London, the *Sunday Telegraph*.

Many writers, journalists and travellers before me have documented the issues covered in this book. Not being an academic myself, their work has been invaluable to my own understanding of these matters. In particular, I am indebted to the authors of the various books from which I have quoted, fairly extensively at times: Sakuntala Narasimhan, *Sati: A Study of Widow Burning in India*, HarperCollins Publishers, India; Dr Arvind Sharma, *Sati: Historical and Phenomenological Essays*, Motilal Banarsidass Publishers, Delhi; Dom Moraes, *Rajasthan: Splendour in the Wilderness*, Himalayan Books, New Delhi; Sekhar Bandyopadhyay, *From the Seams of History*, Oxford University Press, India; François Bernier, *Travels in the Mogul Empire*, D. K. Publishers Distributors (P) Ltd, Delhi; Meena Menon, Geeta

Seshu and Sujata Anadan, *Trial by Fire*, a booklet published by the Bombay Union of Journalists.

Over the years, this collective body of work has added depth and detail to a wider canvas that spans centuries. What I have tried to do is merely an addition to this tradition of recording events as they happen and affect the lives of individuals in contemporary society. In doing so, I have been able to reflect on the possibilities we face, as women, in my own lifetime and for that I am grateful, despite the knowledge that the road ahead is likely to be rough. Still, it is good for us to know that we are all part of a process to which many have contributed and that we are not alone, historically speaking, in that sense.

Mala Sen
London, November 2000

Preface

In 1987, after a young Rajput woman was burned alive on her husband's funeral pyre and then proclaimed by thousands to be the new *Sati Mata* – a 'Pure Mother' who is considered by many to possess spiritual powers beyond this mortal world – attention was focused, once again, on the widespread violence against women in modern India. The widow was eighteen years old and had been married, by arrangement, to a man she barely knew. After her death, she was projected as the epitome of Indian Womanhood, of pure feminity: the faithful and devoted wife, the potential mother of sons, self-sacrificing to the end.

This role model has dominated the psyche of Indian women for centuries and many women aspire to these levels of 'perfection', convinced that their preordained duty in life is to live and die for their husbands, putting their interests before their own at all times.

Another section of public opinion was outraged, and condemned the act, accusing the in-laws of premeditated murder. The stage was set for a political debate that would span the next decade and more, churning up issues that affect the very existence of women in modern-day India, focusing attention on the ruthlessness of a feudal order that persists in 'the world's largest democracy' as we, supported by the rest of the world's media, are prone to describe ourselves.

In telling the stories of three women – Roop Kanwar, Selvi and Karrupayee – I have tried to draw attention to the violence of their life-experiences which, I believe, reflect the experiences of countless women who remain trapped within the values of tradition. In contrast, I have also met many women who persist in their fight for a change in an oppressive social order by challenging its very foundations. Such women, who cut across the spectrum of caste and class, are beginning to reshape their own destinies and, in doing so, will bring about revolutionary changes in Indian society which are long overdue. In India, these women still remain in the minority but their influence is growing as it spreads across the barriers of silence, giving women a new sense of their own potential and collective strength. I have written about some of these women in the course of my narrative, and they speak for themselves through this journey.

In the spring of 2000, as I was trying to complete this book, I received a series of press clippings – from my sister and other close friends in India – which painted a horrifying portrait of a country reeling from the effects of social, political and economic turmoil. A wave of religious murders was attributed to Hindu fanatics, covered by the umbrella of government protection. Cyclones and floods had devastated the land, leaving millions destitute. Women continued to be burned to death for reasons related to dowry demands from their in-laws. It was depressing and disturbing reading.

Among the clippings was one reporting on the drought in Rajasthan. A headline caught my eye: 'Wedding Wells: Water is what makes marriages here' (the *Times of India*: 29 April 2000). The article stated:

> In the marriage bazaar of drought-hit western Rajasthan, a prospective groom's worth is no longer weighed by his wealth but the distance of his dwelling unit from the village well. How far does the groom live from the source of water is what most parents of marriageable girls ask.

It told the story of men like twenty-one-year-old bridegroom Mangraj, who live in *Dhaanis* – far-flung hamlets – several kilometres away from a source of water, where the only supply comes from government tankers that deliver just once in fifteen days.

The writer of the article, Brajesh Upadhyay, had interviewed the bridegroom's uncle Prabhu Singh, a schoolteacher, who told him that the girl came from a 'source village' and that:

> Mangraj owns a truck and also a few camel carts to fetch water so problems are less. If there was some other man from a source village [where water is stored and supplied to other villages] Mangraj wouldn't have stood a chance. For her this marriage would have meant double the work she is used to. The girls married in *Dhaanis* have a hard life ahead and parents rarely agree to send them there.

The region referred to is Barmer, in the heart of the Thar desert, where I had travelled in the past and seen women cleaning household utensils – even rubbing *themselves* down – with sand rather than water in order to avoid the long trudge to the nearest well. It struck me as ironic that a drought in Rajasthan had benefited this woman, enabling her parents to avoid an excessive dowry demand from her future in-laws due to the lack of water in their village.

As a friend of mine once stressed, the concept of dowry is not an 'Indian thing'. To take one example, Bombay was given to Charles II by the Portuguese when he married Catherine of Braganza. It was her dowry. The burning of women is not exclusively Indian either. In the past, women were burned alive on woodpiles throughout the Western world, having been labelled 'witches' because they were independent thinkers and refused to abide by the rules laid down by church and state. The preference for sons rather than daughters is also a common global phenomenon.

Although this book tells the story of three Indian women, it is not an exclusively Indian tale. Nor is the rise of nationalism and religious fundamentalism confined to India. As Samuel Johnson said, 'Patriotism is the last refuge of a scoundrel.' With the rise of Hindu fundamentalism in recent years, as the sub-heading of a cover story in *India Today* (24 August 1998) stated, under an article headed 'The Ugly Indian': 'Bribery, lawlessness, sloth, filth, caste conflict and religious hatred. After 51 years of Independence, we the people aren't a pretty sight.'

Later, in April 2000, another friend who lives in London sent me a couple of clippings from the *Sunday Telegraph*. The abuse and violence against women in India was the theme of both articles written by Julian West. The first (23 April 2000) headed: 'Indian village is shunned for a killing too far' told the story of a twenty-three-year-old mother who had been stripped naked and beaten to death. West wrote:

Relatives who witnessed the brutal attack say that her 'crime' was to have carried an empty water pitcher – a bad omen in India's superstitious villages – and to have let one of her children run in front of her assailants' tractor.

Killings such as this are normally written off as the more extreme examples of the abuse and violence suffered by women in India's 600,000 villages every day.

But this time, the largest *mahapanchayat* in living memory in India was summoned. The reason was simple – the residents of neighbouring villages feared that if their district gained a reputation for beating and murdering women, their sons would be unable to attract brides, who by custom must come from outside their own village and sub-caste.

This was not the first time that Nagla Bhuja (near Agra) had witnessed such an event. Twelve years ago, Ms Devi's assailants, Virendra and Vijaypal Singh, brothers from the village's most feared and wealthy family, who are now in custody, had been accused of murdering another local woman.

Although they were never convicted of that crime, the legacy of it is that 12 ageing bachelors in Nagla Bhuja are all desperately seeking wives.

The second article, written by the same journalist, was headed: 'Indian women take up guns to fight abuse' (7 May 2000). It told the story of women in the conservative heartland of India, Uttar Pradesh, who had decided to defend themselves against domestic and caste violence. The lengthy report concluded:

Of India's 300 'serious' shooters, barely a handful are female, and of those only the women of Johri are villagers. The notion of a woman using a gun is so unusual that it is likely to confer celebrity status. After being abused and raped, Phoolan Devi became a 'dacoit', or armed robber. Having gained notoriety as the 'Bandit Queen', she later became a politician.

Dr Sharma [a founder member of the Johri gun club] hopes that the idea of women using guns will catch on. 'When you light something in the dark it doesn't matter if it's only one candle. Even from that one light there can be many candles.'

The photograph accompanying the article showed sixty-one-year-old Prakashi Tomar, who had beaten four men, including a policeman, to win two gold medals in India's state shooting championships.

Reading this report, I wondered if the answer to repression and violence lay in retaliation. I would like to believe that it does not, but, over the centuries, history has shown that 'eye for eye, tooth for tooth' is the way of men. Perhaps women will find alternative ways of empowering themselves and creating value systems of their own. Meanwhile, self-defence is not considered to be an offence. *That*, at least, is universally accepted. Only time will tell how we evolve as a society in modern times. For the moment, we must weather the storm.

Mala Sen
London, November 2000

CHAPTER ONE

A sudden surge in the sale of coconuts alerted the District Revenue Officer to the fact that something was going on somewhere in the region. He reported his observations to the Officer-in-Charge at Thoi *chowki*, the small police outpost responsible for maintaining law and order in this cluster of villages in Rajasthan, the north-western Indian state bordering Pakistan. The police in turn made their own enquiries and pinpointed the village of Deorala as the destination for these coconuts; the site of some religious ritual, coconuts being the traditional offering at temples, shrines and tombs. It was not a day of any significance in the Hindu calendar, so was a matter for some concern. Caste and communal conflicts – riots resulting in much bloodshed and the rise of Hindu fundamentalism – have dominated the Indian political scene since the mid-eighties, and officials have learned to remain alert and watchful. Consequently, at about 1.45 p.m. that afternoon, Head Constable Rathi and two other policemen were dispatched to the village.

Deorala is neither remote nor feudal in the strictest sense. A tar road leads off the main highway to the village, connecting its population of some 10,000 people to neighbouring towns and cities. It is considered modern in that its inhabitants live in brick and cement houses. Running water in individual homes is commonplace, as is electricity. There are two secondary schools – one for girls and the other for boys – adult education facilities and a proper hospital. Some villagers have owned television sets for over twenty years.

Yet, that day on 4 September 1987, a young Rajput woman was burned alive on her husband's funeral pyre before a crowd of several thousand people, predominantly men. Women, I was told, do not attend such ceremonies. The sound of drums and brass bands and the wail of religious chants drowned the entire village as Roop Kanwar walked to her death, dressed in her bridal finery of red and gold. Within hours her body was reduced to ashes behind a cloud of *gulal*, festive pink powder, showered in fistfuls around the pyre. Roop Kanwar was eighteen years old. She had been married for just eight months and her husband, Maal Singh, was twenty-four.

Villagers say it was a divine and voluntary act of self-sacrifice, of sublimation. They have tried to erect a shrine in her name, and they refer to her as *Sati Mata*, Pure Mother. She had no children, so the term is a religious metaphor. They say she received the power of *sat* (or purity) from God and envy her her place – her status – in the universe.

There was a public outcry over Roop Kanwar's death in the urban centres of the country. Ordinary people and politicians took sides. There was uproar in parliament. Rajasthani women's organizations took to the streets of Jaipur in protest, demanding the arrest of Roop Kanwar's murderers. As a consequence, police were mobilized to prevent any further celebration of what many saw as a barbaric and archaic tradition.

Roop Kanwar's eldest brother-in-law, it was reported, had lit the funeral pyre. Some claimed she had been doped with opium, mixed in a glass of warm milk and crushed almonds, earlier that morning when her husband's body was brought back from the hospital in a jeep that threw up clouds of dust in the narrow village lanes that led to their home. The first to gather around the house were village women. Some had come out of curiosity, to catch a glimpse of the young widow, and others to participate in the singing that began spontaneously. They sang *bhajans* that celebrated the everlasting love of God but gave little hope to the earthbound despair of the living. When the whiff of rumour descended, when they heard that the widow had locked herself

2

in her room and was considering sati, the hymns turned to shouting as slogans rent the air. Chants of *Sati Mata ki Jai* (Long Live *Sati Mata*) could be heard throughout the village, the villagers were creating a new goddess. We will never know what impact this atmosphere had on Roop Kanwar, sitting in her locked room, contemplating her future in a society that has no place for widows.

As a bride, new to the village, Roop Kanwar had been well-respected, even envied. She had walked through the local bazaar, her nails painted bright red, dressed in city clothes coveted by all. Everyone also knew that she had decked her bedroom with red velvet from Jaipur. She was a city girl who came and went according to her will. She had not been born into village life and was known to have studied up to the tenth standard. She was literate, fashionable and married to a rich farmer's son who, everyone also knew, had a B.Sc. degree, although he had been unemployed since. His mother had mental problems and was rarely seen in the village, but she had three handsome sons and a daughter who did the housework, so the family were considered privileged. Roop Kanwar had brought additional wealth to the family in the form of her dowry, a large colour TV, an enormous fridge-freezer, a gas cooker, a vast double bed and forty *tola*s of gold as well as fixed deposits worth 30,000 rupees in her name. The gold and money were meant to be her own security, but the rest was a contribution to the family she had married into on 17 January 1987.

During her short-lived married life of just over seven months, Roop Kanwar had spent barely three weeks with her husband – the period immediately after the marriage ceremony and a few days before his death. Rumour had it that her husband was mentally disturbed – like his mother – suicidal, impotent and unemployed despite his college degree, and that this was why Roop Kanwar preferred to live with her parents in the city. Rumour also had it that she had a past love, a young man from Ranchi where she had been born. This man was not a Rajput, but from another caste, and her family thought he was a bad influence on her. They were said to have moved from Ranchi to Jaipur to put an end to the affair. Although Roop Kanwar's parents were not informed of her intention to commit sati, they celebrated her death after the event and supported her in-laws, proud of their own place in Rajasthan's culture and history of valour. Their daughter had put them on the map. They were no longer just business people who ran lorries between Jaipur and Ranchi, they were the parents of a new goddess, of the most celebrated *Sati Mata* of their time. Scores of reporters, often accompanied by photographers, travelled many miles to seek their comments in Transport Nagar, a run-down, filthy, diesel-fume-choked part of Jaipur, where pigs for slaughter swill in mud puddles black with engine oil.

On the day of Roop Kanwar's death, news of the event was quick to spread in the surrounding villages, through the gossip of bus-drivers who plied the route to Deorala and young men who exchanged views in tea shops that lined the outskirts of villages along that route. They all spoke of the impending event, of the women who had gathered around the house, of the widow's intention to commit sati because of her deep love for and loyalty to her husband, who had been born of their soil.

As a result of the gossip, many more flocked to the village laden with coconuts, the customary and most expensive offering on such occasions. This was what alerted the Revenue Officer and consequently the police. It was about 2.30 p.m. by the time Head Constable Rathi and his two colleagues arrived at the village on their bicycles. 'The funeral pyre had been reduced to burning embers by then,' he told me many years later when we met. That is also what he stated in his First Information Report (FIR) recorded some hours after his intervention that day, at Thoi police *chowki*, the closest outpost to the village. He stated that by the time he got there, the crowd had dwindled to about two hundred people, among them seven Rajput youths who marched around the pyre, their *talwar*s held upright, still shou-ting slogans: '*Ek do teen char, Roop Kanwar ki jay jaykar* (One,

4

two, three, four, all hail Roop Kanwar)' and '*Jab tak suraj chand rahega, Roop Kanwar ka naam rahega* (As long as the sun and moon remain, Roop Kanwar's name will remain)'. Every now and then they seemed to remember Maal Singh and chanted, '*Sati ki pati ki jai* (Long live the husband of the Sati)'. Somewhat overwhelmed by the atmosphere of religious fervour himself, Rathi started taking down the names of potential witnesses, people who told him they had witnessed the supernatural powers of Roop Kanwar as she walked to her death. Some said her eyes had glowed red, that her body had generated a great internal heat – so intense that it would have scorched anyone who tried to touch her. He was told, mostly by children, that the widow had seemed unsteady on her feet, as if drunk or drugged. She had stumbled several times as she followed her husband's body, surrounded by armed youths. Adults insisted that she had been in a spiritual trance. Rathi was also informed by several people that Roop Kanwar's eldest brother-in-law, Pushpinder Singh, who was fourteen at the time, had lit the funeral pyre. Under the law, this amounted to either murder or culpable homicide but the Head Constable made no arrests. He merely filed his FIR recording the events, leaving his superior officers to act if they wished to do so. They did nothing.

The responses came from the local Rajasthani press. Several Hindi dailies carried the story on their front pages the following day, 5 September. They romanticized the event. With a combined circulation of about 1.5 lakhs within the state, these newspapers began to shape public opinion. *Rashtradoot*, for instance, carried what amounted to an editorial that covered most of its back page on 6 September, with photographs of sword-wielding Rajput youths circling the pyre and devotees paying homage to the site. It read: 'By sacrificing her life, an eighteen-year-old woman, Roop Kanwar, has re-enacted the spectacle of sati, a tradition written in golden letters in the history of virtuous Rajput women devoted to their husbands. Steeped in the glorious Rajput tradition, this brave girl has moved the common people by following the Indian

cultural tradition of sati even forty years after independence.'
The report went on to state that Roop Kanwar had 'worshipped'
her husband, treated him 'like God' and had died with a smile
on her face, although none of the newspaper's reporters had been
present on the day. It was widely assumed that Roop Kanwar
had died voluntarily, painlessly and without protest, strengthened
by divine force. Such reports and comments not only glorified a
gruesome death, but gave rise to a sense of communal Rajput
pride in the 'purity' of their women, re-emphasizing the legendary
Rajput sense of honour and reinforcing Rajput manhood. The
central government in Delhi, headed by Rajiv Gandhi at the time,
and the national press remained silent.

Such was the impact of the local media that thousands more
from all over the state and elsewhere joined the growing queue
of pilgrims to the *Sati Sthal* (sati site) at Deorala. Encouraged by
this phenomenal response, the embers of the funeral pyre were
kept alight and Rajput youths from the village continued to
parade around it, now in three-hour shifts, night and day. People
came with prayers and offerings. Rumour had it that all ailments
could be cured by the *Maha Sati* (Great Sati) provided one had
absolute faith. Stories of miracles abounded. People left their
spectacles and crutches behind, convinced that they would no
longer need them.

Meanwhile, the living room on the ground floor of Roop
Kanwar's in-laws' home had been converted into a temporary
shrine. An enlarged colour photograph, taken of the couple on
the day of their ill-fated wedding, was surrounded by burning
incense and decked with a garland of fresh flowers each morning.
Her ornate *chunari* (veil) embroidered with real gold thread,
hung like an awning above it. For some strange reason, a silent,
brand-new TV set had been placed prominently in one corner
and all the other furniture moved to another side. Devotees
crowded round the barred window and threw fistfuls of coins
and notes on to the floor. By now, the family was collecting funds
for the construction of a temple in Roop's name which was to be
built on the *Sati Sthal*. Within a very short time, over 30 lakhs

had been collected and a group of trustees was elected by the village *panchayat* (council of elders).

As the number of pilgrims flooding to the village on a daily basis grew, local vendors had a field day. Makeshift stalls sprang up overnight, lining the route visitors took as they entered the village. Everything was on offer. Coconuts, flowers and incense abounded. Food-stalls, fruit-carts and toy-stalls all did a brisk trade. A young man from Jaipur who owned a photographic studio used trick photography to superimpose the faces of the dead couple on to a picture of the burning pyre. He too made a small fortune. In a clumsy picture, mounted on a white and gold cardboard frame, Roop Kanwar sits upright on the pyre, smiling as she did on her wedding day, her husband's head on her lap, as hand-painted flames straight out of Bollywood film posters engulf them. In the sky above, the goddess Durga throws her shaft of light towards the heroic couple. These pictures sold for seven rupees at first but the price shot up to twenty-five rupees as demand grew.

In this climate of growing religious hysteria, a small group of women petitioned the Rajasthan High Court in Jaipur, demanding an end to any further celebration of the widow's death. They became the first voices of protest. They had heard that there was to be another mass ceremony in the village on 16 September, the thirteenth day after Roop Kanwar's immolation. It was referred to as the *Chunari Mahotsav* (The Festival of the Veil), the day that the bride's veil, which hung above the photograph in her in-laws' home, was to be placed on the pyre as a last tribute. Legend had it that this *chunari* would rise and disappear into the sky for all to see. Tens of thousands were expected to attend the spectacle.

By law, the women petitioning the High Court in Jaipur had a strong case. The practice of sati had been banned since 1829 by an East India Company regulation. Lord William Bentinck, Governor-General of India at the time, had endorsed the move and the Abolition of Sati Act had been in force since then. On 15 September 1987, just one day before the planned *Chunari Mahotsav*, the Rajasthan High Court ordered the state government to 'prevent the glorification of sati in the form of any public function'. However, the judge stated that what a family wanted to do within the confines of their own home could not be prevented. By this time, thirteen women's organizations had banded together and marched to the Chief Minister's residence in Jaipur, where he had refused to see them. At the time, their actions went unreported in the press, as did the Minister's reaction. I learned of these developments through friends who were active in such organizations. There was much anger against government apathy.

There was anger too in the pro-sati Rajput lobby which demanded religious freedom and the right to honour age-old traditions. The whole of Rajasthan was polarized into pro- and anti-sati groups, with the former in the vast majority. At public meetings Rajput men spoke out venomously against women who opposed sati. They condemned and attacked them for being modern, corrupt and godless; women who had been westernized and were no longer real Indians; women who smoked cigarettes, drank alcohol and wore sleeveless *choli*s with their saris, women who had abandoned tradition, having been corrupted by city values, women who had been westernized and were no longer authentic Indian women. Hindu pundits and *sankaracharya*s (teachers) also entered the arena, interpreting various Hindu scriptures to suit their own political position. Chaos, violence and disorder threatened to topple the state government. In this atmosphere, on 16 September, the *Chunari Mahotsav*, the Festival of the Veil, took place on a massive scale, in defiance of the court order against it. It was a public demonstration of Rajput power, and the central government in Delhi could no longer ignore the situation. Various ministers made statements and some flew to Jaipur to discuss matters with the state government but the Prime Minister, Rajiv Gandhi, remained conspicuously silent.

By this time, reports had begun to appear in all the major national newspapers, and Deorala witnessed a sudden influx of reporters and photographers from all over the country, keen to interview anyone who was prepared to talk. Writing for the

Indian Express, Vishal Mangalwadi, an author and social worker, described his experience of Deorala in an article headlined 'Making a Carnival of Murder':

> As I walked through the red sandy street of Deorala village on September 16, 1987, I was part of a 3km long, 3 lakh strong stream of humanity which had come to honour Roop Kanwar … The local newspapers said that the state government had banned all public transportation going to the village (because of the High Court ban on the ceremony) … It was indeed impossible to take a bus, since hundreds of buses pouring into Deorala were all overloaded, with 30–50 people sitting on top or hanging by the sides. The only way to reach [*sic*] in time for the ceremony was to take a taxi. But the rates had doubled.
>
> Hundreds of overcrowded taxis were going to the village with 5–7 people sitting on the roof of the canvas-top Mahindra jeeps that serve as taxis in Rajasthan…

He then described his journey to the village, past police road blocks that allowed pilgrims through but seemed keen to keep journalists out. He got through them with the help of his taxi-driver, who managed to convince the police that Mangalwadi was a VIP from Delhi, eager to witness the miracle. The article described the scene at the village vividly:

> … we had to walk through 800-odd newly set up shops that were doing roaring business, having commercialised the cruelty of 'sati' into a carnival … The *Sati Sthal* was a sea of heads and a mountain of coconuts. The cries of '*Sati Mata ki Jai*' were rending the air as the devout were contributing their mite to the growing wealth of the capable organisers of this festival. The ceremony had already been held two hours earlier than announced to pre-empt the possibility of police interference. Though I could not see a single police uniform in the crowd, order was being maintained (and police kept away) by the Rajput youth who, I was told, had brought 1000 swords to meet the challenge of the police, if an attempt was made by the State to

implement the court's instructions. Sword wielding, barefoot and grim looking Rajput youth were guarding the funeral pyre. Tens of thousands of women and young girls were worshipping the photographs of 'Mahasati' Roop Kanwar and invoking her blessings. The Sati's father-in-law, Sumer Singh, a teacher in the local school, was blessing the visitors. Her family was hosting a 'brahma bhoj' (holy feast) for 1001 Brahmins...

Mangalwadi found that most people he spoke to 'insisted that Roop Kanwar's act was a voluntary act of heroic courage. A sacrifice that had made her a goddess and given her the power to answer the prayers of her devotees.' He says that there were a few dissenting voices, and he attempted to interview them. These were village women who were against the practice of sati and cynical about its religious merits. He met with hostility:

> By now quite a crowd had gathered around me. Uma Devi, the widow, sensing the crowd's mood, disappeared. I was being given angry looks by young men and shouted at by 4–5 women at the same time. One praising the 'sati', another praising the scriptures, the third denouncing the government, still another describing the powers and benefits of the 'sati' who had been freed from all curses and had already attained 'moksha' ('perfection' or 'the silence of Gods')...
>
> As I endured this bombardment by Rajput women, something in me began to tell me that 'mahasati' Roop Kanwar had indeed performed a powerful feat. Her act has made a mockery of an impotent State which cannot enforce its own laws...

He was stating a fact, but concluded his article based on the hearsay evidence of his driver:

> Muralidhar, my taxi-driver, was a new man on our return journey from Deorala to Jaipur. The miracle of the *chunari* disappearing into heaven had not happened and he also learnt from the villagers that divine power had not ignited the fire in the funeral pyre. Roop Kanwar had been buried under a heavy load of firewood so that she could not escape. The fire was lit once and

died out. Partially burnt, Roop Kanwar screamed and begged for mercy and help. Out of the 90-odd people who gathered for Maal Singh's funeral, most did not know that they were going to witness a 'sati'. Those who could neither bear to see the pain of Roop Kanwar nor had the courage to help her, quietly moved away in shame as the fire was cruelly relit by those determined to murder her ...

Other national newspapers carried similar reports under various headlines: 'Sati Glorified As Cash Pours In', 'Rajputs Play Politics Over Sati Issue', 'Sati Setback for Indian Womanhood', 'Anti-Sati Law Mere Paper Tiger', 'Outrage Upon Outrage', 'Sati: Who's Guilty?', 'Burn Scriptures Extolling Sati' and so on.

The Government could no longer dither. On 19 September, under pressure from Delhi, police arrested Roop Kanwar's father-in-law, Sumer Singh, her two brothers-in-law, Pushpinder Singh, just under fifteen at the time and accused of lighting the pyre, Bhupinder Singh, under ten, together with members of Roop Kanwar's own family who lived in the village – the husbands of two aunts and their sons. Other arrests followed, and the police were looking for Dr Magan Singh, who had attended to Maal Singh and was alleged to have administered drugs to Roop Kanwar after her husband's death. Dr Singh was a close friend of the family and lived next door to them. When Maal Singh fell ill on 2 September, Dr Singh was called to the house. The next morning, he advised the family to take Maal Singh to the government hospital in Sikar, a town over eighty kilometres away, despite the existence of a village hospital which was just as well equipped. Dr Singh accompanied Sumer Singh and his son in a jeep and used his influence to get the patient admitted. When Maal Singh died in the early hours of the next morning, Dr Singh used his influence once again to avoid a post-mortem. All this was on record. Having talked to several people in the village, the police suspected that Maal Singh, who had a psychiatric record, had committed suicide by consuming some form of poison, 'probably rat killer which is commonly used in such cases and easily available', a senior officer in Sikar told me several years later. In addition, it was alleged that Dr Singh had fabricated admission records at the hospital in Ajitgarh where he worked to show that Sumer Singh had been an in-patient, suffering from stress, the day Roop Kanwar was burned alive. If this was so, it meant that a fourteen-year-old boy had presided over the sati ceremony. The police found this hard to believe and the suspicion surrounding the doctor mounted when they found his house in the village padlocked and deserted. He was to remain on the run for the next eight months.

As facts, rumour and gossip unfolded in the press at the time, it became clear that the debate surrounding Roop Kanwar's death was to rage for years to come. Yet, it was not until 28 September, over three weeks after the event, that the Prime Minister, Rajiv Gandhi, finally made a short public statement, saying 'Sati is a national shame.'

CHAPTER TWO

During this time, throughout September 1987, I was in Delhi working on a film for Channel Four television in London. My research had come to a virtual standstill. Any further progress depended on permission from various government departments that had, in turn, to filter through the Ministry of Foreign Affairs. It was a frustrating and uncertain time for me, waiting on telephone calls that never came when promised, making countless trips to Shastri Bhavan where the government offices were based, fighting the urge to flip and become confrontational. (*That*, I knew, would never work with government officials, who, full of their sense of self-importance, would only respond to the 'humble approach'. Any outburst or deviation from this approach would lead to even further delays or an outright refusal.) There was little I could do but wait.

I was staying in Nizamuddin, a wonderfully peaceful part of Delhi, with an old friend, Praful, a well-known journalist who worked for the *Times of India* at the time. Because of his work, each morning an enormous pile of newspapers landed on his first-floor balcony in bundles as the delivery boy rode past on his bike, aiming well over the iron gate. The boy never missed, and the rolled-up newspapers, in both English and Hindi, were there soon after dawn each day. After my friend left for work, some time after nine, I had the flat and the papers to myself. With the day stretching ahead, housebound as I was on many occasions – waiting on telephone calls – reading newspapers helped pass the time. The death of Roop Kanwar and national reactions to the event began to fill many columns and I found myself collecting press clippings – reports, editorials and letters from the public that reflected mixed feelings about the issue. A single woman's death had triggered a barrage of argument, a string of emotional reactions in a country where dowry deaths had become commonplace, particularly among the relatively affluent and middle-class. Women burned to death in some part of the country every day but Roop Kanwar's alleged participation in the rite of sati had struck a deeper chord, churning up history in a way that rarely happens.

The arrest of Roop Kanwar's in-laws and others in the village who had participated in the ritual of her death created a furore in Rajasthan and political pandemonium in the country as a whole. Prominent politicians were divided on the issue. Although the Abolition of Sati Act had been on the statute books since 1829, after Independence, no one had ever been charged with murder or successfully prosecuted in a court of law, under its provisions, which allowed for life imprisonment and/or a fine. Amidst the uproar over the Roop Kanwar case, the Law Secretary, S. R. Bansal, was quick to rule that the 1829 Act was 'only a regulation passed by the East India Company and could not apply in the present case'. Meanwhile, the police had charged those arrested with two separate offences listed in the Indian Penal Code (IPC): section 302, which deals with premeditated murder, and section 306, which deals with the abetment of suicide. The punishment for the former was a life sentence or the death penalty and for the latter, a maximum of ten years' imprisonment and/or a fine.

On 1 October 1987, under pressure from Delhi, the State Governor of Rajasthan, Vasant Dada Patil, signed the Rajasthan Sati (Prevention) Ordinance 1987. This provided for the death penalty or life imprisonment for abettors of sati, and severe punishment for any attempt to commit sati or glorify it by organizing ceremonies or constructing memorials. The ordinance also provided for the setting up of special courts to try such offences, shifting the burden of proof on to the accused. However, a report headed 'Death rap for sati abetters', circulated by the Press Trust of India that day, stated that, according to official sources, the punitive clauses of the ordinance would not be applied in the Roop Kanwar case.

Section 19 of the ordinance stated:

> ... nothing in this ordinance shall affect any temple or other structure constructed for the glorification of sati and in existence immediately before the commencement of this ordinance or the continuance of any ceremonies in such temples or other structures in connection with such sati.

Another section empowered district magistrates to confiscate all funds collected for the purpose of 'glorifying sati', but did not specify whether this would apply to the Deorala case. It was well known that the organizers of the *Chunari Mahotsav* ceremony, held on the thirteenth day after Roop Kanwar's death, had netted a small fortune. Estimates in the press reports varied, but the figures involved were between six to seven million rupees, proving that sati-worship is a lucrative business.

In effect, therefore, the new ordinance had little relevance to the case of Roop Kanwar. Designed as a deterrent for the future, it was the government's way of demonstrating its will to act in the face of rising criticism, an attempt to protect the 'modern' image of India in the twentieth century. It was also a gesture to regain credibility in the global community, where legislation and lip-service are the basic tools of political survival when it comes to issues involving human rights and the blatant persecution of women, among several other forms of traditional exploitation.

The rite of sati has been an important element – and at times the pivot of political argument – in the history of Indo-Western relations. In his book of essays on the subject Dr Arvind Sharma, of the Department of Religious Studies at the University of Sydney, has this to say about attitudes to the practice:

> [Sati] aroused a wide gamut of reactions ranging from admiration to outright condemnation, and abolition. Over the long history

of Indo-Western contact, the emphasis shifted. In what has been called the first period – from the 4th century BC to 1757 – the Western reaction was a mix of admiration and criticism. In what has been called the second period – the 1757–1857 period – the reactions of condemnation and prohibition manifested themselves with vigour, leading to the abolition of sati in 1829. In what has been called the third period – the post 1857 period – two opposite trends appeared. On the one hand an approach of broad-based condemnation was developed, which used sati as a justification for the perpetuation of the British Raj in India. On the other hand, a streak of admiration also reappeared. In this period, scholarly investigation into the origin of sati also made considerable headway.

According to Dr Sharma, the Greeks provide us with the first account of the Western reaction to sati. In 316 BC the Hindu general Keteus died in the battle between Antigonus and Eumenes. Keteus had two wives. Both wanted to commit sati, but the older wife was pregnant and prevented from doing so on account of her condition, at which:

The elder wife went away lamenting, with the band about her head rent, and tearing her hair, as if tidings of some great disaster had been brought her; and the other departed, exultant at her victory, to the pyre, crowned with fillets by the women who belonged to her and decked out splendidly as for a wedding. She was escorted by her kinsfolk who chanted a song in praise of her virtue. When she came near to the pyre, she took off her adornments and distributed them to her familiars and friends, leaving a memorial for herself, as it were, to those who had loved her. Her adornments consisted of a multitude of rings on her hands, set with precious gems of diverse colours, about her head golden stars not a few, variegated with different sorts of stones, and about her neck a multitude of necklaces, each a little larger than the one about it. In conclusion, she said farewell to her familiars and was helped by her brother onto the pyre, and there, to the admiration of the crowd which had gathered together for the spectacle, she ended her life in heroic fashion. Before the pyre was kindled, the whole army in battle array marched around it thrice. She, meanwhile, lay down beside her husband, and as the fire seized her no sound of weakness escaped her lips. The spectators were moved, some to pity and some to exuberant praise. But some of the Greeks present found fault with such customs as savage and inhumane.

The Greeks also had a theory to account for the custom. They believed that the rite of sati was designed to dissuade wives from poisoning their husbands when they found better lovers – an experience that was within the realm of their own understanding of human behaviour from their own society.

Much later, during the seventeenth century, numerous accounts of sati were recorded by various travellers who came to India from the West. Among them was François Bernier, a French physician at the court of Aurangzeb, who, in his book, *Travels in the Mogul Empire*, said of the Moguls:

> The *Mahometans*, by whom the country is governed, [do] all in their power to suppress the barbarous custom. They do not, indeed, forbid it by a positive law, because it is a part of their policy to leave the idolatrous population, which is so much more numerous than their own, in the free exercise of their religion; but the practice is checked by indirect means. No woman can sacrifice herself without permission from the governor of the province in which she resides, and he never grants it until he shall have ascertained that she is not to be turned away from her purpose: to accomplish this desirable end the governor reasons with the widow and makes her enticing promises; after which, if these methods fail, he sometimes sends her among his women, that the effect of their remonstrances may be tried. Notwithstanding these obstacles, the number of self-immolations is still very considerable, particularly in the territories of the *Rajas*, where no *Mahometan* governors are appointed.

Rajasthan gets its name from the 'territory of the *Rajas*' and, literally translated, means 'The Land of Kings'.

Bernier goes on to describe the events he witnessed:

When travelling from *Ahmed-abad* to *Agra*, through the territories of the *Rajas*, and while the caravan halted under the shade of a banyan tree until the cool of the evening, news reached us that a widow was then on the point of burning herself with the body of her husband. I ran at once to the spot, and going to the edge of a large and nearly dry reservoir, observed at the bottom a deep pit filled with wood: the body of a dead man extended thereon; a woman seated upon the same pile; four or five *Brahmens* setting fire to it in every part; five middle-aged women, tolerably well dressed, holding one another by the hand, singing and dancing round the pit; and a great number of spectators of both sexes.

The pile, whereon large quantities of butter (ghee) and oil had been thrown, was soon enveloped in flames, and I saw the fire catch the woman's garments, which were impregnated with scented oil, mixed with sandalwood powder and saffron; but I could not perceive the slightest indication of pain or even uneasiness in the victim, and it was said that she pronounced with emphasis the words *five, two*, to signify that this being the fifth time she had burnt herself with the same husband, there were wanted only two more similar sacrifices to render her perfect, according to the doctrine of the transmigration of souls: as if a certain reminiscence, or prophetic spirit, had been imparted to her at that moment of her dissolution.

But this was only the commencement of the infernal tragedy. I thought that the singing and dancing of the five women was nothing more than some unmeaning ceremony; great therefore was my astonishment when I saw that the flames having ignited the clothes of one of these females, she cast herself head-foremost into the pit. The horrid example was followed by another woman, as soon as the flames caught her person: the three women who remained then took hold of each other by the hand, resumed the dance with perfect composure; and after a short lapse of time, they also precipitated themselves, one after the other, into the fire.

I soon learnt the meaning of these multiplied sacrifices. The five women were slaves, and having witnessed the deep affliction of their mistress in consequence of the illness of her husband, whom she promised not to survive, they were so moved with compassion that they entered into an engagement to perish by the same flames that consumed their beloved mistress.

Bernier also describes another reality:

It is true, however, that I have known some of these unhappy widows shrink at the sight of the piled wood; so as to leave no doubt on my mind that they would willingly have recanted, if recantation had been permitted by the merciless *Brahmens*; but those demons excite or astound the affrighted victims, and even thrust them into the fire. I was present when a poor young woman, who had fallen back five or six paces from the pit, was thus driven forward; and I saw another of these wretched beings struggling to leave the funeral pile when the fire increased around her person, but she was prevented from escaping by the long poles of the diabolical executioners.

A liberal at heart and deeply fascinated by all he learned through his travels in India and his involvement with the Mogul court, Bernier was scathing in his attack on high-caste Hindus:

I have not yet mentioned all the barbarity and atrocity of these monsters. In some part of the *Indies*, instead of burning the women who determine not to survive their husbands, the *Brahmens* bury them alive, by slow degrees, up to the throat; then two or three of them fall suddenly upon the victim, wring her neck, and when she has been effectually and completely choked, cover over the body with earth thrown upon it from successive baskets, and tread upon the head.

At first, Bernier saw himself as a silent, helpless observer:

In *Lahore* I saw a most beautiful young widow sacrificed, who could not, I think, have been more than twelve years of age. The poor creature appeared more dead than alive when she approached the dreadful pit: the agony of her mind cannot be described; she trembled and wept bitterly; but three or four of the *Brahmens*, assisted by an old woman who held her under the arm, forced the unwilling victim toward the fatal spot, seated her on the wood, tied her hands and feet, lest she should run away, and in that situation the innocent creature was burnt alive. I found it difficult to repress my feelings and to prevent their bursting forth into clamorous and unavailing rage; but restrained by prudential considerations, I contented myself with silently lamenting the abominable superstition of these people...

Later on, because of his involvement with the Mogul court, he was to get personally involved:

One of my friends, named *Bendidas, Danechmend-kan's* principal writer, died of a hectic fever for which I had attended him upward of two years, and his wife immediately resolved to burn herself with the body of her husband. Her friends were in the service of my *Agah* [employer], and being commanded by him to dissuade the widow from the commission of so frantic an act, they represented to her that although she had adopted a generous and commendable resolution, which would redound to the honour and conduce to the happiness of the family, yet she ought to consider that her children were of a tender age, that it would be cruel to abandon them, and that her anxiety for their welfare ought to exceed the affection she bore to the memory of her deceased husband. The infatuated creature attended not, however, to their reasoning, and I was requested to visit the widow as if by my *Agah's* desire, and in the capacity of an old friend of the family. I complied, and found on entering the apartment a regular witches' *Sabat* of seven or eight old hags, and another four or five excited, wild, and aged *Brahmens* standing around the body, all of whom gave by turn a horrid yell, and beat their hands with violence. The widow was seated at the feet of her dead husband; her hair was dishevelled and her visage pale, but her eyes were tearless and sparkling with animation while she cried and screamed aloud like the rest of the company, and beat time with her hands to this horrible concert. The hurly-burly having subsided, I approached the hellish group, and addressed the women [sic] in a gentle tone. 'I am come hither,' said I, 'by desire of *Danechmend-kan*, to inform you that he will settle a pension of two crowns per month on each of your two sons, provided you do not destroy your life, a life so necessary for their care and education. We have ways and means indeed to prevent your ascending the pile, and to punish those who encourage you in so unreasonable a resolution. All your relations wish you to live for the sake of your offspring, and you will not be reputed infamous as are the childless widows who possess not courage to burn themselves with their dead husbands.' I repeated these arguments several times without receiving any answer; but, at last, fixing a determined look on me, she said, 'Well, if I am prevented from burning myself, I will dash out my brains against a wall.' What a diabolical spirit has taken possession of you, thought I. 'Let it be so then,' I rejoined, with undissembled anger, 'but first take your children, wretched and unnatural mother! Cut their throats, and consume them on the same pile; otherwise you will leave them to die of famine, for I shall return immediately to *Danechmend-kan* and annul their pensions.' These words, spoken with a loud and resolute voice, made the desired impression: without uttering a syllable, her head fell suddenly on her knees, and the greater part of the old women and *Brahmens* sneaked toward the door and left the room. I thought I might now safely leave the widow in the hands of her friends, who had accompanied me, and mounting my horse, returned home. In the evening, when on my way to *Danechmend-kan* to inform him of what I had done, I met one of the relations who thanked me, and said that the body had been burnt without the widow, who had promised not to die by her own hands.

Such intervention did not always work. J. B. Tavernier, the seventeenth-century traveller, narrates how a widow of twenty-two at Patna (now the capital city of Bihar) 'held her hand in the flame of a torch till it burnt to cinders in order to convince the officer that she was a willing party'.

Aurangzeb, the last of the great Mogul emperors, died in 1707, bringing about the disruption of the Mogul Empire. In his book of essays, Dr Arvind Sharma says:

> One of the chief beneficiaries of this disruption were the British. These developments opened up a new chapter in the role of sati as a factor on the Indo-Western encounter, for the establishment of the British Raj lead [*sic*] to the abolition of sati first in Bengal and then in the rest of the country ... The British, along with other European nations, originally ventured into Bengal as traders. In the confusion following the dismemberment of the Moghul Empire they involved themselves in local politics and consolidated their position by defeating the local Nawab at the Battle of Plassey (1757). With the acquisition of the Diwani of Bengal in 1765 from the Moghul Emperor they became administrators, in addition to being traders. As traders they had largely been spectators on the Indian scene, now they became actors. In due course this change of status showed in a change of attitude towards sati. Whereas the earlier attitude had been one of passive reaction, of observation and criticism, it could now be one of active intervention, of prevention and abolition. Moreover, just as the flag had followed trade (reversing for a while the famous dictum that trade follows the flag), the cross followed the flag.

Dr Sharma goes on to trace the development of Christian missionary involvement with sati:

> In November 1793 Rev. William Carey of the Baptist Mission arrived in Calcutta. After nearly six years, in the spring of 1799, he saw widow-burning one evening. It was in a place thirty miles away from Calcutta. He tried to stop the ceremony and to reason

with the widow and the Brahmin priests. 'I talked till reasoning was of no use, and then began to exclaim with all my might against what they were doing, telling them it was shocking murder. They told me it was a great act of holiness.' Carey was greatly agitated, his spirit was in anguish, and he vowed like Lincoln later concerning the auction of slave women 'to hit this accursed thing hard', if God should spare him. Carey started immediately. He sent careful investigators to every village within a radius of thirty miles of Calcutta, to learn how many widows had been immolated there in the previous twelve months, and their ages, and the children they had left behind them. 'Four hundred and thirty eight was the damning total in this specific area alone, the toll of a single year's superstition, cruelty and waste.' The Serampore Missionaries under the leadership of Carey implored the Government to forbid the rite by law. Carey made use of his position as a lecturer in the College of Fort William to collect from the pundits there various texts from the Hindu *sastras* on which the practice of sati was allegedly based. The missionaries placed all these documents, together with the statistics of sati they had already compiled, in the hands of George Udney – a member of the Supreme Council and an ardent abolitionist. Udney's submission on sati was the first official notice regarding female immolation which had appeared in the records of the government. As a result, Wellesley's government asked the judges of the Nizamat Adalat to 'ascertain in the first instance, by means of a reference to the pundits how far the practice above noticed is founded on the religious opinion of the Hindoos'. But Lord Wellesley's reign was ending, and with a swarm of critics in London and in Calcutta, he feared to risk a reform so challenged and so controversial.

As a result of these activities, the missionaries began to mould public opinion both in India and Britain and on 22 June 1813, William Wilberforce raised the matter in the House of Commons, quoting the statistics of sati which the Baptists had compiled. The theme of his speech was the propagation of Christianity in

India. The movement towards abolition had begun with European religious reaction taking the direction of condemnation, declaring sati to be a heathen practice. Referring to this time, Dr Sharma states:

> Between 1815 and 1818 the number of satis doubled, from 378 in 1815 to 839 in 1818 in the Presidency of Bengal. The 1815–1818 records – 'truly awful records for any Christian Government' – had a disquieting effect on officials. In 1818, 'when the pyres blazed most fiercely', Raja Rammohun Roy launched his journalistic attack on the rite, 'which aroused such anger that for a while his life was in danger'.

Raja Rammohun Roy was a Bengali intellectual, social reformer and prolific writer on such issues. He came from a class that represented the interests of Indian middlemen, providing a link between European traders and the Indian peasantry of Bengal. By 1818, the British had established themselves well enough to want to deal with the growers themselves, cutting out the power of the middle class. They did not succeed in this. In order to rule and to impose new laws, the British needed the support of the Indian intelligentsia, and Rammohun Roy fitted the bill. He was passionate in his opposition to sati, having witnessed the immolation of his brother's wife, which he had tried to stop. Analysing his role in the affair, Dr Sharma says:

> Amidst the kudos which is showered on Raja Rammohun Roy for his role in the advocacy of the abolition of sati, one crucial fact is often overlooked: that when Lord William Bentinck sought his advice on the matter of the British prohibiting the practice of sati, he advised Lord William Bentinck *against* such a step.
>
> By 1828 Lord William Bentinck had ascertained the opinion of the judges and officers of the Government but had no way of ascertaining native Indian opinion on the question of abolition of sati. But he had heard of Rammohun Roy as an advocate of the abolition of sati and sought a meeting with him. The manner in which this came about was thus 'narrated by Rev. Dr K. S.

MacDonald, at a meeting in 1879, on the information supplied
to him by Ananda Chandra Basu, the oldest pupil then living of
Rammohun':

Lord William Bentinck, the Governor-General, on hearing that
he would receive considerable help from the Raja in suppressing
the pernicious custom of widow-burning, sent one of his *aides-
de-camp* to him expressing his desire to see him. To this the Raja
replied, 'I have now given up all worldly advocations, and am
engaged in religious culture and in the investigation of truth.
Kindly express my humble respects to the Governor-General and
inform him that I have no inclination to appear before his august
presence, and therefore I hope that he will kindly pardon me.'
These words the *aide-de-camp* conveyed to the Governor-
General, who enquired, 'What did you say to Rammohun Roy?'
The *aide-de-camp* replied, 'I told him that Lord William
Bentinck, the Governor-General, would be pleased to see him.'
The Governor-General answered, 'Go back and tell him again
that Mr William Bentinck will be highly obliged to him if he
will kindly see him at once.' This the *aide-de-camp* did and
Rammohun Roy could no longer refuse the urgent and polite
request of his lordship.

The meeting eventually took place and was noted in the *Indian
Gazette* of 27 July 1829, and Lord William Bentinck provided
the gist of the discussion himself:

I must acknowledge that a similar opinion as to the probable
excitation of a deep distrust of our future intentions was mentioned to me in a conversation by that enlightened native, Rammohun Roy, a warm advocate for the abolition of *Sati* and of all
other superstitions and corruptions engrafted on Hindu religion,
which he considers originally to have been a pure Deism. It was
his opinion that the practice might be suppressed quietly and
unobservedly by increasing the difficulties and by the indirect
agency of the police. He apprehended that any public enactment
would give rise to general apprehension, that the reasoning
would be, while the English were contending for power they

deemed it politic to allow universal toleration and to respect our religion, but having obtained the supremacy their first act is a violation of their profession, and the next will probably be, like the Muhammadan conquerors, to force upon us their own religion.

This need to be seen to be independent of British influence dominated men like Rammohun Roy who did not approve of governmental interference in the sphere of Hindu social life. However, when Lord William Bentinck took it upon himself to abolish sati in 1829, Rammohun Roy came out in open support of the Act and became an active and vocal campaigner, using Hindu scriptures to challenge the notion that sati played a part in the enhancement of Indian society.

Post-1829, the debate surrounding sati was clouded by larger world events, two world wars and the fight for independence from colonial rule, which cost millions of lives. Post-independence, from 1947 onwards, particularly in the 1980s, India witnessed the rise of fundamentalism and sati became, once again, the cornerstone of regional pride. Forty years later, in 1987, Roop Kanwar's death reopened the controversy.

As the sati debate gathered momentum in the Indian press in the wake of the Roop Kanwar case, a fact-finding team representing the Women and Media Committee of the Bombay Union of Journalists (BUJ) travelled to Rajasthan for six days, trying to unearth facts and document the aftermath of the incident. After their return, they published a report in the form of a small booklet entitled *Trial by Fire* which in itself was to make headline news. The team came to the conclusion that Roop Kanwar had been murdered. This added weight to the anti-sati movement started by the women in Jaipur who had petitioned the Rajasthan High Court demanding an end to the post-sati celebrations. By the time the BUJ team got to the village of Deorala, the police had already made several arrests, so it is not surprising that they met with stiff resistance from the villagers:

The fact-finding team's first impression was that there was a conspiracy of silence in Deorala. Not a single villager admitted to seeing the sati. There were a number of people at the sati sthal and villagers poured in by bus, taxi and camel cart. The rest of the village appeared strangely deserted. No one seemed to belong to Deorala. '*Hum is gaon ke nahin hain, door se aaye hain* (We are not from this village, we have come from far away)' was the stock reply to queries.

The three women, Meena Menon, Geeta Seshu and Sujata Anandan, then went to Roop Kanwar's in-laws' home:

From the outside the house seemed deserted. We were told by the villagers standing outside that no one was allowed in and that only Maal Singh's ailing mother was in. We went in never-theless, a man appeared from the inner room and told us firmly to leave at once. No photographs would be allowed, he warned. We insisted that we had come only to meet the mother. We were told that she was lying inside and had not eaten since the arrest of her sons, especially nine-year-old Bhupendra [*sic*] Singh and their father. Some women who emerged from the inner quarters, said that *sati* had occurred in the past in the village – it is not uncommon. But the families of the women had never been harassed by the government. '*Sarkar ne humko bahut dukhi kiya hai* (The government has given us a lot of trouble).'

Strangely, the women refused to identify themselves, only saying that they were relatives. Further on in the village, two women in a house invited us in. They were friendly and wel-coming. In contrast, however, the man of the house told us in menacing tones, 'You've come to worship *sati mata*, please leave after that. There is no work for you here.'

Under the circumstances, it was not at all strange that the women refused to identify themselves. From their point of view, the village and their homes had been invaded by the police and press alike and they were defensive, afraid of being involved as witnesses, reluctant to assist the authorities in what they saw as the persecution of their men. It was, as one of the prosecution lawyers for the case put to me many years later in Jaipur, 'a clash between twentieth-century ideas and a fourteenth-century situation'. He was right.

The lives of Rajput women remain deeply rooted in feudal custom. Medieval structures and practices persist within the family and the place of women, according to their age and marital status, is strictly defined. There are rules of behaviour for the unmarried daughter, the new bride, the mother-in-law and the widow. The widow, for example, must always be the last to eat and so must eat alone, apart from the rest of the family. She must never be seen in public. She cannot attend social functions, not even those involving only the family. She must keep her head covered at all times. She is, for all intents and purposes, a social outcast. This reality has not changed for centuries. In *Travels in the Mogul Empire*, François Bernier records the fate of widows in his time:

> I have been often in the company of a fair *Idolater*, who contrived to save her life by throwing herself upon the protection of the *scavengers* (sweepers of the lowest caste) who assemble on these occasions in considerable numbers, when they learn that the intended victim is young and handsome, that her relations are of little note, and that she is to be accompanied by only a few of her acquaintance. Yet the woman whose courage fails at the sight of the horrid apparatus of death, and who avails herself of the presence of these men to avoid the impending sacrifice, cannot hope to pass her days in happiness, or to be treated with respect or affection. Never again can she live with the *Gentiles*: no individual of that nation will at any time, or under any circumstances, associate with a creature so degraded, who is accounted utterly infamous, and execrated because of the dishonour which her conduct has brought upon the religion of the country. Consequently she is ever afterwards exposed to the ill-treatment of her low and vulgar protectors...

In 1987, the three women of the fact-finding team from Bombay came to similar conclusions:

In our view, the debate over whether Roop Kanwar's death by *sati* was voluntary or not is both specious and irrelevant. Even if it is ultimately proven beyond doubt (as it has not been so far) that she herself expressed a desire to immolate herself on the funeral pyre of her dead husband and that she went to her death willingly, without the use of force by anyone else, it must be remembered that she was a product of the society in which she grew up and lived.

In that society, and in much of Indian society, the status of women is so low that there is very little question of women exercising their free will in any aspect of their lives ... Would Roop Kanwar or any other 18-year-old girl like her have been allowed to 'voluntarily' choose her own husband or elect to work or opt for remarriage? Indeed, are the majority of women in India free to choose what they will do from day to day, whether or not to study, whether or not to get married, whether or not to seek employment, whether or not to have children, whether or not to give birth to female children, whether or not to shoulder the entire burden of domestic work singlehandedly, whether or not their daughters will go to school? Seen in this context, the arguments put forward by defenders of this practice of a woman's right to exercise her own free will to commit *sati* stand exposed.

In addition to the general oppression of women and their lack of choice in most aspects of their lives, there is the factor of cruel treatment meted out to widows in many parts of the country – this is certainly so in Rajasthan and the Rajput community. The pathetic status of widows and the special tortures (psychological and physical) devised to torment them for the rest of their lives have their roots in the belief that a woman can have no life unless she is attached to a man; after marriage this man is the husband and when he dies, she also is as good as dead, whether or not she remains alive.

Under the circumstances, if a woman thinks that immediate death by *sati* is preferable to a prolonged absence of life, and acts upon this conviction, it can hardly be seen as an exercise of

free will. A choice can be made only between viable alternatives;
for many women, there are no alternatives.

The BUJ report, based on interviews with a wide-ranging group
of politicians, police, city activists and village women, was to
make a significant impact on the media. Their conclusion that
Roop Kanwar had been murdered in cold blood influenced the
direction the feminist movement was to take: demanding that her
killer be convicted and sentenced accordingly. The confrontation
between anti-sati campaigners and the powerful pro-sati, predominantly male, Rajput lobby was to intensify with women
playing an active part on both sides. The debate surrounding sati
was reopened on a national and international level, 158 years
after the British had first legislated against the practice.

CHAPTER THREE

Having come up against a wall of silence and hostility in the village of Deorala, the three women representing the BUJ returned to Jaipur to confront the Chief Minister of Rajasthan, Harideo Joshi, and register their protest against the government's handling of the situation. They were told by women activists in Jaipur, who had initiated the protest movement, that Joshi had been 'brusque and indifferent' when he had first been made aware of the incident on 6 September, two days after Roop Kanwar's death. However, eleven days later, in a televised speech that was broadcast countrywide, he had condemned the incident – probably under pressure from Delhi – adding his own comments. He stated that Roop Kanwar had committed sati 'voluntarily' and warned against interfering with the religious beliefs and rites (he could have meant 'rights') of communities throughout the country. He emphasized that these rites/rights had to be 'respected and protected'. The women in Jaipur were outraged by this response. As Kavita Srivastava said to me many years later, 'How can he say that it was *voluntary*? He wasn't even there – and neither were any other government or police officials. He has clearly decided to support the pro-sati Rajput lobby in order to further his own career.'

On 29 September, when the BUJ team met Joshi, he denied his earlier assertion, saying, 'Words have been put in my mouth ... It is not right for me to comment on whether it was voluntary or not.' By this time, the Union Minister of State for Home Affairs, Mr P. Chidambaram, had flown in from Delhi in an attempt to defuse a politically volatile situation and warn local politicians to remain cautious in their remarks to the press. Despite this, the disarray and contradictions within the ruling Congress Party were apparent to all. Opposition leaders cashed in by supporting the Rajput lobby, quoting the scriptures and warning the government that all attempts to interfere with local sentiments would be 'severely restricted, and with arms if necessary'. The women involved in the protest movement were ridiculed and condemned. At a rally in Deorala attended by some 2000 Rajputs on 27 September, the leader of the Bharatiya Janata Party (BJP), Om Prakash Gupta, referred to these women as *bazaari aurate* (street women) who were unmarried and would remain so. 'How could these women know about *pativrata* (devotion to one's husband) or the desire to commit sati? They can barely tolerate the heat of the sun! How will they then stand near a pyre, let alone experience the burning of a woman committing sati?' he asked an enraptured crowd. They cheered and shouted slogans in Gupta's support as he went on to describe such women as 'Western' women who lived in air-conditioned houses in Jaipur, Delhi and Bombay. He characterized the protesters as women who frequented clubs, drank alcohol, smoked cigarettes and had 'loose morals'. His sentiments were echoed by other Rajput leaders who shared the platform that day and subsequently spoke to the press.

Angered by what they had experienced and seen, the BUJ team returned to Bombay and produced *Trial by Fire*, despite all the hostility and lack of support they had encountered. They concluded:

We are convinced that the state – the government, the administration and the police – failed to carry out their duty in this matter. Further, politicians (belonging to both the ruling and the opposition parties, in Rajasthan as well as at the centre) keeping a gimlet eye on electoral gains and losses either steered clear of the whole issue as long as they could or actively participated in ceremonies glorifying sati and made provocative pronouncements about the freedom of religion and the sanctity of religious practices.

Even the minister who holds the Women's Portfolio in the union government, Margaret Alva, was conspicuous by her absence in Rajasthan at a time when a burning women's issue was the talk of the state: she did not even issue any major statements on the subject. In fact, P. Chidambaram, the union minister for home, who was sent to Rajasthan rather late in the day on a fact-finding mission was the first central government spokesperson to speak out unequivocally against what happened in Deorala. Few have joined him since.

The BUJ booklet had a tremendous impact on the press and other journalists picked up from where they had left off. At least among women in India – thinking, socially conscious women – Roop Kanwar's death was not to be forgotten easily. She had become the symbol of an oppression many felt, in a world that does not respect women who live without men.

Meanwhile, in Deorala, the village council of elders and land-owners, supported by local Rajput politicians, had set up a committee to perpetuate their celebration of the widow's death. At first they called themselves the *Sati Dharam Raksha Samiti* (loosely translated as the saviours of the sati tradition), but after the Rajasthan Sati (Prevention) Ordinance, signed by the State Governor on 1 October, they dropped the word 'sati' in order to avoid prosecution and called themselves the *Dharam Raksha Samiti* (Keepers of the Faith). It was farcical. Their sentiments and aspirations remained the same but the word 'sati' had been left out for purely pragmatic reasons. They continued to campaign, and defied the authorities by celebrating the Thirteenth Day Ceremony, where no one was arrested and thousands celebrated. The government was seen to be powerless in the face of religious fundamentalism.

A prominent supporter of the *Dharam Raksha Samiti* was Kalyan Singh Kalvi, president of the Rajasthan State Janata Party.

He spearheaded the pro-sati Rajput movement while trying to remain 'politically correct' by saying, 'I am against sati as a practice. It should be punished as suicide. But once it is done, what is the point of harassing innocent people? Again, once it is committed, there are certain rites which must be done. No one can interfere with these rites.' When the BUJ team met him, he recounted the events leading up to Roop Kanwar's death as if he had no doubt about their authenticity. He told them that a number of his relatives had been in the village at the time; that Roop Kanwar had become oblivious to all around her the moment she 'attained *sat* (purity)'; that she had generated so much heat then that her aunt was nearly 'scorched' when she tried to touch her; that her brothers-in-law did not know of her intention to commit sati until she emerged from her room dressed in her bridal finery. Kalvi was proud that one of his nephews, on seeing Roop Kanwar 'lead' the procession, 'immediately took up a sword and stationed himself behind her'. He went on to say his nephew had kept close to the widow and had witnessed everything. In their booklet, the BUJ women say: 'Kalvi said this with great emphasis to impress upon us that his rendition was possibly the most accurate.' Yet, throughout the entire police investigation that went on for months, no one ever questioned this nephew nor did they ask Kalvi, a senior and powerful politician, where they might find him.

In the last week of October 1987, two women who edited and produced a feminist magazine in Delhi called *Manushi* travelled to Deorala to cover the story. Their article, published in a special double issue of their magazine, was revealing. Madhu Kishwar and Ruth Vanita made the following observations:

> The Sati Sthal is situated at one end of the village, in an open ground. It is a temporary structure, a platform topped by a pavilion. When we reached there, four schoolboys who looked between seven and fifteen years old, were walking round and round it with sticks in their hands, chanting slogans. They wore

shirts and shorts with outsize turbans perched incongruously on their heads.

Nearby, a group of young men were selling coconuts and other offerings, and distributing *prasad*. At a little distance, another group of young men were selling reprints of the now famous photo collage showing Roop Kanwar on the pyre with her husband's head in her lap.

Clusters of women sat around talking, among them a number of schoolgirls. They were very different from the film stereotype of the village woman as a shy secluded belle. They assumed we were journalists and kept staring at us for about forty-five minutes with overt hostility. Since we refrained from asking any journalistic questions or taking photos, they finally called us and started cross-questioning us with great confidence. Their hostility melted into the warmth and hospitality characteristic of an Indian village only after they were somewhat assured that we were not seeking to extract any statements from them. None of the women were veiled and they talked, joked, teased and laughed unabashedly in the presence of men.

The scene around the *Sati Sthal* was political rather than devotional. The Thirteenth Day Ceremony of the Veil had already taken place and the gathered crowd, mostly local residents, felt proud in their victory over police and state. Most of the slogans being shouted at the *sthal* had the rhythm and structure of electoral slogans and not 'the remotest connection to any kind of religious chant'.

Kishwar and Vanita spent the day wandering around Deorala talking to people, observing various rituals. In the evening, they attended the daily worship – the evening *arti*. I read with fascination their description of the scene:

The ground was floodlit. The schoolboys were replaced by young men with naked swords in hand. The *arti* sung was 'Om Jai Jagdish Hare', an *arti* of recent origin in modern Hindi which has been popularised by Bombay cinema to the extent that it has now assumed the status of a sort of national *arti*, sung indiscriminately on all occasions. It has nothing at all to do with sati, and certainly is not of Rajput or Rajasthani origin.

A majority of those gathered at the worship were young men and women, most of them educated. That the *arti* was a recent imposition on village culture was evident from the fact that most of those who sang it had no notion of the tune and only a few of them knew the words, with the result that the rendering was ragged and unintelligible. The *arti* was performed by educated youths whose idea of religious ritual seemed more influenced by Hindi films than by any local religious tradition.

The fascination with the sati cult has been attributed to the superstitious ignorance of illiterate village women, but it is noteworthy that the entire cult being created in Deorala is in the hands of men. Women participate by standing at a respectable distance, and joining in the singing.

By this time, October 1987, the pro-sati Rajput lobby had gained ground against the women protesters. A rally organized by the *Dharam Raksha Samiti* (referred to by the villagers as the *Samiti*) had already attracted approximately 70,000 Rajput men, who gathered in Jaipur on 8 October to protest against new laws and demand the release of all those arrested. In the face of these developments, the *Manushi* journalists from Delhi felt the same sense of isolation from the villagers as had the women from Bombay a few weeks before.

In all, thirty-two men, including Roop Kanwar's two brothers-in-law who were referred to the juvenile courts because they were under age, had been arrested and were referred to as 'the accused persons'. These included members of her own family as well as her husband's. The charge sheet stated that Roop had been taken to the funeral ground from her in-laws' house under 'armed escort'. 'Four persons were walking around her, brandishing swords.' She was made to sit on the pyre and her husband's head was placed on her head; a layer of firewood was 'erected on her up to her shoulder so that she might not get up'. She tried to speak but the members of her husband's family and others started shouting 'Jai Jai' (Long Live) and 'within minutes' they had lit the pyre. The charge sheet stated that evidence existed to show that Roop Kanwar had tried to sit up and speak once again after the pyre had been ignited, but that the accused had 'collected dried thorny bushes from the nearby field and again lit the fire, burning her alive. Cases had been 'registered against the accused' under various sections of the Indian Penal Code (IPC). The charge sheet included allegations that members of her family had started collecting funds from the day after her immolation; that 'they gave a religious cover to the burning of Roop Kanwar to save themselves from the onus of criminal conspiracy'. Doubt was cast on the 'mysterious death' of her husband, Maal Singh. The charge sheet stated that the police were still trying to 'apprehend a medical doctor (Magan Singh) who reportedly treated him and tried to make false records showing that the father-in-law of Roop Kanwar, Sumer Singh, was an in-patient in the hospital at the time of her burning'. This report, distributed by the Press Trust of India, was picked up by many national dailies.

Both the press and the women's movement had prodded and pushed the authorities, and neither were popular in Rajasthan. They had focused on many issues connected with the situation, emphasizing that big business was involved; that temples and religious rituals were money spinners for the very rich. For instance, it became well known that some of the country's biggest business houses – names like Goenka, Birla, Somani, Modi, Jain and Poddar – came from the Shekawati region, where Deorala is situated. For years they had financed the largest sati temple in Rajasthan – the Rani Sati Temple at Jhunjhunu. Rituals and celebrations at the Jhunjhunu Temple were to become a testing ground for politicians and devotees in the following year. Much was to happen before then.

By May 1988, the polarization of opinions engendered by Roop Kanwar's case was complete. On the one hand there was the protest movement, led by women up and down the country, supported by and large by progressive, well-known journalists and writers and on the other, self-appointed religious leaders who quoted the Vedas and other ancient Hindu scriptures in support of their pro-sati stance. Among the most volatile of these, was the *Shankaracharya* of Puri. An article published in the *Indian Post*, headlined 'Solving Water Crisis the Sati Way' began:

> The controversial Sankaracharya of Puri, who is in the news because of his support for sati, has now come out with an incredible solution to Hyderabad's water problem.
>
> At a felicitation function of some Telugu Brahmins in the city last Saturday, he is reported to have said that the water problem could be solved if any woman in the city committed sati.
>
> In fact, the Sankaracharya not only defended sati at the function but also challenged any newsman, if present among the audience, to argue with him on the issue. However, no newsman was present.

The term *Sankaracharya* or *Shankaracharya* comes from Adi Shankara, a Hindu ascetic (literally the first Shankara) who lived in the eighth century, and laid down sixty-four *acharas* – observances – which, according to Sakuntala Narasimhan, the author of *Sati: A Study of Widow Burning in India*, included the prohibition of sati. Narasimhan comments, 'Oddly enough, it is one of these spiritual heirs of Adi Shankara who is now in the forefront of the pro-sati movement, claiming that widow immolation is part of Hindu dharma. There is no logical explanation of how a religious descendant of the original Shankara who forbade sati burnings can take a stance in favour of sati.' Of course, the concept of a 'spiritual heir' is so nebulous that it is wide open to abuse. Anyone can claim to be such an heir. However, throughout India, the tradition of *Shankaracharyas* – *acharya* being a teacher or a learned person – has been revered for centuries and although both their role in society and political power have dwindled considerably, they still have considerable influence over their followers. No longer a united bunch of ascetics, the *Shankaracharyas* are divided among themselves and have opposing political allegiances to different political parties and politicians. From the eighth century onwards, these teachers represented a revivalist Hindu movement which sought to stem the flow of desertion from Hinduism to Buddhism, and, much later, to Christianity. As many began converting to Buddhism in order to escape the tyranny of the rigid Hindu caste system, the *Shankaracharya*s set out to reform the religion in order to reverse this trend. They were consulted regularly by the rulers of their time, and gained much prominence. Hence their popularity with respect to 'traditional values' – a much-cited phrase in the twentieth century.

This is what the *Shankaracharya* of Puri relied on when he turned to later scriptures which evolved in the sixteenth and seventeenth centuries – a time of turbulence and unrest – and quoted from these in support of his stance. Sakuntala Narasimhan records some of his remarks in her book, published after Roop Kanwar's death:

The modern-day equivalent of the ancient lawmaker then described how a woman should become a sati: 'She should go near her husband's pyre, with flowers, fruit etc. In her *aanchal* (the end portion of a sari) give the symbols of her fortunate marital status to other fortunate women and then placing a pearl in her mouth, should pray to *Agni* the fire god, and enter the flames. At the moment of her entering the fire, Brahmins should chant mantras, to the effect that this woman who is entering the flames should be awarded with entry into heaven via her husband's pyre.'

A pregnant or a menstruating woman, he conceded, should not burn herself. Neither should a woman with small children. He added, 'Should a menstruating woman desire to become a sati, she should immolate herself five days later along with her husband's footwear. If such a woman feels that she cannot possibly wait four days before immolating herself, she should grind ten kilos of rice grain with a grinder in an earthenware container. This will purify her blood. Then she should donate 30, 20 or 10 cows – 30 if it is the first day, 20 if it is the second, 10 on the third – bathe five times in mud and that very day immolate herself.'

At the time, in 1988, the *Shankaracharya* of Puri seemed to revel in the fact that he was creating a storm and attracting the attention of the national press. He spoke out in favour of the practice of sati whenever he had an audience. Opposed to him were other spiritual leaders, among them Swami Agnivesh, who had ingratiated himself with politicians in the past. He challenged the *Shankaracharya* of Puri to an open debate on the scriptures, but was arrested on his way to the public event by police who claimed that he was a 'law and order risk' and might 'inflame the situation'. It became obvious to all who followed these events that the government had decided to woo the Rajput vote. The death of a single widow, however dramatic, did not warrant a tilt in the electoral balance.

In the midst of all this, Dr Magan Singh, who had been on the run for several months, was reported to have been arrested in Jaipur. Dr Singh was the first physician to treat Roop Kanwar's husband when he fell ill on 2 September; he had accompanied Roop Kanwar home from the hospital and was widely believed to have administered certain drugs to keep her calm. He had hastened 'procedures' by recommending that no post-mortem be conducted, and was also said to have fabricated hospital records to show that Sumer Singh, his friend and neighbour in the village, had not been present that day when his daughter-in-law had walked to her death.

The newspapers were quick to pick up the story. Headlines read: 'Doctor held in Deorala sati case', 'Doctor may give clue to sati', and so on. As reporters hounded Dr Singh, he remained reclusive, refusing to speak to the press. There were contradictory claims about the circumstances of the doctor's arrest. Some reports said he had been picked up by local police at his home in the village. Others, including the police, insisted he had been arrested from the Jaipur Collectorate while attempting to make some kind of deal with local administrators. A report in the *Times of India* stated:

The police version seems more plausible. Dr Magan Singh had

exhausted all possible avenues of escape. His application for anticipatory bail had been rejected no less than four times by the Rajasthan High Court. He was also suspended from his government post at Ajitgarh. The home department had recently recommended termination of his services to the medical and health department. The court had also ordered attachment of his property.

Despite all the uproar, all those arrested in connection with Roop Kanwar's death were released on bail within a few months of their arrest, and the case was to drag on for the next nine years.

CHAPTER FOUR

As summer turned to monsoon in 1988, the *Samiti* in Deorala announced that the first anniversary of Roop Kanwar's death would be 'observed and honoured' according to the Hindu lunar calendar, on 22 September instead of 4 September. Many commentators thought this a politically astute move, planned to test the government, individual political leaders and the power of the courts.

Not many miles from Deorala, in the same Shekawati region of Rajasthan, stands the vast and imposing Rani Sati Temple in Jhunjhunu, the country's largest and most influential sati temple, dedicated to Narayani Devi, a young girl of seventeen who is said to have lived in the fourteenth century. There are many conflicting legends about her. According to Sakuntala Narasimhan,

> The legend is that the nawab coveted the white mare that her betrothed rode on, and in the confrontation that ensued Tandhan Das (her husband) was killed, leaving his faithful servant as the only survivor apart from Dadi Narayani Devi and the mare. When the servant asked her whether he should take her back to her father's or to her father-in-law's, she is said to have replied that she would become a sati and that wherever the horse stopped while carrying the ashes of the couple, a temple to their memory should be raised.

Other versions, stories told by villagers, differ. Some say she died on the battlefield defending her husband's honour against a band

42

of dacoits who tried to steal the mare and killed her husband, and she is therefore regarded as a warrior goddess rather than a woman who merely lived for her husband. Nevertheless, she is worshipped as a *Maha Sati* – Great Sati.

The legend is nearly 700 years old but the temple, in its present form, is of this century. Supported, financed and frequented by influential businessmen from Calcutta and Bombay, its estimated annual income is approximately twenty lakh rupee, and it also has assets worth close to eighty lakhs. Each year the trustees organize a *mela* (fair) to celebrate the sacrifice of this particular goddess, and many prominent politicians and businessmen usually attend. The date set for these celebrations was 10 September in 1988, and the whole of Deorala waited to see what the state would do to intervene in the light of the Sati (Prevention) Ordinance, which had been passed after Roop Kanwar's death, and now applied to the whole of India, excluding Jammu and Kashmir, a war-torn and predominantly Muslim state in the north-east of the country.

Under pressure from women's groups, the State Government had to be seen to act. An official circular was sent to the temple authorities, quoting sections of the law, virtually banning the annual *mela* and forbidding any 'glorification of sati'. In response, the trustees of the temple – many of whom live in Calcutta – challenged these orders in the Calcutta High Court. A similar circular had been sent to all the other sati temples in Rajasthan – approximately 100 in all – but the political battleground was to be the Rani Sati Temple at Jhunjhunu, the most prominent site for sati worship during the season of celebrations and fairs that take place after the rains every year.

On 18 August 1988, the Calcutta High Court passed an interim order allowing the 'annual puja', or worship in the temple complex, scheduled for 10 September. This ruling had been made in response to a private petition filed by one of the trustees of the Jhunjhunu temple, who claimed that it was his 'ancestral place of worship'. He demanded that he and his family be allowed to hold their annual 'family puja'. Two judges sat on the bench and ruled in his favour, directing the Central Government in Delhi and the State Government in Rajasthan 'not [to] cause any interruption or harassment to visitors and devotees who may be visiting the said temple for daily worship, *sewa* and *puja* of the deities inside the temple'. The Rajasthan government appealed to the Supreme Court in Delhi, stating in their petition that this 'private' puja could create the stage for the 'glorification of sati' which was now against the law. As the lawlords debated, all eyes turned to Jhunjhunu, aware of the militant mood among the Rajputs, although it was predominantly the Banias and the Aggarwal community who attended this particular fair. The issue was no longer caste and creed but the right to worship sati.

During this time, Kalyan Singh Kalvi, the Rajput popularist leader who had made several volatile speeches in public and offered many a spirited defence of those accused of killing Roop Kanwar, gave an 'exclusive' interview to the *Illustrated Weekly of India*. Headlined 'In Defence of Sati?', the blurb in block letters said: 'Kalyan Singh Kalvi, president of the Rajasthan Janata party, leap-frogged into the national consciousness by his shocking view of sati. Sanjeev Srivastava met him recently and discovered that his views remain unchanged a year after Roop Kanwar's murder.'

Through the course of a long interview, Mr Kalvi remained defiant and contemptuous of both the government and the law:

Q: According to reports Roop Kanwar was drugged and forced to the funeral pyre with sword-wielding Rajput youths surrounding her.

A: This is all crap.

Q: Even the police case? And the large number of arrests made in this connection?

A: It [the case] is one of the biggest farces in the annals of India's legal history. Never have so many persons been arrested and charged with murder without even a shred of evidence. There is not a single eyewitness. All of them will be acquitted.

Q: Then why were they arrested?

A: To please the political masters in New Delhi. In fact, only 20 persons were initially arrested and the news was conveyed to the then Chief Minister, Harideo Joshi, who was in New Delhi at the time of these arrests. Through some mistake the state authorities conveyed to Doordarshan [State controlled TV] that 56 persons were arrested and the same was announced in the news bulletin. In the confusion that followed the authorities felt that the safest way out was to further arrest some 30-odd persons rather than send a clarification to Doordarshan. That was the manner in which the trial was conducted – by the media and certain leaders in Delhi.

Q: Which leaders and political masters are you talking about?

A: Those who have nothing to do with Hindu culture interfered the most in this affair. We shall not forgive them.

Q: Who are you talking about?

A: You know who. Sonia Gandhi, Margaret Alva and Chidambaram. None of them is a Hindu.

Q: I am not sure but I think Chidambaram is a Hindu.

A: Is that so? Then don't mention his name. In any case, the women were really responsible for all the hullabaloo.

[In reference to the dispute concerning the sati *mela* at Jhunjhunu which was still being considered by the Supreme Court, the interview continued.]

Q: Do you think sati *mela*s should be allowed?

A: I told you earlier that we should have some respect for tradition. The Jhunjhunu *mela* is held to commemorate the memory of Narayani Devi, a brave woman who was injured fighting dacoits who had killed her husband. If she mounted the funeral pyre of her husband, I would view it as a supreme sacrifice.

Q: But the anti-sati law bans any glorification of sati. Should this *mela* be allowed or not?

A: The matter is in court. But how can you change public opinion through acts and ordinances? If we don't worship a faithful woman, should we revere those who deceive their husbands and murder them?

Q: But don't you think such glorification would amount to inciting other young girls with impressionable minds to commit sati?

A: Nonsense. There have been about 30 cases of sati reported from Rajasthan in the post-Independence period. Do you think that if Kalvi decides to preach the message of sati today people will follow him? Or that if someone preaches against the practice, it would dissuade a genuine sati?

Q: But surely laws and social reform movements help?

A: Yes, but merely preaching and sermons do not. Did Gandhiji ever advocate that congressmen should become corrupt? But see the state of the party only 40 years after his death.

Q: That is surely a vague example.

A: No. You have failed to appreciate the point.

[Further on in the same interview Kalvi's motives are challenged.]

Q: It is believed that you have supported pro-sati activists only to humble the leader of the Opposition and BJP stalwart Bhairon Singh Shekhawat. You wanted to upstage him as the leader of the Rajput community.

A: It is another attempt at sidetracking the main issue. Kalyan Singh is not just any politician who speaks something but feels differently. What my head, heart and lips say is in complete co-ordination.

Q: What do you mean?

A: That I am not a hypocrite, unlike so many other politicians.

Q: Who are the hypocrites?

A: Many of them. Practically everyone thought that my political career was finished, following my statements in the wake of the Roop Kanwar incident last year. But the same people are now congratulating me for my far-sightedness in pointing out the defects in the anti-sati legislation.

Q: Why now?

A: Because so many powerful interests are associated with the Rani Sati Temple in Jhunjhunu. When their worship is stopped they feel the pinch. Many of them are Congress leaders.

Q: Can you name them?
A: Why should I? They will themselves come out in the open sooner or later. Their number is in the hundreds. That is all I can tell you now.

In the months that followed, Kalvi was indeed to supersede his opponent, Bhairon Singh Shekhawat and, on the strength of his power base within the Rajput community, eventually become a cabinet minister in the Central Government, under the leadership of Chandra Shekhar's coalition, which replaced Rajiv Gandhi's government after Congress were defeated at the polls. It was a turbulent time for the country as a whole. Kalvi's allegations about ministerial involvement in the Jhunjhunu affair were difficult to challenge. For instance, it was well known that the State Governor who signed the Sati (Prevention) Ordinance on 1 October 1987, Vasant Dada Patil, had himself been the chief guest of the fair that year.

By early September 1988, the Supreme Court had upheld the Calcutta High Court's decision to allow worship within the Jhunjhunu temple but ruled against the *mela* usually held in the grounds outside. It was a somewhat vague ruling, allowing worship but not celebration, adding that there should be no *chunari* ceremony – offerings of veils to the deity – during such worship, as this was a symbol of sati celebration. Somewhat confused, the authorities watched as hundreds and then thousands of pilgrims began pouring into the small temple town. Reporters representing various national dailies also converged on the scene. A report published in the *Telegraph*, a Calcutta-based newspaper, gives just one example of the atmosphere at Jhunjhunu:

Undeterred by the risks of being implicated in court cases, the temple trustees are making all possible efforts to make Saturday's fair the usual big show. Loudspeakers fitted all over the complex blare out bhajans in praise of Rani Sati. At the entrance, the temple notice board displays the order of the Supreme Court passed in the appeal against the Calcutta High Court verdict. The massive complex has been given a facelift.

Bedrolls, cots, bedsheets are also being piled up. Over two hundred labourers have been brought to the temple from Bhagalpur for help. A large kitchen has been set up where about 50 cooks are busy cooking throughout the day. Meals are available for the guest house occupants at the rate of eight rupees per head. (The temple complex includes some 400 rooms it rents out.) A special shamiana (festive tent) has been erected where about 500 people can eat at a time. Snack stalls provide South Indian dishes and tea and coffee round the clock.

Several journalists noted that although a police *chowki* – a temporary checkpost hastily assembled – had been set up in the road leading to the fairground entrance, constables stood around watching from a distance while chants of *Rani Sati ki jai* rose from the open courtyards of the temple and filled the air. This in turn led to the chanting of slogans in the grounds outside. The temple trustees had won the battle.

Greatly encouraged by this turn of events, Roop Kanwar's father-in-law, Sumer Singh, backed by the *Samiti* in Deorala, announced he would be 'honouring' his daughter-in-law's death anniversary by conducting daily recitals from the *Bhagavadgita*. Insisting it was a 'family puja' in compliance with the law, he added that all devotees and supporters of his family were welcome. Begun in the week leading up to 22 September, the move was clearly calculated to attract a crowd, which it did. Once again, hundreds flocked to the village. While women protesters petitioned the courts in Jaipur and Delhi, the Rajput community celebrated Roop Kanwar's first death anniversary in Deorala. Neither the police nor the civil authorities intervened and no one was held responsible for this flagrant flouting of the law.

As a result of this and the Jhunjhunu *mela*, as well as the release on bail of all those accused of Roop Kanwar's murder, Deorala closed ranks. Only pilgrims were welcome. The hostility towards journalists and activists from women's groups who visited from time to time was so severe that any form of meaningful investigation seemed impossible.

Sumer Singh and his sons had become local heros within the tradition of 'valour' in Rajasthan. The doctor, Magan Singh, shut down his practice as his licence had been withdrawn pending his trial, and he spent much of his time with relatives in Jaipur, remaining elusive in relation to the press. Sumer Singh, however, supported by Kalyan Singh Kalvi and members of the *Samiti*, toured various parts of the country, including Bombay, in an attempt to muster public support. The publicity that followed added to the group's political clout in the village.

Not a single dissenting voice was heard within Deorala. Those who had been arrested were all well connected. Among them were the village pandit, Babulal, the village barber, Bansi Nai and the woodcutter, Bodu Khati. The barber had been called in to shave Maal Singh's head and body before the funeral on 4 September 1987, and was seen by the courts as a key witness because of his proximity to the family and the dead man in the hours preceding the ceremonial walk to the pyre that day. Bodu Khati had supplied the wood for the pyre and was said to have responded swiftly when asked to provide more as the flames began to dwindle. He was said to have rushed to an adjoining field and cut long sheaves of dry grass to rekindle the fire before adding more logs to the pile. This made him a potential accomplice in the eyes of the law. The family priest, Babulal, had presided over religious rituals, chanting prayers while Roop Kanwar burned to death. He too had been charged as an accomplice. All these men, including the doctor who came and went from the village, were well-known figures whose families had lived there for generations. They interacted with everyone – or at any rate with everyone who mattered – mostly landlords and wealthy farmers who could afford to pay for firewood, a professional shave or the services of a priest.

Deorala is a relatively prosperous village. It is dominated by Rajputs, and lower-caste families make up a tiny minority. Traditionally, they have been subservient to the will of high-caste men and their families, working at menial lowly paid jobs in people's homes as sweepers, or in the fields as seasonal labourers. It can safely be assumed that they were too scared or intimidated to speak out, and we will probably never know for certain what they heard or witnessed at the time. Their lives in the village would not have been worth living had they indulged in even a passing conversation with outsiders. They too had learned to shun the press and women who visited from the city.

It was inevitable that as time passed and other issues attracted the attention of the media, public interest began to fade. A handful of activists from women's groups kept up some pressure and petitions and counter-petitions lay suspended in the legal system, as did the trial of those arrested. Thirty-two people had been charged, including two minors whose cases were transferred to the Juvenile Court in Jaipur. The rest were to be tried by the Additional District and Sessions Court in the small, dusty town of Neem-ka-Thana, not far from the Deorala. Prosecution lawyers were seeking to transfer the case to a more cosmopolitan centre because Neem-ka-Thana was located in a Rajput strong-hold, steeped in traditional values, where a communal fun-damentalism was on the rise and witnesses could be easily intimidated.

At the end of 1988, I was in London working on a script for a film which had finally cleared the various hurdles of government permission in India. Deadlines were tight, and I knew I had to concentrate on the work in hand and put all else out of my mind. I filed away a pile of press-clippings at the time, thinking that one day I would like to visit Deorala and travel in Rajasthan, to try to understand this terrible, brutal legacy women had inherited in the country of my birth. In school, as a child in Calcutta, I remembered that the nuns had told us sati had been abolished by the British, opening up the way for social reform – just as they had built the railways – bringing progress and development. Nothing more was taught on the subject.

The script I was writing was based on the life of Phoolan Devi, a low-caste village woman from Uttar Pradesh, who had been systematically abused and gang raped by high-caste men. In 1981, she made international headlines when, having joined forces with a band of rural bandits, she was accused of murdering twenty-two such men as an act of retribution. Her life too was full of almost unbelievable tales of oppression, and in trying to understand her experience, I had become aware of the alarming rise in acts of violence against women all over India. Both Roop Kanwar and Phoolan Devi, in completely different ways, had focused the glare of international publicity on the position of women in India, creating a horrifying portrait of the country.

Tens of thousands of women in India die each year, mostly soaked in kerosene by their husbands or in-laws and then set alight. Those who survive live with hideous scars. Commonly referred to as 'victims of dowry deaths', they have become stat-istics. So have the tens of thousands of girl babies killed each year, often by their own mothers, simply because they were not boys. Considered a lifelong burden, their lives are easily snuffed at birth or soon afterwards, and the authorities rarely intervene. Among the middle classes, female infanticide has also become increasingly common in the form of abortions, following scans that detect the sex of the unborn child. That too has become big business in towns and cities, with unscrupulous doctors making vast fortunes. It is a complete cycle of violence and oppression – from birth to death – and women themselves seem to have helped perpetuate this practice in the name of religion and tradition. Many have seen their own lives as not worth living, and have tried to spare their daughters from a similar fate.

CHAPTER FIVE

In the years that followed Roop Kanwar's death I worked on various projects, mostly as a researcher on documentaries for British television. Although some of this work took me back to India – and to parts of Rajasthan – there was never enough time or money to travel to Deorala. It remained a thought for the future. As I continued to gather all the material I could around the idea, I knew I needed a publisher in order to get an advance payment. That would enable me to travel in India again, alone this time, in an attempt to understand the full complexity of the tyrannical hierarchy in a country that was fast moving from a secular philosophical base towards a frighteningly fundamentalist one in which women were brutalized, maimed and killed in increasing numbers each year. It was not that their voices had not been heard, or their experiences highlighted from time to time – case histories and interviews in the press and in feminist magazines had become commonplace – but mostly such women remained nameless, faceless and powerless, enslaved by generations of oppression.

There are, of course, powerful exceptions to the rule, but these are educated women who only make up less than ten per cent of the total population. Many less-privileged women are being killed ritually, both at random and systematically, and India has now reached the point where there are more men than women. 917 women to every 1000 men was the ratio I last saw on a sheet of government statistics. Multiply that by 1 billion and that makes and enormous gap. As a consequence of this gender imbalance, sexual crimes against women – rape, gang rapes and child molestation – too are on the increase. The more I read about all this, the more depressing and horrifying it became. After all, I too was an 'Indian Woman', and beneath the skin-surface, the class-surface, lay the reality of powerlessness against the will of men. I had felt this helplessness more in relation to race in Britain, rather than in terms of gender as a child or teenager in India, but the feeling of vulnerability was the same.

Having come to England in 1965 for personal rather than economic reasons, the sudden shock of living in a rabidly racist society was like a slap in the face. I had never met such English or white people in India. Those who knew my parents there had a genuine affection for the country. Some – like my own paternal grandmother – had married Indians and stayed on after independence. Others simply stayed on under a new order. The landlords, employers and other people I came across in London were nothing like them. Theirs was a world in which I fast became aware of the ever-present threat of violence. So in some ways, I wanted to understand my own past, my own failed marriage and subsequent love affairs with men – colonised men, traditional men – through exploring my heritage.

My preoccupation with the subject of female oppression in India grew, and then in the winter of 1993, I received a letter from Adam, a friend living in the small mountain town of Kodaikanal in south India. He asked if I had heard about 'Selvi's accident' and said she was still in hospital, in a 'bad state'. He mentioned burns and kerosene without explaining the circumstances of the incident. I remember feeling chilled as I read and reread those words. I tried to tell myself not to jump to conclusions. Most people who live on low incomes in India cook on kerosene stoves, and accidents are common. A great-aunt of mine had once been badly scarred that way years ago, having turned her back on the lit stove that stood about a foot high on the marble kitchen floor. She had bent down to pick up something, and the back of her sari had caught fire within seconds, engulfing her in flames. I remember visiting her in hospital in

Calcutta with my mother when I was about seven, and I never forgot the iron cage that surrounded her body, which was covered by a white sheet. She lay in that state for several months, in great agony, but she eventually recovered. Another aunt, married to my mother's cousin, had killed herself in a state of alcoholic depression. She had thrown kerosene all over herself and lit a match. This aunt had been a singer of classical Bengali music. She had recorded songs by Tagore and performed at concerts, but suddenly – or perhaps over a number of years – stopped feeling that life was worth living. I didn't know her very well but heard from other members of my family that she had been the victim of an unhappy marriage. Suicide too was commonplace in connection with kerosene. I imagined Selvi in all these situations and decided to call Adam.

There was no answer so I reread his letter and thought of Maria Selvi and Kodaikanal – known as Kodai for short – and Adam, the English painter who had moved there permanently many years ago, leaving a well-paid, professional job behind him in England. My thoughts revolved around Selvi and the way I'd seen her last. She had been warm and generous, supportive and understanding at a time when I'd been at a low emotional ebb. We had laughed and shed tears together, walked through the steep slopes of the hill-market, and confided our fears and doubts to each other. Although Selvi had worked for me from time to time as a 'servant', we had become close. She would cook wonderful south Indian lunches while I sat trying to write, hoping the mountain mists would bring some inspiration. They didn't, but I looked forward to her visits and we often ate together on the sunlit porch, exchanging local gossip and points of view.

Selvi told me that she had been married by arrangement to a man more or less her own age when she was in her late twenties, and that she had a daughter called Ramya – a shy and withdrawn child of about five at the time. She and her husband didn't get on. He was unemployed and drank heavily, she said, while she did as many part-time jobs as she could find. Kodai was a seasonal town, as many mountain resorts are, and for much of the year there was little work. The focus of her life was her daughter, whom she wanted to educate well, knowing that an education and financial independence could give her some status in life beyond the clutches of men. This was about all I knew of her life at the time. I had heard gossip about Selvi's 'loose morals' and 'avarice' from others, but also knew that she was hard-working in a way that was inspirational to me; a survivor pained by the shadows of the past. Her reputation, I thought, probably came from the fact that she was quite beautiful, with velvet-smooth skin and dark eyes almost the same colour, which lit up with mischief and laughter when we discussed local scandals. Some mornings she had come to work in tears, her daughter in tow, swearing she had had enough of her husband. As the hours passed, she would calm down, seeming to gain strength just from being away from her own environment, and then she would return to her husband in a defiant mood. She took pride in her appearance, and always looked immaculate in a variety of lovely, soft-flowing saris which made her look much more affluent than she was. She had a real passion for clothes. I had never met her husband but had heard that he was exactly as she described him. Over the years, Selvi and I kept in touch, and exchanged greeting cards for Diwali or Christmas or Pongal, the Tamil New Year. I realized I had not heard from her at all that year.

After several attempts, I finally got through to Adam on a crackly line. He said he only had second-hand information through his neighbour, a mutual friend for whom Selvi worked from time to time. From what he could gather, there had been an argument and Selvi's husband had set her on fire. She had run to her parents' home a few yards down the steep hill on which she lived, her sari ablaze, the flames fuelled by the wind. Her younger brother, Gilson, had thrown a blanket over her and rolled her on the floor to extinguish the fire. She was now in a local clinic, badly burned but alive; no longer in a life-threatening situation; afraid to report the matter to the police. Skin grafts would be necessary. She needed money. I asked about her face and Adam said, 'That's OK. She was attacked from behind.'

It was not until the spring of 1996 that I saw Selvi again. I had been commissioned to research a series of six documentaries for Channel Four television in London. My brief was to look for 'strong, successful role models in India', women who 'defied the victim image' of Indian women. I had travelled in the north and then worked my way south, ending up in Kodaikanal on a beautiful morning in early March. No trains or planes ply that route so I had taken the overnight 'Deluxe Bus' from Bangalore, about a twelve-hour journey. The mixture of mist, sun and rain makes the last stretch unpredictable in terms of journey time, as the bus slows down to an unsteady jolting pace, puffing its way up the winding mountain road, past landslides and roadworks, blasting its horn round dangerous-looking bends. The oncoming traffic seems to whizz past at great speed on the downhill run. Adam and Selvi would both be expecting me.

I had a window seat, and stayed awake most of the night, aware of the young man in the seat next to me, who was flirtatious and eager to talk, full of questions. A lascivious grin spread across his face when I lit a cigarette. Somewhat nervous of his hands, that seemed to wander in his sleep, and his head, that kept hitting my shoulder from time to time, I'd kept alert. At dawn, the bus stopped for about half an hour at a small, dusty market town called Batlagundu (a name that has never ceased to amuse me, for some reason) before starting on the mountain climb. I'd done this journey many times before, and knew that the breakfast in the noisy, bustling south Indian café would be good; steaming *idlis* and *vadas*, *sambar* with drumsticks and fresh-ground coffee. The 'Women's Latrine', as the sign read, had to be avoided at all costs. An innocent-looking doorway, painted white and red, led into an open dumping ground of human waste. High walls surrounded the yard in which people squatted wherever they wished. The sight of bare bottoms, and the stench of the place, swarming with flies, first thing in the morning, definitely had to be avoided. One had to learn the art of controlling both bowels and bladder on such journeys.

As the bus chugged up the mountain, I watched the changing

landscape with fascination and a feeling of elation. After the heat of the plains, it was wonderful to feel the air cool and thin, as memories and images of times past whirled through my head. We passed the fruit belt and the coffee belt as we rose upwards into the mists that engulf Kodai. The man next to me had given up all attempts at conversation after I'd yelled at him in the early hours of the morning, telling him to keep his hands to himself in front of a busload of sleepy passengers. He'd looked confused and offended, and then looked away. We didn't speak again and at the café in Batlagundu we sat, pointedly, at separate tables.

When we finally pulled into the narrow, winding streets that lead to the bus station in Kodai, I noticed how run-down everything had begun to look in the last few years. Busloads of tourists from the plains had taken their toll. Plastic bags, soft-drink cartons, abandoned newspaper wrappings and empty biscuit packets littered the hillside, and the mix of engine oil and mud on the streets around the bus station made walking through slippery sludge with a heavy suitcase a risky feat of navigation and balance.

A local taxi-driver I knew recognized me and came to my rescue, helping with the suitcase. We drove straight to Adam's place, to Roseneath, a vast and beautiful forest enclave of four bungalows spread over some five acres, and protected from tourists by a network of log fences and tall impenetrable shrubs, not to mention dogs who moved in a pack against all strangers. I had arranged to rent the small bungalow next to Adam's, whose tenant lived in Bombay and only came up once a year for the season, which began in May or June. Roseneath belonged to the church, and all who lived on it were tenants, including Miss Roberts, who managed the property and chose the tenants. An Australian missionary who had worked as a nurse in India throughout the Second World War, Miss Roberts was now almost ninety. As she grew more frail, she relied more and more on Adam, who had become the unofficial manager over the years because of the work he put into the place on a voluntary basis. He kept the grassy slopes trim and the vegetable patches growing, checked the water levels each day in the sump Miss Roberts had designed to hold rain water, generally fixed things when they went wrong and kept a watchful eye on the place. In summer, Adam also supervised local fruit-pickers who came to gather pears and plums that were either sold or converted into jams and wines by those who lived on the compound. An idyllic place in many ways, Roseneath was where I had first met Selvi and where she still worked for a friend who lived in one of the larger bungalows. I knew she had recovered and was back on her feet, but little else.

Stiff from the bus journey and generally exhausted by the travelling up north, it was a great relief to sit in the sun drinking fresh south Indian coffee in Adam's semi-wild garden as he spoke of mutual friends and recent events. He told me Selvi would come at around nine that morning, after dropping Ramya off at school. He added, 'She's eager to talk to you. I think some sort of deal was made with the husband and she now lives alone and he keeps away.' I sat in silence, formulating questions in my mind as Adam helped move my stuff into the bungalow next door, which would be my home for the next month or so.

Full of smiles and laughter, Selvi suddenly arrived a few minutes later looking radiant. We hugged each other, exchanged words as we embraced, and then I stood back to look at her, reaching out for her hand. She withdrew a few paces, her right hand wrapped in the folds of her sari. Her expression changed in a second as she lowered her eyes and said in a voice full of sorrow, 'It is so ugly. I feel so ashamed when people look at it.'

'Your hand?' I asked. 'Let me see it. Does it hurt?' She shook her head and slowly withdrew her hand from her sari to hold it out towards me. It was a shocking sight. Badly mutilated. The little finger had gone, melted down, and only a tiny stub remained. The rest was a mass of scars, a roughly healed network of black skin and pink flesh without the pigment. I still had my hand extended but was afraid to touch hers.

'It's all right,' she said. 'It doesn't hurt. In fact, I can't even feel parts of it.' As I ran my fingers gingerly over and around her hand she said, 'This is nothing, Ma, when we go inside I will show you the rest. Now don't worry. I am so happy to see you.' I saw her struggling with tears, trying to regain her smile, so I turned away, my throat tight, and offered her some coffee. We sat in the sun for a while after Adam returned but Selvi, who used to love the sun, shifted as it moved through the clouds, keeping to the shadows of trees and bushes. Her skin got 'overheated' in the sun these days, she said, despite the chill in the air. She preferred to be indoors.

Adam handed me the keys to my bungalow, which I had not even seen the inside of yet, and a flask of coffee, saying he was going into town later – a ten-minute walk down the hill – and could get me what I needed for the day. The walk back up the steep hill was hard going, and I usually took a taxi back. Selvi immediately offered to do any household shopping I needed. Overwhelmed by their warmth and generosity of spirit, I was glad to be away from London. I was glad to be in India. Glad to be in Kodaikanal.

Once indoors, Selvi lifted her sari, and I saw that the whole of her lower body, from both legs all the way up to her midriff, was in a terrible mess. The backs of her knees had not healed in over two years and oozed a sticky, watery substance. Her explanation was that as she had to walk everywhere, uphill and downhill every day, the scar-tissue had no time to heal – and never would unless she could afford to pay privately for skin grafts at a hospital in Madras. That would cost at least 35,000 rupees and she earned less than 400 a month. She could not afford it, and said she had learned to live with her wounds.

Apart from the part-time job Selvi had with Adam's neighbour, Navroz, whom she was extremely fond of, and whose children she had helped to raise, she had no other work. 'The children have grown up and left home, Madam is in America and Master is not here so much.' Renowned for her ability to cook 'European' food, having worked for white teachers at the International School – the central focus and largest employer of the town – she could no longer get a job. I asked why. 'Because when they see my hand, they don't want me to touch their food. They think it is ugly and dirty.' There was no self-pity in her voice, no tears in her eyes as she added in a practical tone, 'I too think it ugly. Not dirty, Ma, but ugly. People think ugly and dirty same thing. No?' I nodded and then shrugged.

To relieve the tension of emotion and painful realities, Selvi proceeded to inspect the kitchen as I followed her through the two rooms. She had worked for Nelam too (the tenant who lived in Bombay) and knew the bungalow well. She knew where everything was and how the combination of plugs and wires worked. There was gas in the cylinder and plenty of pots and pans so the kitchen was declared functional. I watched her take pride and gain strength from her own brisk efficiency, and felt overwhelmed by her warmth and courage. Next to the kitchen was a beautiful semi-enclosed section. Half the wall was an open window with no glass pane, just a sheet of transparent plastic rolled up like a blind outside and tied with string. 'Use this when it rains,' she said, adding, 'only if the rain is coming inside. All depends on the wind.' I nodded again, having understood the mechanics of the kitchen and the 'sun-room' as we came to call it. Outside, the landscape was lush and the sound of birds, frogs and insects gave the day a sense of pace and the passing of time as they emerged and used the surrounding space at specific times each day and night, giving a rhythm to the natural order of things.

I invited Selvi to share Adam's flask of coffee with me and to tell me about friends I hadn't yet met. Kodai is a small hill town where most people know each other. I pulled out a wicker chair for her in the sun-room and sank into another. She continued standing. When I asked her why, she said it was painful to sit. She could stand or lie flat in relative comfort but sitting down was painful. 'Like the back of my knees,' she said. 'It's like that, what to do?' I suggested alternatives. There was a divan in the adjoining room where she could lie down, or we could try padding the chair with pillows. She chose the latter saying, 'No sun in there, Ma. Very cold. Neelam not been here since last year.

Tomorrow we build one fire in that room. Take out the damp. You ask Adam for wood.' The pillows on the chair seemed to work and as we drank coffee she told me about the economic hardships of her life.

I told her I was working on another possible film project about 'successful' women, but really wanted to write a book about something else. I asked if I could tell her story in my book, once I was able to raise some money to work on it. Meanwhile, I could pay her by the hour or day to interview her. She laughed and said, 'I will tell you anything you want to know for your book for *no* money! I want to work here in Roseneath. I will cook and you will write!' We both laughed and she said, taking charge once again, 'Tomorrow, Sunday, I will bring Ramya and come here. I will make *idli* in my house – you have no steamer in this kitchen. Then I will buy *dal* from market – give me ten rupees – then we will start using this kitchen.' She proceeded to tell me that she knew all the shopkeepers and would get things much cheaper than I could. 'We will save money,' she stated emphatically.

In the days and weeks that followed, Selvi came every day and we talked for hours, often with a tape recorder running. She wanted to tell her story, but was also afraid of the backlash. She had decided not to prosecute her husband because she was afraid of his vengeance, especially if he had been on a drinking spree, a common occurrence in her experience. About the local police she said, 'You have to have money – big money – no point otherwise. They only work for bribes and my husband's family can pay them more than I can.' Her family had negotiated a 'deal' with his family after the 'accident'. It had been agreed that no complaint would be made if he kept away from Selvi, Ramya and Kodaikanal. Selvi had not seen her husband since the night he had tried to kill her. She wanted to keep it that way.

As Selvi unravelled her tale to me, I took notes at first, then decided to run my Walkman in order to keep pace with her fluctuating emotions of anger, sorrow and despair, leavened with laughter.

CHAPTER SIX

On my second day in Kodaikanal, Selvi came as planned with her daughter, Ramya, who looked even more withdrawn and shy than I had remembered. She had witnessed the attack on her mother and had not seen her father since the night of the 'accident', the term Selvi used whenever she referred to the incident that had changed her life. Unwrapping the perfectly shaped *idli*s she had steamed at home, Selvi was exceptionally well dressed that day, in a pale lavender sari with a fern-like print, a green blouse to match and fresh flowers in her neatly plaited hair, pinned in a loop at the nape of her neck, in a style that is the hallmark of women from south India. She had done the shopping and brought me a string of flowers too, for my hair, which hung loose and somewhat dishevelled at that hour of the morning. A gift, I realized, as she carefully counted out the change and accounted for my ten rupees spent on *dal*, some mustard seeds and a handful of red chillies.

As Selvi set about reorganizing the kitchen, I looked at Ramya, dressed in her Sunday best, leaning against the kitchen door, observing her mother in silence and throwing the odd glance at me. I tried to converse with the child but she just hung her head in a coy fashion, wide eyed, as she twisted strands of her short, bobbed hair into the corners of her mouth. I couldn't get a word out of her so decided to do something useful myself by clearing up the rest of the place, emptying ashtrays, dusting down wood surfaces, aware of her eyes firmly fixed on my movements as an uneasy silence prevailed. Selvi interjected by telling Ramya to go out and look for Bonnie, one of the two puppies Adam had recently acquired. The other one was called Clyde. 'Bonnie is the only one she is not afraid of,' she said to me. I wondered if she meant among the dogs in the compound or people in general.

Having put the *dal* on to boil, Selvi said she could now get down to telling me what had happened that night sixteen months ago. She didn't want to speak about it in front of her daughter and said we should switch to something else when Ramya returned. I told her I understood and we moved to the sun-room. As I put a tape in my Walkman and attached an external microphone, I saw her adjust herself and her sari as if she were about to appear on TV or have her photograph taken. I couldn't help being amused as I told her to try and ignore the machine; it was only for my own record, to help me remember details, something she could play back and listen to herself. I played her a track from a popular Hindi film I'd been listening to on the bus and gave her the headphones. She relaxed but as soon as the novelty of that wore off and I sat down opposite, asking her to describe the night of the 'accident', she regained her formal posture, adjusting the pleats of her sari, straightening her back.

The language Selvi spoke to me in was a kind of local patois, descriptive, blunt and dramatic but I've decided to transcribe the meaning of her words into standard English so as not to distract the reader from the trauma of her experience. Selvi's first and natural language is Tamil, of which I speak no more than a few words and understand even less when it is spoken rapidly, as it normally is. An ancient Dravidian language with roots of its own, Tamil is completely different from the languages of north India, where I had grown up through the school and college years.

Selvi began to speak in a barely audible voice, in sharp contrast to her usual, confident tone. 'It was 27 November 1993, around seven-thirty in the evening. There was to be an "ear-ring cere-mony" in my elder brother's house. It was for his son who was three years old that day ...' She drew a deep breath and paused, so I asked what an ear-ring ceremony signified. She didn't know.

It was an old ritual of celebration within the family. 'I had been dressed and ready to leave since five, Ma,' she continued. 'My husband knew I had offered to help Raja's wife, my sister-in-law, with the cooking and other arrangements for welcoming the guests. He had promised Raja that we would go over early and that he would help with other things – like carrying extra chairs they had borrowed from neighbours for the occasion. He knew this was an important day for my family.'

By now I had lapsed into silence, concentrating on the details of her story, aware that she was no longer self-conscious about the silently spooling tape. She took another deep breath and went on, 'I can't tell you how I managed to pass those two hours, Ma. Walking, walking. Up and down, between the two rooms of my house, getting more and more angry. When he finally walked in, soon after seven, I said, "Where have you been? You said we would go at five. Look at the time!" Then I saw he was drunk, and this made me even more angry. We shouted at each other, both very angry. When he threw a metal tumbler on the kitchen floor, still shouting, I decided to keep quiet. I didn't want him to hit me – something he had done many times before – and I didn't want him to break anything either! I remember sitting down on the corner of the bed with my back to him. I was looking outside through the open door and saw it was getting dark. We were very late and I didn't want to take him to Raja's house drunk. This is what I was thinking, Ma, and for some minutes it became very quiet. Then I felt something wet near my ankles – like water. I put my hand back, without turning around, and felt the wet edge of my sari. Before I had time to think, I felt this burning sensation and saw the fire rising, upwards, towards my face ...' I saw tears well up in her eyes as she paused to regain her composure. After a few seconds she continued, 'I remember rushing towards the bucket of water I always keep in the kitchen – you see, we have no tap water so I bring water from the pump in the road below our house every day – but he pushed me hard and kicked the bucket over. I remember running out of the house with this terrible fire all around me. I ran to my mother's house.

My brother, Gilson, threw a blanket around me and was rolling with me on the floor. Everyone looked shocked and no one said anything. When the fire was out, I looked at myself and started screaming. I was naked. The nylon sari I was wearing had been reduced to nothing and my skin looked like burned fish skin, with pink flesh showing here and there. Nobody moved. They were all staring at me in shock. Then I remember them all shouting at each other.

'Nobody was doing anything to help me. I remember getting up and grabbing Gilson's *lungi* from the washing line outside the house to cover myself, and then running as fast as I could to the hospital, near the lake. Nobody followed me. I was thinking, "I'm going to die. What will happen to Ramya?" These thoughts made me run faster. I knew my face and head were all right but everywhere else was – I don't know how to tell you, Ma, like this ...' she said, holding her arms up above her head and making a hissing sound. She had third-degree burns that covered more than half of her body.

The 'hospital' Selvi had run to, barefoot and half-naked, wrapped in her brother's *lungi*, was a free clinic run by a lone doctor with few facilities. She had been there before for routine ailments and knew his one-room establishment next to the lake beyond the town centre would still be open. 'Don't write anything bad about this doctor, Ma,' she said. 'He was very good to me and I don't know what I would have done without him. He made me lie down on a bed and I saw him rushing around, very shocked. He was trying to put a needle in my arm but couldn't find any place on either side, he said, so he had to put it in my left foot. A tube was attached to that and a bag of liquid on a stand hung over my head. He gave me some tablets to swallow. That's all I can remember about that night, Ma.'

A friend of mine and Selvi's part-time employer, Navroz, who lived in the bungalow below Adam's and whose children Selvi had helped raise, visited her the next day, having heard of the incident. He recalled, many years later, that it had been a horrendous sight. The Kurinju Clinic, named after the rare and beautiful mountain flower that only blooms once in every twelve years was, in reality, a dingy basement room. 'She was just lying there, face down on an unclean bed, covered with a filthy-looking *lungi*,' he said. 'Apart from the drip she was attached to, the only treatment she had received was the sprinkling of some silverish powder all over her body, a local remedy for minor burns, I think. She was in much pain and in a state of shock. She was alone, the sole patient in this room that looked as if it hadn't been swept in weeks, with not a single nurse in sight. It was hard to look at her.'

Selvi went on to describe the next few weeks as a struggle between life and death, being in states of consciousness that fluctuated between nightmares and reality, always aware of the terrible agony that consumed her body. She couldn't remember if visits and conversations were real or imagined. She had to lie on her stomach all the time, not even able to turn sideways, never sitting up because the burns that covered her back were so severe. When people spoke to her, she heard their voices but faced the floor that surrounded her *charpai* – a sagging, rickety cot of coarse woven jute, as she recalled, with sparse bedding and a very thin, lumpy mattress. When her arms, also badly burned, strayed to the edges of the cot in her sleep, she would awake with the shock of pain, as the prickly jute rubbed against her wounds. 'This lasted for about five months, Ma,' she said, looking wistfully out of the window, as if trying to calculate the length of time she had endured this terrible ordeal.

As Selvi spoke, tears filled her eyes from time to time but she wiped them away with the edge of her sari with quick, almost impatient gestures, as if annoyed by her own emotions. I could find no adequate words of comfort so remained mostly silent, struggling to remain calm and unemotional myself. When she paused, having relived that night, I stopped the tape and instinctively rose to embrace her. As I put my arm around her shoulder, saying something foolish like, 'Don't worry. It's all over now . . .' she burst into tears and wept with the intensity of a child. It was impossible to hold back my own tears by now, as I knelt down beside her and held her with a firmer grip. I wanted to do something, anything that would help heal her grief but realized there was little anyone could do to blot out the memory of such pain. Besides, it was not 'all over' at all. She couldn't find a regular job and felt like a social outcast, trying to hold her head high amid the gossip that surrounded her in the town where she had been born. In Selvi's world, a woman who is abused or abandoned by her husband is viewed with deep suspicion. It is generally assumed that she is to blame, that she must have 'provoked' the man in one way or another. Rumour and gossip run rife, and Selvi lived in that shadow. I realized this was partly why she was always so careful about her appearance and projected a kind of confidence that many took for arrogance. In reality, she felt deeply insecure and vulnerable, torn between anger and despair, trying to put on a bold front for the sake of her own self-image.

As she regained her composure, she said that she wanted to check if the *dal* was properly cooked and to add the spices. I said I would have a quick bath and get dressed. It was well past noon, and the sun-baked room felt warm and comfortable after a cold damp night, which I had passed weighed down by heavy blankets, listening to the sound of persistent rain hitting the tin roof.

Back in the bedroom, the air felt chilly. The bed was still unmade and my clothes were scattered all around my open suitcase. I decided to skip the bath and sort out the room instead before lunch. Heating water for a bath was a lengthy process and would take about an hour, providing there was electricity. Power cuts were frequent, as was water shortage. In order to heat bath water, the naked metal rod of an immersion heater had to be hung inside a plastic bucket, and I had to remember not to touch the water, as one does habitually to test its temperature, in order to avoid electrocution. Thinking of Selvi and all she had told me, I felt quite exhausted as I started unpacking. I too had experienced something of the vengeance, violence and selfishness of quick-tempered, self-absorbed men, but nothing that could possibly compare with what she had endured. Was it just a question of degree? This question haunted me for years to come.

When I returned to the kitchen, dressed for the day with my hair put up in a bun, Selvi promptly picked up the string of jasmine she had kept fresh in a saucer of shallow water and proceeded to pin the flowers around the nape of my neck. Her mood had changed, and she looked calm and confident once more, the natural smile of warmth and affection back in her eyes. Ramya was sitting on the steps that led to the back garden with Bonnie, Adam's playful Alsatian puppy, whom she was trying to entice into a game, scratching swirling patterns in the dust with a twig. I noticed the care with which she had been dressed for the day. A pink ribbon in her hair complemented the colours of her freshly starched frock, knee-high white socks and shiny black plastic shoes. I complimented her on her appearance and asked if they had been to church that morning, knowing that Selvi's family had converted to Christianity some generations earlier. Before Ramya could reply, Selvi intervened and said, 'Church? No, Ma, I never go to church. Even the priests make money from the poor!' We both laughed, and I chased Bonnie into the living room as she darted past, to stop her from ripping up the floor.

I had strict instructions from Adam not to let any of the dogs into the house. Neelam, he told me, had had the floor covered with wall-to-wall rush matting at great expense, and he was responsible for the upkeep of the place, having negotiated the deal for me. She didn't normally sub-let the bungalow, and had left things the way she expected to find them on her return, everything neatly in its place, sparse but elegant. Interesting wall-hangings, several colourful cotton-covered cushions, a divan and two white wicker chairs next to the old-fashioned funnel-furnace which released smoke from the woodfire into the night air through a pipe connected to the tin roof, keeping the room warmer than an open logfire. It was an elementary form of central heating, introduced by the missionaries who had inhabited the bungalows in the years gone by. Temperatures dropped sharply after the sun went down. I needed to get some wood.

Having chased Bonnie back into the garden, we sat down to

lunch. Selvi tried to cajole and prompt her daughter into reciting English nursery rhymes but she ate in silence, glancing at me from time to time, a solemn expression on her face, distrust in her eyes.

Chapter Seven

At around ten each morning, I found myself looking forward to Selvi's arrival. She would take Ramya to school and then turn up at more or less the same time every day, depending on what else she had to do. Most days she cooked and we had lunch together, after which she left to collect her daughter again in the mid-afternoon. It was obvious that she felt relaxed and secure at Roseneath. She knew all the tenants as well as all those who worked for them, but seemed particularly fond of Miss Roberts's gardener, Susai, a weather-beaten old man, his face furrowed by age. With his *lungi* hitched up to his knees, whatever the weather, he wandered around in a world of his own, digging up weeds, constructing new flower beds, repairing fences or building new ones. From time to time, I heard them talking, animatedly in fast-flowing Tamil. I always wondered what they spoke about but never got round to asking. Selvi seemed to be in her element with him.

I liked the old man too. His face seemed to reflect a quiet and deep understanding of life. It was obvious that he had had much experience of its hardships but he kept his own counsel for the most part. I used to observe him with mixed feelings of affection and amusement. For instance, when it rained, he used a large plastic bag, much like a bin-liner, cut along one side to serve as a makeshift raincoat, which he hung from his head, sticking to the self-imposed routine of his work on the compound, seemingly oblivious of the fact that he was getting drenched anyway, as the plastic flapped around him in the wind. He became a regular visitor at the back door, and Selvi always made him a cup of tea or coffee mid-morning, tracking me down wherever I was on the compound to ask if I wanted one too. I felt the harmony of Roseneath myself, enjoying the casual way in which people came and went: unexpected friends or local traders selling various kinds of local produce, from avocados to firewood. Susai took it upon himself to leave me bundles of kindling he had gathered on the grounds. He never said a word about it, but simply added to the small pile I collected myself and kept under the shelter of the front veranda. Every now and then I would notice that the pile had grown, which meant that I had a steady supply of dry twigs without making any effort myself. It was a tranquil, almost magical atmosphere. Roseneath had a definite rhythm of its own, fenced off from the public and from the motorcycles that roared up and down the hill beyond its boundaries. Adam referred to Susai as the 'Garden Gnome'!

'What did your husband do that night, after he had set you on fire?' I asked Selvi soon after our first long talk about the 'accident'.

'He fled from the house, I'm told. No one knows where he went. Probably spent the night in the village below, drinking. He must have been frightened by what he had done. I know he took the first bus down to the plains – to Trichy – the next morning. A friend of his told me.' I asked if she had seen or heard from him since. She said he had returned a month later and visited her at the Kurinju Clinic, full of apparent remorse. 'He said he'd hire a car, take me to Trichy and put me in a proper hospital. I refused. I told him to stay away from me and Ramya – and Kodaikanal. He said he'd look after me and raise money for an operation. I told him I never wanted to see him again.'

'What happened then?' I asked.

'He said he wanted to "look after" Ramya, and I said, "If you go anywhere near my daughter I will make a statement against you to the police." He knew I meant it and hasn't been back to Kodai since then.' I asked if that was the last she had heard of him. 'No. I know he is living with his brother's family in Trichy.

Some months after he came to see me in the clinic, he wrote me a letter. He said he wanted to take another wife because I had refused to return to Trichy with him. He said he wanted to take Ramya to Trichy, saying he would look after her and send her to school but would have nothing more to do with me. He told me to ask my parents for anything I needed in the future. He would send me no money – not even for Ramya while she remained with me. He said all that without even asking how I was!' Selvi was in a strong mood that day, laughing with contempt at her husband's nerve. 'He will never get Ramya,' she said, and I knew she meant it. Recalling his conversation with her in the clinic she suddenly said, 'You know, Ma, that man is so bad, so mean-minded, he even said to me then, when I was in so much pain in that hospital, "You know how much I care for my daughter. Look at all the fruit I used to buy her every week." *Fruit*, Ma? I know fruit is expensive but imagine saying that of all things. He never bought her any clothes – not even once in her life – and he talks of *fruit*!'

In the weeks that followed, as Selvi spoke of her past, linking it to her present predicament, it became clear that the issue of dowry had overshadowed her life although she never used the term in describing her own experience. She had been bartered and sold to a man she did not love for the sake of 'respectability', for the sake of preserving her 'family's sense of honour'. Speaking about her marriage, she said I had to first understand the background, asking me not to discuss these matters with anyone in Kodai as, so far, it was a family secret. 'You can write it in your book because that is in English and you live in London,' she added, making me aware of how far apart we were, geographically and in terms of social realities. She asked me not to mention her husband by name, nervous of repercussions. I said I wouldn't, that his name didn't matter.

At the age of sixteen, she told me, she had fallen in love with a young man of about nineteen. He was one of the town's local 'heroes' at the time, as she put it, smiling at the memory. His family had other plans for him and did not approve of their relationship. They arranged his marriage to 'a girl from the plains whose family was richer than ours'. In the face of this, their affair intensified, and Selvi discovered after some time that she was pregnant. The man panicked and stopped seeing her, having accepted his parents' proposal of marriage to the other girl.

'I remember feeling very ashamed and frightened,' Selvi said, trying to recall that time. 'I remember I got quite ill with worry and my parents couldn't understand what was wrong with me. One day, my mother decided to take me to see a doctor. I started crying and told her what had happened. Both she and my father were very angry at first, but then they decided that I should stay at home and have the baby, which my mother would say was her fourth child. So you see, Ma, my son became my brother . . .' Her voice broke and her eyes filled with tears.

Fourteen years later, Pradeep still lived with Selvi's parents thinking of her as his elder sister, and of his uncles as his brothers, but he called her 'Selvi-Appa' or 'Selvi-Pa' ('*Appa*' meaning 'Father' in Tamil). 'So you see, there is something special between us. He spends a lot of time in my house and looks after Ramya as an elder brother would, but he eats and sleeps in my parents' home. He calls them Amma and Appa . . . I never want to take that away from them. They are getting old now and my father has worked hard all his life, as a stonemason. He has done all he can for us.'

By the time Pradeep was eleven, Selvi was still unmarried and gaining a 'bad reputation' for projecting defiance and self-confidence. She had been earning her living by working for various foreigners, teachers and others connected to the International School, through whom she had learned to speak her own brand of English – spoken as rapidly as she spoke Tamil. It was, at times, hard to understand but I was getting used to it and beginning to speak the same way myself, when talking to her. She liked cooking and had learned much from the Americans she had worked for. She could make American apple pie, chocolate-chip cookies, chocolate fudge and excellent roast beef, seasoned with garlic, none of which she ate herself. She confessed that

Ramya loved the fudge, but both sugar and chocolate were expensive. We decided she should make some the next day – for Ramya and the rest of us. I said I would get the sugar and chocolate from Meenakshi Stores when I went into town later that evening. I had to go for bread and cheese anyway and both the bakery and the cheese factory delivered only after four or five each afternoon, generating long queues at the shop.

Selvi said she loved her work and the interaction with people who treated her with more kindness and consideration than 'Indians treat their servants – or *dogs* for that matter!'. Through the efforts of a past employer, who had returned to America, she had been able to build a small, two-room concrete house on the hill, less than a hundred yards from her parents' home. 'Susan Madam was a very kind lady,' she said, referring to her employer's former wife. 'She got money for me from some church fund and also did a lot for me herself. She made sure the house was in my name. When I die, it will go to Pradeep. She helped me with all the papers and told me to keep them in a safe place.'

Selvi's house on the hill had become her dowry. The marriage her parents had arranged for her, when Pradeep was around eleven, was to a man who had no home of his own. His parents had died and he lived with his brother in Trichy – short for Tiruchirappalli – a bustling, dusty temple city not far from Kodai, famous for its rock fort and the temple on top of the rock. A deal had been struck. No money would change hands. Having been told the truth about her past, he would accept Pradeep as Selvi's brother and, in return, would move into her home after they were married, and seek employment in Kodai. Meanwhile, Selvi, who had a full-time job then, would support him.

'He came to Kodai with nothing, Ma. Just his *lungi*! No proper clothes or shoes, nothing warm to wear. I bought him everything, thinking, "He's my husband, I must do this." I wanted to make him happy and make my marriage work. He was not much older than me and had had a hard life himself. For a few months, when I was pregnant with Ramya and for a while after she was born, we were happy. Sometimes he brought in a few rupees, working with my father as a stonemason, but he didn't work regularly and often disappeared for days on end ...' she said, her voice trailing off.

'Did he have a job in the plains when you married him?' I asked.

She said she wasn't sure. 'He said he had a driving licence and worked as a long-distance truck driver but then, he lied about so many things. I had no idea what he did when he went to Trichy. He usually came back drunk and never seemed to have any money. I learned not to argue with him and just think of Ramya and myself. I had quite a good job then but I remember there were always fights between us at the end of every month, around the 27th or 28th when I got paid. Apart from that, we left each other alone. I told him I didn't want any more children.'

They had been to his brother's home together for short holidays but Selvi had always felt uncomfortable there, trying to play the role of a dutiful sister-in-law to his elder brother and his wife while concealing the hostility she felt towards her husband. 'I went for Ramya's sake. She had her cousins to play with, and she enjoyed the bus ride. I myself feel sick on winding roads and have often thrown up on such journeys, leaning out of bus windows, feeling very embarrassed. I began to dread the whole experience, so stopped going. Once or twice he took Ramya for a few days at a time, during holidays and festivals. I told him I couldn't take time off work, so he accepted that.' I asked if she had ever feared him and she said with a shrug, 'Not really, but he had some odd habits. For instance, he would sleep with a long stick under the mattress sometimes after we had fought or argued about something but I learned to ignore him. He was usually drunk when he did these things so I would stay awake till he went to sleep, knowing he would remember little about it in the morning.' After a long pause she added, 'Now, of course, I know he is capable of anything when he's been drinking. I often wonder what he will do next.'

From what I could see at the time, Selvi still lived in fear of her husband, anticipating his return one day. I suggested she formalize the situation by getting a divorce. Through some mutual friends I had met a young Tamil lawyer, Dannapal, who had set up a small practice and lived in Kodai. He had agreed to meet Selvi, discuss the situation with her and possibly represent her, free of charge. To Selvi, I explained, or tried to explain, the concept of court injunctions and the protection women could seek through the law. She looked dubious but agreed to meet Dannapal, adding, 'It will be good to have someone like him to turn to, Ma, but I tell you one thing, I will not go to court.'

'Not even to keep him away from you and Ramya by *law*?' I emphasized.

'What law?' she promptly shot back. 'The police here only work for bribes. It is best not to involve them in anything.' She was quite emphatic.

She went on to say that it was for precisely this reason that she had refused the doctor's offer of a transfer from his clinic to a proper hospital, where free government-sponsored skin grafts may have been possible. She would have been questioned by the authorities. The police would have been involved and she had decided to avoid that at all cost. She feared retribution on the one hand, and, on the other, did not want to make any false statements about the 'accident' which would exonerate her husband. She knew that her knowledge of the truth, of what really happened that night of 27 November 1993, was the only weapon she had to keep him at bay. It was her only power over him, her way of ensuring a permanent separation from the man she had married to appease her family. I could see the practical sense in what she was saying, but said I thought she should talk with Dannapal anyway. I could ask him over to lunch one day, when he was free, in order to introduce them. It could do no harm. She gave me an affectionate pat on the shoulder and said, 'I'll cook a nice fish curry with coconut milk. You think he'll like that?' I said it was a great idea but had been warned against buying fish in Kodai because it had to be trucked up the mountain, on blocks of melting ice, covered in sawdust for preservation, and might not be fresh. We didn't want to poison Dannapal!

Selvi laughed and said, 'You leave that to me. At six-thirty in the morning, the fish in the market *is* fresh! Ramya loves my fish curry and I will choose the fish myself.' All I had to do, I was told, was to call Dannapal from Adam's phone and fix a date. Selvi had her own way of dealing with situations and retaining her pragmatic approach to life. I had learned to admire that in her.

Dannapal was an extremely down-to-earth, sympathetic young lawyer in his early thirties. Interested in cases of social concern and public interest, he spent well over an hour talking to Selvi, discussing the overall situation and considering the ramifications of different options. They spoke in Tamil but I could keep pace with the discussion because, from time to time, one or other of them would involve me by breaking into English.

Although Selvi's meeting with Dannapal would turn out to be useful in the long term, there was little he could do at the time. She wanted to take no legal action against her husband and he too agreed that the police were corrupt, especially in cases involving domestic violence, and that courts throughout the country had 'a gender bias that is so deeply traditional, it makes one despair'. Like me, he felt that Selvi should at least legalize her separation from her husband and gain legal custody of her child. She said she would think about it.

Their discussion over, Selvi took charge once again and asked me 'You want to eat now? I need about ten minutes more in the kitchen. I put the beer in a bucket of water to keep it cool. It's in the bathroom – because no sun ever comes there!' Dannapal laughed and said he'd love a drink before the fish curry that already smelt so good.

Selvi laid the lunch out on the veranda, having warned me before not to ask her to eat with us. 'It will look bad, Ma. Anyway, I've cooked extra and will take some home for Ramya and me to eat tonight.' She was right. In India, as in many other countries, the class divide runs deep and workers do not normally eat with their employers. The 'correctness' of such behaviour seems to be universally accepted and those who break the rules are considered either eccentric or of dubious intention. We had agreed to play it 'straight'.

Over lunch, in the course of general conversation, Dannapal asked me what I did. I told him of the job that had enabled me to revisit Kodai, but also spoke of what I really wanted to investigate. We spoke of the circle of oppression that many Indian women were trapped in, throughout the cycle of life from birth to death. We discussed the Roop Kanwar case as well as the dramatic rise in the incidence of dowry deaths and female infanticide. He told me that the killing of female babies was a 'terrible and almost insoluble problem' in the south, and that the state of Tamil Nadu had the worst record in India. He suggested I make a preliminary trip to the temple city of Madurai, just three hours from Kodai by bus, and gave me the names and addresses of individual activists and organizations trying to combat the problem. Meeting Dannapal had, unexpectedly, given me an important lead for my own project.

After he left, Selvi, who had overheard most of the conversation, offered to accompany me to Madurai in order to translate from Tamil to English, so that I could communicate better with the people I met. She had become my self-appointed co-researcher and I was grateful. There wasn't much time, as I had to leave for Bombay in four days. Undaunted, she said, 'Let's go tomorrow morning. I'll get Pradeep to collect Ramya from school and take her to my mother's house.' It was agreed that we would make a day trip down to the plains, in a taxi, as we needed the transport at the other end. We walked into town together and went our separate ways. 'Tell the taxi to come any time after nine tomorrow morning. I'll be there,' she said, as she waved goodbye to me outside Meenakshi Stores.

Chapter Eight

Back at Roseneath that evening, having booked the taxi for the next morning, I decided to settle down and study my file of press clippings. I needed to be better informed on the facts surrounding the practice of female infanticide, particularly in the state of Tamil Nadu, before my journey down to the plains with Selvi. Roseneath had lulled me into a state of relaxed contentment which had to be shaken off. 'No chat by the fire with Adam tonight,' I told myself, as I followed the beam of my torch along the pathway to his cottage, with Bonnie leading the way. She always greeted me on my return from a trip into town, her tail wagging furiously in the hope of a biscuit or some other treat.

I found Adam in his living room, fire ablaze, painting a large poster which, he said, would then be mounted on wood as a billboard for Ravi Stores. The owner, Ravi, was a friend of his and ran a small shop located just opposite the iron gates of the International School, a lucrative spot for selling chocolates, sweets, chewing gum, biscuits, cigarettes and so on. He was expanding his business, and the sign read: 'Tea, Coffee & Fruit Juice Available Here'. Adam was wondering whether to add illustrations of some fruit or coffee beans to liven it up. I told him of my conversation with Dannapal and my plan for the next day. He asked if I had any fixed appointments. 'No,' I said, 'only names and addresses.'

'That's OK,' he replied, concentrating on his brushwork. 'It's the way things work here. People just turn up. It's normal.' His response was reassuring. I had begun to doubt my own impulse and wondered if I should have written letters or sent telegrams first. There was no time anyway, I told myself, as I returned to the chill of Neelam's bungalow to light a fire for the night.

I sat up for hours that night, reading one horror story after another. Dannapal had said Tamil Nadu's record was the worst in the whole of India. How much worse could it possibly be?

An article published in one of the country's most well respected current affairs magazines, *Outlook*, caught my eye. Headed 'Lambs to the Slaughter', the sub-heading read: 'With hefty dowry demands in caste-ridden Bihar, over 1.6 lakh female infants are killed in the state every year.' The article began:

> The rates are fixed. A local *dai* in Katihar is paid Rs 100 for the delivery of a son and Rs 25 for a daughter. If the daughter is killed, the fee goes up to Rs 50.
>
> 'Yes, we kill baby girls for a pittance,' says Adila Devi, a midwife in this eastern district of Bihar. 'Poor people like us cannot protest. Many a father has been known to refuse us payment after we have killed the daughter but who do we approach for justice?' Having helped deliver babies in the Teja Tola, Fasiya Tola and Budhuchak areas for over 40 years now, the sexagenarian midwife claims to have 'done away' with more than 150 infant girls.

The photographs accompanying the article were equally shocking. A woman demonstrated on a doll, swaddled like a baby, how an infant was strangled. Another midwife stood in a wheat field, pointing to an unmarked spot on the ground to indicate where the last baby she killed was buried. The writer of the article, Soma Wadhwa, went on to say:

> The methods of killing are as simple as they are varied. The baby girls are usually strangled with a length of rope. Sometimes the *dai* snaps the spine by bending it backwards. A handful of fertiliser pushed down the baby's throat also does the job. A lump of black salt placed in the newborn's mouth, experienced *dais* say, takes an hour to kill the infant.

The less-experienced midwives, however, choose to suffocate the baby by stuffing her into a clay pot and sealing the lid with fresh dough. The baby dies within two hours. 'This way one doesn't actually have to see the baby dying,' Phool points out. For witnessing an infant's death can make even the most experienced *dai* shudder, she says. 'Strangling makes the tongue hang out and urea makes her eyes bulge. It's a ghastly sight – even the most hardened of us cannot sleep for days after the deed is done.'

It is not so much the act but the aftermath that seems to haunt the midwives. 'The fear that some wild animal might drag the infant carcass out of the undergrowth where I have dumped it makes me break into cold sweat,' says Seema Devi. Most *dais* in the area, she adds, dispose of the bodies in the nearby Kolasi ghat and Chaumukhi stream. 'It torments me to think that I have deprived so many souls of last rites,' she murmurs.

But Phool is quick to pin the 'sin' on the father of the child. 'We hardly have any choice in the matter,' she argues ... Significantly, these unreported deaths carried out by the Chamars (the lowest in the caste hierarchy) are an upper-class malaise in caste-ridden Bihar. The superior status of the Rajputs, Bhumihars and Brahmins in society finds expression in demands for hefty dowries. And intrinsic to the dowry system is a bias against the female. Girls are seen as 'burdens' that must be 'offloaded'.

Feeling my stomach churn, I flipped through the rest of the file. An extraordinary headline from the *Indian Express*, a national daily, made me stop. It read: 'After 115 yrs, a village celebrates the wedding of a girl it did not kill.' The article described Jawan Kanwai's marriage in the Rajasthani village of Deora:

> The last time the village saw a Rajput girl's marriage was in 1883. There is no one alive who has ever witnessed a *baraat* [the groom's wedding procession] come to the village. The purohit [priest] for Kanwar's marriage was the first of his Brahmin family to conduct such a ceremony.

The girl's father, Indra Singh, the article said, was now the

Sarpanch (headman) of the village, and had taken the 'bold step' not to kill his daughter, as was traditional, twenty years ago, after her birth fifteen days after the death of his son, who died at a young age due to natural causes. The article continued:

> Emboldened by Indra Singh's decision to keep his daughter, his uncle and his brother also have a daughter each. As of today, the 150 Rajput families in the village have five daughters. But female infanticide persists. Most admit to it even if they do not acknowledge any particular incident. Some still offer the bizarre, well-worn reason: 'The water of the village well is such that only sons are born here. If things have changed now, it's because the water now comes from the tube well.'

Although I had carted this file around with me from one hotel room to another in the north, I had never actually read through it, waiting to get back to London in order to put a treatment together for potential publishers. Reading through some of it that night put me into an emotionally wretched state. I began to feel my own vulnerability and worthlessness in a society that regards women as fundamentally low-life beings. I started thinking that I was lucky to be alive. For the fact remains that this attitude towards women is not merely a backward village phenomenon. The rich abort their female children, so don't have to face either the revulsion or the nightmares of the *dais*. In urban centres, this too is on the increase. Many Indian women tend to tolerate their daughters but, without exception, adore their sons. It is common knowledge, and a common experience. There are, as always, exceptions but these are few and far between.

It was past midnight and I had to find something relevant for the next day. All I had on Tamil Nadu at the time was an article headed: 'Cradles of mercy' published in *India Today*, probably the country's most popular news magazine with the largest national and international circulation, published in English and several other regional languages. It began:

> A line of cradles lies inside one of the primary health centres in

Tamil Nadu's Salem district with little Kalyani contentedly asleep in one of them. This baby is fortunate in not having ended up contributing to the statistics on female infanticide – murdered by her parents through starvation, suffocation or a dose of lethal poison. If she is still alive it is thanks to the state Government's drastic action in curbing the crime of female infanticide. The inviting cradle is just one of the Government's many measures to persuade parents to leave a female child in the state's care rather than kill her and to counter all the consequences of a popular proverb: 'Raising a female child is like watering your neighbour's plant.'

The article went on to say that the state of Tamil Nadu was fast gaining notoriety for female infanticide, which was so wide-spread across the caste/class spectrum that the government had been forced to act. In addition to the 'Cradle Scheme', the Chief Minister, Jayalalitha, had announced 'a 1-per cent reservation in jobs for the cradle babies as a provision for when they grow up'. So far, eighteen babies, all no more than two to three days old, had been left in these cradles by parents who had not even waited to be seen. The law too had been modified so that 'Anyone arrested on charges of infanticide is charged under Section 302 of the IPC (Indian Penal Code) which has life imprisonment as its maximum punishment. Already 12 people have been arrested – of whom one has been sentenced to life imprisonment.' I wondered if the person sentenced was a man or a woman. The article didn't say. I checked the date and realised the article had been published two years earlier, on 28 February 1993. This was something I could enquire about the next day. Had the 'Cradle Scheme' worked? Dannapal had not even mentioned it.

I made a few notes, realized that the fire had gone out and the air had turned icy, so decided to climb into bed and refer to Sakuntala Narasimhan's book, *Sati: A Study of Widow Burning in India*, which made references to this issue as well. I found the section I was looking for:

The British outlawed infanticide in 1804 and declared it to be murder, but a tribal chief who protested against the British edict is on record as having claimed that the practice was '4,900 years old'.

As with other enactments that sought to wipe out customs rooted in deviant social attitudes, passing a prohibitory law did not ensure that female infants were no longer shunned. Thanks to the severity of the clutches of the dowry system, certain communities in different regions of the country (parts of Tamil Nadu, Rajasthan) have seen, even in the 1980s, the systematic infanticide of girl babies because the family could see no way of mustering enough savings to facilitate the girls' marriages when they grew up. More recently, there have been allegations of female infanticide in the family of a member of the state legislative assembly of Rajasthan (an investigation was ordered by the crime branch). The law notwithstanding, reports of female infants being given poison berries or being abandoned to die, keep surfacing.

As long as women's lives are trivialized, even modern technology cannot help getting hijacked to serve culture-based prejudices. Thus, with amniocentesis techniques becoming available in recent years, and abortion made legal, the clamour to know the sex of the unborn child has led to a medical procedure meant primarily to discover foetal abnormalities being used for large-scale selective abortions of female foetuses. In one survey that is often quoted, out of 8,000 foetuses aborted following sex-determination tests, 7,999 were reported to be female, the lone exception being that of a Jewish woman who wanted a daughter. In 1987, following demands from women's groups for a ban on these tests, the state of Maharashtra made it illegal to use prenatal diagnostic techniques for ascertaining the sex of the unborn child. The root cause of female foeticide, however, remains – the stranglehold of the custom of dowry and the very strong cultural preference for sons in certain communities. A nation-wide ban on sex-determination tests is yet to be imposed, so all that a family in Maharashtra need do to circumvent the law is to step across into another state and get the test done. ('Better pay Rs

500 now than Rs five lakhs later on' – as dowry – is how these sex-determination tests are promoted.)

Giving birth to girls is in fact considered no less than a crime in several communities and the mother pays a heavy price for it, although science has made it clear that the sex of the offspring is not determined by the mother...

By this time, the rain had descended once more and as I listened to its patter on the tin roof, I realized that I was feeling very cold. The blankets on my bed seemed to weigh a ton – like old-fashioned army or hospital blankets left over from World War II – and as I switched off the light and tried to sleep, headlines from the press-clippings I had just flipped through began to scream at me in my state of half-dream, half-sleep: 'Born to Die', 'Lambs to the Slaughter', 'Cradles of Mercy', 'Woman kills granddaughters', 'Man dumps month-old daughter in sewer', 'Father dumps newborn in river', 'Praying for the son, preying on the daughter' ... I remember waking up in a cold sweat in the early hours of the morning and thinking, 'Selvi will be here in a few hours.' I climbed out from under the heavy blankets – which had felt like a strait-jacket through the night – and decided to make some coffee and watch the dawn turn the night into day. It was cold. I was looking forward to a day in the heat of the plains.

CHAPTER NINE

Both Selvi and the taxi arrived within minutes of each other and we set off for Madurai, the sound of horns blasting around each bend as we seemed to plummet down the mountain road at high speed. Mohan, the taxi-driver whom I had known for some years, seemed in an enthusiastic mood. He had to see his 'cousin-brother' on some important business in Madurai, he informed me, asking if I planned to take a lunch break. He could go then. I said we were only passing through the city and had to find a village called Kallupatti somewhere in the district rather than within Madurai itself. He looked somewhat downcast for a while and stopped driving at his manic pace. 'That's better,' said Selvi, who had been clutching the back of the front seat, as she settled back to gaze at the ever-changing landscape as it flashed past our open windows. My side of the car hugged the rockface for most of the journey and I found myself enclosed in my own thoughts, staring into a space beyond the rock, oblivious to its constant presence and close proximity. In the background, Selvi and Mohan spoke in rapid Tamil. Exhausted by the night before, I fell asleep with my head against the open window frame, feeling the luxury of the mountain breeze on my face, steadily getting warmer as the sun rose and we continued to descend into the plains below.

I woke with a start, drenched in sweat. We were parked in a noisy market street, under the full blaze of the sun and I still had my woollen shawl wrapped around me. Next to me, Selvi was eating a slice of watermelon she must have bought from a vendor.

'We are in Madurai, Ma,' she said. 'I didn't want to wake you. Mohan has gone to find out about the road to the village.' I straightened and realized that I must have looked a complete mess. My hair had come loose with the wind and felt all tangled and dusty. My clothes felt wet and clung to my body. I realized I had slept so deeply that even the intense heat had not made me remove my shawl.

Looking up and down the crowded street, I spotted a billboard which read: 'Air-conditioned Meals' and underneath in brackets: 'First Class Toilet Facilities'. Pointing it out to Selvi I said, 'That's what I need.'

'You hungry?' she asked.

'No,' I said, 'just feeling wrecked! I must tidy up before we meet the priest who is in charge of the programme in the village.'

She laughed, still looking neat and bright-eyed as she opened the car door and stepped out into the sun. 'Mohan can wait,' she said. 'Let's go.'

I searched my bag for a Post-It sticker and asked Selvi to write a note in Tamil, telling him where to find us. We stuck the note on the windscreen and went into the bustling (but air-conditioned) restaurant, much to my relief. We rolled up the windows of the taxi but had no way of locking it. Selvi said it didn't matter. I left my shawl on the back seat but carried my notebook and Walkman.

We ordered two 'Meals', set menus in south India for lunch, served on banana leaves, consisting of various vegetables, lentils and yoghurt, accompanied by both rice and *puri*s, an incredible spread at midday. I managed to have a wash and re-do my hair; Mohan appeared an hour later (probably having met his 'cousin-brother') and we set off for the village of Kallupatti, which he told me was somewhere off the road to Batlagundu (the town of 'goondas' and the infamous 'Ladies Latrine'). I didn't ask what he'd done with his time because I'd needed the break myself. I had recovered from all the negative feelings that come from just being tired – both mentally and physically. In the early hours of the morning, I had seriously doubted the wisdom of this sudden trip. I had not made any appointments to see anyone and the taxi was going to cost me close to 3,000 rupees by the end of the day, an amount I could ill afford at the time. I had to keep an eye on my fare back to Bombay; I would have to fly if I couldn't get a train ticket. All these thoughts had worn me out but now I felt good for having made the decision. This was India – taking chances worked.

As we turned off the highway and travelled through the heat and clouds of dust thrown up by passing vehicles, on village link-roads, I noticed that the area was extremely impoverished. The people we passed on the roads looked very poor, even by Indian standards, and the land was completely arid.

The car was overheating. Mohan said we needed water for the radiator but there was nothing that looked even vaguely hopeful in sight. I gave him my unopened bottle of mineral water, which I had bought outside the restaurant in Madurai. Annoyed and irritated by the possibility of a breakdown in that heat, I asked, 'What were you doing in Madurai? Why did you not think of it then?' Mohan didn't reply as he bent under the hood to empty the bottle into the radiator.

At last, we arrived at Kallupatti, and I told Mohan we were looking for a place called Anbu Illam, run by a Brother James. Selvi said the words meant 'Home of Love'. We found the place with little difficulty. It was well known – and apparently re-spected – by the people whom we asked for directions. Everyone had heard of Brother James and his centre for abandoned chil-dren. Officially, the organization he had established was called 'Reaching the Unreached' and signs in both English and Tamil pointed the way to the open gates of Anbu Illam, constructed with bamboo and held together with rough jute rope. It was like entering an oasis in the desert with much greenery and small huts standing in neat rows under the shade of young coconut palms.

Selvi got out of the car and made enquiries. Brother James was not there but someone else would see me in the office. I was pointed towards a small bungalow-like structure on the com-pound and headed towards it, while Selvi and Mohan stood around near the car as it let off steam through its now open bonnet. I entered a small room with a large desk and two chairs placed formally opposite the larger chair behind the desk. The walls displayed posters and a blackboard. My first impression was that, in contrast to any government office I had ever been in, this room offered information and had no framed portraits of 'leaders' or 'founders'. I sat down in one of the two chairs and felt the cool of the room, shaded by the thatched roof which overhung the small veranda outside. Within minutes, a young Tamil girl came in, silently switched on a ceiling fan and offered me a glass of water. I spoke to her in English. She flashed me a shy smile and left the room through a set of cotton curtains that led to an adjoining room. Silence prevailed, except for the slow hum of the fan above.

To prevent myself from falling asleep again, in this cool and quiet atmosphere, I took out my notebook and started studying the walls, blackboard first. The writing on it was headed CAT-ERGORIES, and listed below were:

> Orphans
> Found
> Parents in Jail
> Infanticide [I noted the number 20 here]
> Street Children
> Parent Suicide
> Handicapped

A framed poem next to the blackboard read:

> I who am fed
>   Who never went hungry for a day,
> I see the dead
>   the children starved for lack of bread
> I see and try to pray
>   I who am strong
> With health and love and laughter in my
>   soul,

89

I see a throng of stunted children
   reared in wrong,
And wish to make them whole . . .
And know full well that
   not until I share their bitter cry
Their pain and hell,
   Can God within my spirit dwell.
(Doctor Tom Dooley)

'Tom Dooley?' I thought. My father had banned me and my sister from playing that song, a hit single when we were both at school in Delhi. He'd said, 'I will not have murderers glorified in this house!' The lines of the song came back to me after so many years, describing Tom Dooley, who was to be hanged the next morning. My father thought the song was grotesque, but we still played it when he was out.

Lost in distant memories, I didn't hear Haja Mohideen enter the room. A big man who spoke in faltering English, Mohideen looked Tamil but, given his name, I wondered if he was. He said Brother James was at the Boys' Village, an earlier establishment set up in 1972, but would probably be back at any time. I tried to explain the purpose of my visit and ask him about the growing problem of female infanticide in Tamil Nadu. He looked cagey and merely said, 'Here we look after all kinds of abandoned children,' pointing to the blackboard. I asked him to tell me a bit about Anbu Illam. He thought for a moment and then, from the adjoining room, brought me a few leaflets and a copy of their annual report for the year 1994–95. He then left, saying he had to attend to some urgent business. I could wait for Brother James if I wished, and should feel free to look around the compound. Putting the leaflets he had given me into my bag, I went back outside into the glare of the sun.

Both Mohan and the car had vanished but I saw Selvi sitting on a bench under a thatched open shed, a parking spot for bicycles and motorcycles. I told her that the priest I had come to meet was not around, and suggested that we walk around anyway to try to talk to the women in the neatly lined row of huts. Because of the heat, most people were indoors. I asked about Mohan and she shrugged, saying that he had left in a hurry, saying that he had to fix the car. I felt annoyed, having thought we might drive to the Boy's Village in search of Brother James. It was approximately nine miles away.

Left with no alternative but to wait, we approached the first hut. Whitewashed in limestone, with emerald-green window frames and a door that stood ajar, it had a well-tended vegetable bed, no more than a metre wide, surrounding its four walls. We knocked and entered the open doorway. An old woman of nearly seventy or so sat fanning herself on a stone floor. Along one wall, four young children slept on separate small *chatai*s – grass mats woven locally. The room was relatively spacious and spotlessly clean despite the fact that one corner served as a tiny kitchen, divided from the rest of the hut by a low brick wall. The sleeping children looked as if they were all under five or six and the woman could easily have been their great-grandmother. Her furrowed face and gentle manner reminded me of Susai instantly. She reflected the same sort of inner calm, the same quiet dignity.

I stood in the doorway while Selvi spoke to the old woman in hushed tones, presumably explaining the purpose of our visit. The woman gave us a warm smile and invited us to sit beside her on the grey stone floor. I noticed that, like the office, this room too had been designed to keep the heat out and it took a few seconds to get used to the dimness after the blinding glare outside. I could see the roof thatch once more, overhanging the two small, barred windows, and the floor felt cool and comforting to my bare feet. I told Selvi not to rush the questions. I wanted to know the woman's relationship to the children and something about her own situation.

As they spoke to each other, I looked around and noticed how sparse the place looked. No clutter of clothes. No adjoining room, and the cooking utensils had been scrubbed so vigorously that they gleamed in the half-light of the far corner. The children were still fast asleep and didn't stir despite the sound of voices, and the old woman flicked a hand-held fan in their direction every now and then to ward off the occasional fly or bee that came in through the bars and buzzed around the room.

After a while, Selvi turned to me and said, 'This lady, Ma, she is a widow and these children are not related to her. It is her job to look after them as if they were her own and she is paid for doing this.'

'How much is she paid?' I asked.

Selvi looked impressed by the reply as she reported back: 'Four hundred and fifty rupees a month for each child. Out of this, she says, she has to feed them and buy their clothes. She also has to make sure that they go to school every day until they are sixteen years old. The school is free and she says she is very happy with her life in this village and that Brother James is a very nice man.' Selvi herself had not been able to earn even the allowance for one child in Kodaikanal, to support herself and Ramya. I too was impressed. As we talked, a fuller picture emerged. The children in the old woman's care were too young to attend school proper, but they spent a few hours each morning in a playgroup with other children of their own age. Before they came home, they were given a glass of milk and something to eat. She only had to cook in the evenings. The one-room cottage was more than adequate for their needs. Showers and toilets were communal and she got much pleasure from the narrow vegetable patch that surrounded her home. She had planted tomatoes, onions, potatoes, coriander and chillies. The coriander had not survived. Next year she would try something else. She asked if we would like to look at her 'small field' – especially the tomato plants. As we circuited her home in the blinding sun, I noticed that others had chosen to plant flowers instead.

I asked Selvi to visit other huts, talk to the women and meet me back in the office. I wanted to check if Brother James was back. I knew by now that Selvi was more than competent in gathering information, and she seemed to be enjoying the interaction with this world that neither of us had encountered. This was different from other charitable institutions I had visited in the past. People still had their own individuality – you could see it just by looking at the flower beds and vegetable patches that surrounded their homes. The pathways were clean and partially paved to keep wet feet from getting muddied on the way back from the bathing area.

The office was empty. I walked around the compound, looking for someone who could give me some information regarding the whereabouts of Brother James, the man who had initiated this immaculate village within a village. Unable to speak Tamil, I missed Selvi's presence but used monosyllabic sentences and hand-gestures instead. 'Brother James?' I asked, twisting my hand in the air at people I passed.

Eventually, I came across a young woman who spoke Selvi's kind of English. She said that Brother James was probably at the clinic some 300 yards down the road, and called out to a boy of about ten, instructing him to show me the way past the gate. 'It is not so far, Ma,' she said, looking up at the sun to indicate that she realized the heat was oppressive. I followed the boy as he walked briskly ahead and out of the gate. I had expected him to point the way but instead he set off down the road, making his way through the sandy verge that lined a narrow tarmac road. The road was for vehicles, mostly bicycles, scooters and motor-cycles that overtook bullock-carts at high speed, covering all around in red dust. My young guide was enthusiastic and chatted away in Tamil until he realized that I couldn't understand a word. After that, he resorted to gestures and the odd word in English. He was bright-eyed, literally bouncing with energy. He told me he lived in the Boys' Village but had friends and an old aunt who lived at Anbu Illam, whom he visited every few days, walking the nine-mile stretch or hitching a lift on carts that plied the route.

As we entered the gates of another compound, containing a cluster of small, low-lying concrete buildings with tin roofs, the boy said, 'Wait. Brother James?' I nodded as I watched him dart off and disappear around a corner. The clinic must have been closed, as I saw no patients. There were signs with arrows pointing in different directions: 'General (Pushparani) Clinic', 'Leprosy and T.B. Clinic', 'Day Care Centre', 'Laboratory' and so on. This compound too looked spotlessly clean, and I realized how filthy my feet were, caked with mud and sweat in ruined sandals. I noticed a water-pump surrounded by stone slabs not far from the gate and decided to rinse my feet. As I was doing this, the boy reappeared, beckoning me to follow with frantic gestures as if time was of essence. He had the gleam of success in his eyes.

After several turns, he led me to a low building, pointed to the open doorway and announced, 'Brother James!' triumphantly. I had developed a strange sort of affection for this child during our walk and wanted to reward him in some way for his efforts. A few rupees perhaps? Thinking he would follow me in, I went ahead. I entered a long, narrow room with tables and benches lining the walls, which were painted a pale sea-green, triggering once more that immediate sensation of relief from the sun. Brother James was the sole occupant. He sat at a table near the door eating from a *thali*. I said, 'Brother James?' He nodded and gestured for me to sit down. He said nothing and asked me nothing as he continued to chew. I felt I had to explain myself so I started out saying something like, 'I'm a journalist. I live in London but work in India ... I'm trying to write a book ... I've just come for the day from Kodaikanal ...' I knew I was talking too fast and suddenly sounded very Western.

Brother James had a kind of detachment in his manner which was both soothing and unsettling at the same time. I felt somewhat foolish without fully understanding why. Seeming to sense my discomfort, he said, 'You must have had a long journey, please help yourself to some food. It's over there,' pointing behind me.

My immediate response was, 'I'm not hungry, I'd just like a bit of your time. You see ...'

He cut me short saying, 'Have a bit. You see we have the leftovers! This is the staff canteen and the lunch hour is over, as you can see. I stopped by because the food is always so good here.'

I went over to the opposite side of the room where three large, well-scrubbed pots stood. They contained *dal* and two wonderful-looking dishes – one with potatoes and spinach and the other with a mixture in which I could see carrots and drumsticks. On a shelf nearby were rows of stainless steel *thali*s, all washed and clean. I picked one out of the rack, helped myself to some food and a couple of *chapati*s that stood in a neat pile, realizing how hungry I really was. I hadn't eaten much of the lunch in Madurai, tired as I was and more in need of a wash then. As I returned to the table, I suddenly remembered my child-guide. Putting the *thali* down, I went to the door and looked around. The boy had vanished and I hadn't even asked for his name.

Back at the table, Brother James asked if there was a problem. I explained about wanting to reward the boy and he smiled, saying, 'Charity in that sense is not the way. We must make people self-sufficient. That kid has a good life.' I agreed. Feeling far more relaxed, we talked as we ate. I told him of my intended project. I asked him about the problems surrounding the issue of female infanticide and asked him what he knew about it through the people who had been housed in his institutions. I asked him to tell me a bit about himself and then asked if I could record our conversation. He had no problem with that so I switched on my Walkman and enjoyed my lunch while he spoke, interjecting the odd question.

He was a man of few words, but precise. He said, 'Poverty is the root and literacy is a weapon of survival. The women are not to blame. They kill their children because that is what their husbands tell them to do. Without their marital status, they have little in this society – and they know it. I am concerned about the dispossessed, whoever they be.'

I asked him a bit about himself. He told me that he had left a teaching post in England in 1952 to start his missionary work in Colombo, Sri Lanka, where he remained until 1962. He then moved to Madurai, where he started an Industrial Training School for street boys, which gave them 'a basic education and a skill', and then found jobs for them when they left. 'After ten years, I handed over to the Indian Brothers and moved into the countryside about thirty-five kilometres away. There, I set up a base for destitute village boys between the ages of six and fourteen and called it 'St Joseph's Boys' Village'. Now everyone knows it as just 'The Boys' Village'. This began in 1972 with twelve boys in a disused chicken hut with no water or sanitation. Over the next ten years, this grew into a purpose-built village for 100 boys who lived in small communal dwellings, with their own chapel, library, playground and farm.'

Time was running out. I would have to start the return journey to Kodai within a few hours if I was to get back by midnight. Getting somewhat restless, I asked him about Anbu Illam, the children and their foster mothers. He smiled, saying with pride in his voice, 'That is our latest project and it's where I live too. The Boys' Village is now run and administered by Indian Brothers. In Anbu Illam at the moment, we have forty-eight foster mothers and 250 foster children. Recently, another foster village has been opened in Bodi, not so far from here, which has a capacity for a further eighty-six children. It's a beautiful spot. Perhaps you should go there.' I explained the shortage of time and said I was specifically interested in the issue of female infanticide. He said, 'It is endemic in this area,' and suggested we walk back to his office in Anbu Illam where he could give me some material that might help.

Pointing to the sink he said, 'You can wash the *thali* out there and return it to the rack. We have one strict rule here, everyone does their own washing up!' I laughed and did as he said, deeply impressed by the man and all he seemed to have achieved. Later on, in one of the leaflets I had been given earlier, I read that he belonged to the De La Salle sect and that his full name was James Kimpton. I thought he looked as if he were only in his fifties, but didn't want to ask. I was struck by his confident but unassuming manner and the fact that he didn't look like a priest at all. He was wearing a white T-shirt and safari-style shorts.

As we set off back up the road, he told me that he had also initiated a saving scheme for all the female children in their care, a deposit account in a bank which would gather interest and mature, amounting to 10,000 rupees by the time the children were sixteen years old. This was their dowry.

'But doesn't that perpetuate the system?' I asked.

He replied without hesitation, 'We do what we can to work within existing social traditions. Dowry is an intrinsic part of the system among these communities, and girls without dowries cannot find husbands, so I see no alternative at the present time.'

Back in his office, he suddenly suggested I visit a place called the 'Claretian Home For Female Infants' in the village of Ponnamangalam, which he said was about an hour's drive away. Established by a German missionary in 1988, its specific aim was to rescue female infants from communities where the practice of killing them at birth was rife. They had such children in Anbu Illam too, he added, but said I would gain little information from their foster parents, all single women who were either widowed, unmarried or had fled from violent relationships. I felt I had taken enough of his time. Besides, I had seen the bright blue Ambassador parked near the bike shed as we'd entered the compound, so knew Mohan was back. I told him of Selvi's situation and asked if his clinic had facilities to help her with skin grafts. He said that would only be possible if she was a member of the community. She could apply to become a foster mother, taking on three more children, if she wanted to live at Anbu Illam with Ramya. Then medical help would be possible. I said I understood and would mention it to her.

Back at the taxi, Mohan was full of elaborate explanations about his absence, but I knew the heat was getting to me and feelings of irritability were rising, so I just said, 'It's OK. Just go and find Selvi from that row of huts and don't disappear for the next hour!' Meanwhile, Brother James was leaning on the roof of the car, writing down landmarks that would take us to our destination. We chatted for a while and when Mohan returned with Selvi, he explained the directions to him in fluent Tamil, waving goodbye to us as the car pulled away.

Selvi too was impressed by what she had seen. I told her of

Brother James's offer in relation to her own situation. She thought for a while and then said, 'No, Ma, it is not how I want to live. I have my own family in Kodaikanal and have lived there all my life. I cannot live in the plains.' She went on to tell me what she had learned. She had met a group of old women who had taken her to the communal dining hall where she had eaten a similar lunch to the one I had shared with Brother James at the clinic. The old women had all been midwives at one time or another before moving to Anbu Illam. They had all admitted to having killed newborn infants at the behest of family members involved. They accepted this age-old practice and had no sense of personal guilt, she told me, sharing my amazement at their candour. In this area, she said, unhusked rice was widely used to choke babies to death. She wasn't sure exactly how.

The Claretian Home For Female Infants looked like a much more formal place than Anbu Illam. It had red brick buildings, neatly tended lawns and flower beds and an impressive entrance up a gravel driveway. Leaving Selvi and Mohan in the car, I followed the arrow to the reception, where a sign instructed me to ring a desk-top brass bell. It sounded surprisingly loudly in the silence of an elegant, wood-panelled hallway. Within a few minutes, a woman in a white cotton sari with a narrow border (much like one sees in pictures of Mother Teresa's Sisters) appeared. She was Indian and spoke perfect English. I handed her Brother James's note addressed to Rev. Fr Vincent Anes, CMF, saying I had come from Kodaikanal to meet him. She asked me to wait, saying she would go and look for him. Perhaps he was in the chapel.

I went back to the car and asked Mohan to find a shady spot on the road outside the gates to park, we were blocking the driveway. I saw no role for Selvi at this home. She asked how long I would be, looking somewhat tired, and I replied 'Not long', glancing at my watch to note the time, thinking of the long drive back to Kodai. It was nearly 5 p.m. but the sun was still high in the cloudless sky above. I too was feeling drained by the heat and mentally exhausted, trying to formulate questions I should ask the Reverend Father Vincent. I picked up my Walkman from the car and went back to wait in the cool, wood-panelled hallway, where a ceiling fan had been switched on, emitting a comforting drone that suddenly made me feel sleepy.

I didn't have to wait long. I turned as I heard the shuffle of soft-treading sandals and the swish of robes. Father Vincent held out a firm but gentle hand and asked how he could help. Brother James had not explained the purpose of my visit but he had great respect and admiration for the work he was doing with women and children and would be pleased to assist in any way he could. Did I wish to look around? I said I'd rather talk to him about his knowledge of female infanticide, as practised in the area. He nodded, looking thoughtful. I wondered if I had been too blunt. At Anbu Illam, Haja Mohideen had looked uncomfortable when I'd mentioned it and evaded the issue. But, late in the afternoon, I didn't really want to see infants and toddlers who could tell me nothing.

Father Vincent seemed to understand, and led me to a small room, that looked out on to the trim lawns and flower beds. We sat in comfortable wicker chairs around the curve of a round table. I spoke of the sati in Rajasthan and my interest in writing this book. He thought for a while and then said, 'You see, dowry is the central issue that affects the lives of women in India today.' He told me he had joined the brotherhood in Bangalore, the city in which he had grown up. He had decided to move into the interior, where the problems surrounding 'the girl child' were at their worst. It wasn't that rich people didn't have the same mindset, but they could resort to modern technology and subsequent abortions to achieve the same ends. Here, in the villages, the parents had no way of knowing the sex of the child before it was born.

He asked if I had seen the BBC documentary *Let Her Die*, shown on the international television network. 'Something the government could not ban for a change,' he said with a slight smile, 'because cable TV is beyond their control.' I said I hadn't seen it. 'You must,' he said. It had been a landmark report, he said, following a lengthy, front-page article in *India Today* some time in 1993. What had impressed him was that it had been a candid account, intensively researched by Emily Buchanan, who had covered 'the whole canvas, from Ludhiana in the Punjab, where businessmen wanted sons, to Rajasthan and then to Tamil Nadu, where women were under tremendous pressure to produce sons – and accept the killing of their daughters if they failed'.

Father Vincent told me that the Claretian Home For Female Infants had been established on 26 December 1988 by a German missionary called Francis Xavier Dirnberger and that, so far, about 250 babies had been saved. It was a difficult task, he said, as families preferred to kill their children rather than give them away to institutions because of the social stigma attached. It was easier to justify the death of an infant through supposedly natural causes which few doubted, given the poverty in the area. I asked him if the government's cradle scheme had worked. He said, 'That was just a political gimmick. They have never tackled the root cause, which is the dowry system. Girls are considered a burden because they are not bread-winners. Parents have to pay to find them husbands in these parts and poor people can't afford it. They barely have enough to eat. The BBC showed all this.' I said I'd try and get hold of a copy of the documentary in London.

He went on to compare Tamil Nadu to the neighbouring state of Kerala, which, he said, had traditionally been a matriarchal society. There, in communities like the Nair's and Mukkuva's, men moved in with their wives' families so that daughters could continue to live with their parents and look after them in their old age. They inherited ancestral property and the exchange of presents at weddings was nothing like the dowry system else-where. A left-wing coalition, under the leadership of the com-munists, had helped preserve this tradition and the literacy rate among women was the highest in the country. There, the gender ratio was 1,036 women to 1,000 men. Female infanticide was almost unheard of and many couples wanted to adopt female children. Babies from their institution had found homes in Kerala.

Thinking of Selvi and Mohan waiting in the heat of the car, which had felt like a travelling oven, I tried to get Father Vincent to talk about Tamil Nadu. Ever gentle and thoughtful in his manner, he answered my question and said, 'Even here in Tamil Nadu, the practice of female infanticide is prevalent only in certain caste groups. The worst offenders are the Kallars. Literally translated it means "robbers". For instance, in a neighbouring village of Naiks (Barbers) this practice does not exist.'

'Robbers?' I asked. 'You mean literally?'

'Yes, literally,' he replied. 'Robbers. It was their traditional occupation!' We both laughed. 'Now they are either unemployed or work as unskilled labourers.'

He went on to say that in the Kallar community, proverbs and stories handed down through generations perpetuated female infanticide. I thought of Rajasthan and the legends surrounding sati. It was part of an inherited culture. I had been told this over and over again by almost everyone I had spoken to in Rajasthan. Something, it seemed, that had to be accepted.

'Surely times are changing,' I commented, sounding naive and uncertain.

'Slowly, very slowly,' he replied.

I told him what Selvi had said to me in the car about unhusked rice. Was that how they killed babies? Why would a baby swallow unhusked rice? Wouldn't she spit it out?

'They use *jagri* (unrefined cane sugar) to make small balls within which the grains of rice are embedded. The child sucks the sweet and when the sugar melts the sharp edges of the rice stick in the throat.' There was another, more popular method, he told me as he rose from his chair. I followed him out into the garden and felt the day had cooled. There was a slight breeze and the sun had lost its intensity. He showed me a flowering plant in an enormous pot. 'That's the local oleander,' he said, breaking a stem off. I thought he was about to show me around the garden, having had enough of my questions. 'See this white milky substance?' I examined the broken stem and looked at the thick liquid oozing out, forming a sort of bubble. He touched it with the tip of his middle finger and, pressing it against his thumb, demonstrated that it was extremely sticky. It would cling to the inner lining of the body. 'A teaspoon of this, mixed in milk, will kill an infant within an hour or two.' I looked at the plant with its beautiful cluster of pale pink flowers. 'It grows wild in these parts. Some also have berries that are even more poisonous. Local people are known to use them to commit suicide.' I thought of the white mountain lilies at Roseneath. Adam had said they too were used for the same purpose – or in smaller doses to get high. That was known locally as the *datura* plant.

'If you want to get some insight into the Kallar community,' Father Vincent said, as we walked back towards the front gate, 'you must visit Usilampatti. There are several villages in the area but the Kallars are a very tightly knit community and deeply suspicious of outsiders. They are essentially tribal people. You will have to spend time with them, in order to understand their ways.' I asked him where Usilampatti was. It was beyond the city of Madurai, in the opposite direction from where we were, an impossible journey to undertake that day. At the gate, he said, 'Our organization is quite small and the problem is vast. Good luck with your book.' Then, speaking of Herod and the slaughter of babies under the age of two in Bethlehem as recorded by St Matthew, he said, 'At least Jesus was saved. We think of each child we receive as The One.' I asked if he could put me in touch with any of the parents who had given up their daughters. 'That will not be possible. It would be a breach of confidence and greatly undermine our work in the villages. These people wish to remain anonymous, for obvious reasons, and we have to assure them that we will respect their wishes. Even their own children will never know who they are.' We shook hands once more and he gave me an encouraging smile saying, 'I hope you succeed.'

The car was parked under a huge tamarind tree outside the gates. Selvi had fallen asleep on the back seat, the doors were open for air. Mohan was squatting in the shade, smoking a *bidi*. I felt good for not having even thought of a cigarette for the last couple of hours, as I groped for the packet in my bag. I had smoked while talking to Brother James, but it hadn't seemed appropriate in front of Father Vincent, or perhaps it was just the formality of the environment, which had a distinctly austere, convent-like touch.

On the way back to Kodai, silence prevailed. Selvi slept on the back seat, and I enjoyed sitting in front with the full blast of the wind on my face. I was looking forward to the wintry night ahead in my bed at Roseneath, having forgotten the weight of the army blankets. As we began the climb, the car slowed down to a chugging pace. 'Clapped-out engine,' I thought, but said nothing. Mohan already seemed embarrassed by his taxi's performance and muttered something about the engine being too hot. 'Radiator?' I asked. He shook his head, concentrating on the road ahead.

About an hour into the winding road, Selvi suddenly woke up feeling sick. We stopped while she threw up violently over the edge of a drain. I remembered what she had said about her journeys to Trichy with her husband, and apologized for having forgotten this fact. Wiping tears from her eyes and splashing her face with water that emerged in a small stream from the rocks, she smiled and said, 'It's all right, Ma. I wanted to come.' I suggested she might feel better sitting upright in front and she agreed. I told Mohan we should stop smoking in the car.

Back at Roseneath, Adam's bungalow was in darkness. It was past midnight. We had dropped Selvi off on the way but I hadn't seen her house. The road leading to it was so rough and stony that she said she had to walk the last half-mile. 'Don't worry, Ma,' she said, laughing at the look on my face. 'I do this every day – I am used to it.' I thought of the unhealed scars behind her knees. Not only did she negotiate this stretch every day, she walked all the way to Roseneath and back, up and down steep slopes without complaint. For the first time, I realized what a gruelling distance that must be for her. She said that the municipality had bulldozed the track some years ago and laid down these jagged rocks in preparation for the road that was still to come! She threw up her hands in mock despair and laughed at the absurdity of it all. As we saw her disappear out of the glare of the reversing headlights, I asked Mohan to drive me past the Kurinju Clinic. I wanted to know how far it was from her home. Two miles, he estimated. As we drove past the lake where the clinic stood, I tried to picture Selvi running that agonizing mile or two half-naked on the night of the 'accident', barefoot over rough-cut rock much of the way.

The bungalow felt cold and damp. I had hoped that Adam would still be awake. I needed to talk. He would have had the fire on and we could have chatted over a drink. Instead, the dogs accompanied me up the winding slope from the gate, gravel crunching underfoot as we made our way through a thin drizzle in pitch darkness, shuffling through fallen leaves on a moonless night. Though disappointed, I still felt elated at being back in Kodaikanal, at Roseneath. I had wanted to discuss the events of the day with someone. Miss Roberts perhaps? But she must be in bed too by now, I thought.

I remember lying awake under those now familiar heavy-duty blankets, feeling the cold and damp in a way I had not done throughout my time in England, thinking of the people I had met that day. I wondered why they did what they did. What was in it for them? They didn't appear to have much money and certainly didn't live in any great luxury.

The drizzle had turned to rain as I fell asleep, memories of the past taking over. I remembered that same sound of rain in my father's house in Poona just before I left for England. For good? I didn't know. Nothing was for ever. He had been dead for many years but I had vivid memories of him that brought on a feeling of warmth.

I did not know it then, but in the years to come, people like the ones I had met that morning were to be massacred by religious fanatics operating under an umbrella of government protection; bent on establishing Hindu rule in India; challenging the very foundations of a secular society; triggering riots that led to much bloodshed and slaughter in the name of God; creating conditions for perpetual conflict that would pave the way into this millennium.

CHAPTER TEN

The next morning, Selvi arrived in a bright and energetic mood. In a somewhat gloomy state of mind myself, I watched her rattling pots and pans in the kitchen, wiping down surfaces as if a day away from housework had left the place in need of an urgent facelift. With the sun streaming through the open window and the sounds of birds filling the air outside, I realized my underlying tension was because I did not want to return to London just then. I wanted to visit the village of Deorala where Roop Kanwar had allegedly committed sati on 4 September 1987. I needed some first-hand experience of the prevailing social climate, of the balance of political power within it, if I was to even consider writing a book that would include her story. Yet the visit was not possible at the time and I knew it. I had no funds to support such a venture. Just watching Selvi's pragmatic and cheerful approach to life made me feel calmer. I admired her energy. She had been through much mental and physical turmoil but remained so resilient, and had the kind of infectious laughter I seemed incapable of responding to that day. Suddenly, she cut through my thoughts as if she knew what I was thinking and asked, 'So will you write this book, Ma?'

'Yes,' I said, trying to sound positive. 'You have made me want to write it even more than I did before.'

Wet duster in hand, she gave me a hug and said, 'You can write anything you want about me – just don't mention my husband's name.' I said I wouldn't.

*

It was not until the autumn of that year, 1995, that I was able to return to India. Channel Four television had paid me for my research work on the 'Successful Women' project but didn't want to pursue it. I felt relieved. I had spent six weeks travelling in various parts of India before the time spent in Kodaikanal, speaking with women who worked in various professional fields; smart, well-dressed, highly literate, confident, outspoken women with singular ambitions; married to other professionals; sheltered by the lifestyle of middle-class India; often authoritative and judgemental in their manner. I had felt strangely uncomfortable in their presence, aware that once I said I lived in London there was an air of dismissal, a look in the eye that said 'You have been westernized', you are no longer a 'Real Indian'. Many had projected the kind of nationalistic pride that borders on fundamentalism. I remember thinking at the time, 'But isn't this what men say about you? That you have been "westernized" because you crop your hair, wear sleeveless *cholis*, smoke cigarettes – or whatever? None of this was ever articulated but the attitude was obvious. Selvi had no such attitude problem and I felt good in her company. I was glad to be free of the project, much as I needed the money and the job. Perhaps the commissioning editor sensed my lack of enthusiasm and decided it was not something I was capable of doing, or perhaps not worth doing for other reasons. I never really asked. I was grateful for the research fee and decided to return to India.

That autumn of 1995, I found myself on the road to Deorala. The monsoon had been unexpectedly heavy and the motorway was full of pot-holes, deep ditches camouflaged by muddy pools which the taxi negotiated at a snail's pace, lurching, rattling and creaking to the point that one of the windows sank irretrievably into the door frame and left us open to sheets of rain and the mud splashed by passing trucks.

I was travelling with a friend, Prakash, the son of a Rajasthani landowning family, who commuted between his farm in the village of Borunda and the city of Jodhpur, where we had met while I was working on a project for BBC television. Prakash had become a sort of co-researcher then, in 1991, and was on the road with me once again, four years later. As we rattled along in the taxi he said, 'Buy a coconut, just to be on the safe side.' I laughed at first but after some discussion decided it might not be a bad idea after all. We were partners in deception, buying the coconut as an offering for the shrine neither of us thought should have been there in the first place. We had to present the right image, Prakash said, in order to communicate with people who obviously had a vested interest. He was right, so we stopped at a wayside cluster of stalls where we drank tea, ate samosas filled with *dal* and bought an enormous shiny green coconut which cost fifteen rupees – the going rate in Jaipur being about eight. Prakash remarked quizzically, 'So the road to the Sati Temple starts here!'

'The feminists will kill me for this!' I said, as I paid for it.

Prakash laughed out loud, saying, 'Don't worry about such things. We are a nation full of false gestures! Just try and get Roop Kanwar's in-laws to talk to you. That's what we are here for, are we not?'

The next day, 4 September, was the eighth anniversary of Roop Kanwar's death. We had no idea what to expect. Perhaps the village would be overrun by pilgrims. I thought I'd timed the visit well in that respect, having wanted to witness any public response there might be to mark the occasion.

I had asked Prakash to accompany me because I was nervous of entering a village that was known to be hostile to the press. Roop Kanwar's in-laws and others were still on bail, charged with first-degree murder. The case had not been tried in eight years, and although there had been a lull in the publicity, the outcome remained uncertain, and there was bound to be much tension within the village. Besides, I didn't speak the village dialect but Prakash did, and he had agreed enthusiastically to my request that he accompany me. He was young, somewhere in his late twenties, or early thirties, extremely handsome and quite a complex person. He'd travelled in the West, was deeply traditional in many ways but also curious about the world in general or people in general, to be more accurate. He was telling me why he had settled for an arranged marriage for the sake of family tradition, for which he had a great deal of respect. His widowed mother was in the process of choosing his bride, and he had decided to abide by her wishes. Not in the least concerned about appearing macho, Prakash was a sensitive young man, who chose India over the West.

Prakash had had an American girlfriend whom he still admired, but knew he could not live with on his farm. It would disrupt the tranquillity of generations. She would not be happy, unable to adjust to the rigours of Rajasthani custom. And why should she anyway? They came from different cultures. I listened to Prakash intently but didn't quite know what to say. 'Do you think I have made the right decision?' he asked suddenly.

'Yes,' was my immediate response. Asking myself if I was agreeing to arranged marriages, I added quickly, 'If that's what you want.'

'But I'm not sure what I want!' he said, looking into the distance, forehead furrowed. 'I want to do what's right. For myself, for my family.' I was deeply moved by his passionate sense of duty, touched by his dilemma.

As we turned off the potholed, pukka road, the taxi gathered speed on the dust track leading to a cluster of villages separated by about a couple of kilometres from each other. The taxi was throwing up clouds of dust as the driver, frustrated by the earlier pace from Jaipur to the turn-off point, hurtled along at breakneck speed. Prakash told him to slow down. At the rate we were going, we would soon all choke on dust because of the collapsed window, he told him curtly. The driver laughed good-humouredly and reduced his speed by half.

There were no signposts. Villagers directed us to Deorala. Prakash suggested we pull up on the outskirts of the village. 'Let's walk,' he said. 'We'll create less *tamasha* that way and besides, we won't make ourselves popular with the villagers if we throw up all this dust in front of their homes!' He was so easygoing and good-humoured, a pleasure to work with, I remember thinking at the time, increasingly grateful for his presence and quiet, confident manner.

The village looked like any other we had passed on the way. People ambled down dusty lanes or rode bicycles through the sand. They watched us with curiosity and open hostility. Prakash chatted with a youth on the way, asking for directions to Sumer Singh's home instead of the *Sati Sthal*, as I might have done had I been on my own. This was an astute move, as it turned out.

In the lane leading to what had been Roop Kanwar's marital home, we were suddenly accosted by an extremely aggressive-looking man in his forties, wearing pyjama bottoms and a singlet. 'What do you want and where are you from?' he asked authoritatively.

Prakash said, 'We've come from Jodhpur and my friend here is a writer. She lives in London and is writing a book about Rajasthan and Rajput culture. We have come to meet Mart Sahib.' This was not strictly true, but I didn't understand a word Prakash was saying at the time. The man looked me up and down and exchanged a few more words with Prakash in the local dialect before pointing to a brick house less than twenty yards away. His expression hadn't changed much but he walked away with a nod of the head as if giving us permission to proceed.

'What was that all about?' I asked Prakash.

He handed me the plastic carrier bag containing the coconut and my Walkman, saying, 'He's one of Sumer Singh's brothers and says their family own three houses in this lane. They are hostile to the press but I've said you're writing a book about the traditions of Rajasthan, so stick to that!' Feeling quite out of my depth, I decided to let Prakash take over and lead the way.

Stone steps led up to the two-storeyed brick house from which Roop Kanwar had walked to her death. A narrow corridor led into an open courtyard. The rooms flanking either side, overlooking the veranda, were padlocked and had iron bars across the open windows. There was no sign of life. A large wooden bed on the veranda, with nothing on it, gave the impression of a public platform. Prakash indicated for me to wait there as he removed his shoes and entered the corridor. It was a sort of open-plan house with locks on individual rooms. I could hear Prakash talking to a woman and then a child in the inner courtyard. Sorely tempted to light a cigarette, I told myself I mustn't. First impressions were of extreme importance. Instead, I peered through the bars of the windows. The room on the left looked like someone's bedroom. It was sparsely furnished, with a single *charpai*, and some clothes hung on a cord stretched across one corner. They were men's clothes. The other room on the right was the 'shrine'. Portraits of Maal Singh and Roop Kanwar adorned the facing wall. The centrepiece was a life-size enlargement of Roop Kanwar on her wedding day, draped in a red and gold veil (the one offered to the burning pyre on the Thirteenth Day Ceremony after her death). A garland of fresh flowers hung over the imitation gold frame, and I could see the glitter of coins on the floor through the dim light, much like coins lying scattered at the bottom of a fountain. The silent TV set in the corner, which I had read about in press reports, was still there. As I was peering through the bars, Prakash returned with Roop Kanwar's father-in-law, Sumer Singh or Mart Sahib, as all village schoolteachers are apparently called as a show of respect.

Sumer Singh was a quiet, soft-spoken man who had an air of distraction or detachment about him. I had no idea what Prakash had said to him, so merely folded my hands in a *namaste* and said, in Hindi, 'Thank you for seeing us.'

'Visitors are always welcome in my house,' he replied as he settled down cross-legged on the wooden bed, gesturing that we do the same. He turned to Prakash and spoke once again in the village dialect which I could not understand, although his Hindi was perfect. I realized he was sussing me out through Prakash. Fortunately, the earlier project Prakash and I had worked on together was to do with the epic of Pabuji, a legendary figure in Rajput history and folklore. The epic depicted traditions of honour, loyalty, courage, valour and manhood. It also included descriptions of sati and the courage of women. Professor John Smith, a Sanskrit scholar and head of the Department of Oriental Studies at Cambridge University, had written an impressive book on the age-old oral epic, translating, transcribing and commissioning fine illustrations by a traditional painter. We had made a film for the BBC series *Bookmark* in 1991, exploring the legend, its oral traditions, ritual performances and John Smith's remarkable achievement.

Prakash was explaining all this to Sumer Singh as I watched a braying donkey enter the lane and stop in front of the house, grubbing and rooting for something in a ditch. The noise was deafening at such close proximity and we all laughed, lightening the formality of the atmosphere.

Sumer Singh called into the house and a young girl of about eleven or twelve appeared. He introduced us to his daughter, Usha, and asked her to make some fresh tea. Prakash glanced at me, knowing I didn't drink tea but I remained silent. The donkey had moved on and they resumed their conversation. Later, in the taxi, Prakash told me they had been discussing the fate of the crops and the late arrival of the monsoon. Many farmers had lost a great deal after the drought that year, followed by torrential rain which had flooded fields and ruined many an investment.

After the tea arrived, Sumer Singh turned his attention to me and spoke in Hindi. 'I am prepared to spend some time with you,' he said, 'if you are writing a book, but I am sick to death of these paper-wallahs [newspaper journalists].' I assured him that I was working on a book and would not be writing anything for the Indian press. 'That's all right then,' he said, 'but you must come back next week. I cannot be seen talking to you now. There is a big police presence in the village. You see, her death anniversary is tomorrow and the High Court has ruled that we cannot celebrate it. My family are under close watch.' I looked around and saw no police presence but nodded anyway. He was right, however. Within half an hour a police jeep had driven into the lane, throwing up columns of dust. Under pressure from women's groups, who had taken the matter to the courts, the

State Government had been instructed to prevent any form of gathering in celebration of the widow's death.

The officer in the passenger seat of the police jeep greeted Sumer Singh and then addressed Prakash and me in English. 'What is the purpose of your visit?' he asked.

I answered immediately, sensing danger. 'I'm writing a book on Rajput culture and its traditions,' I replied. 'I live in London.' He looked somewhat more relaxed.

Prakash added, 'She is a writer of international fame!' This was far from the truth, but the policeman smiled – I was looking my docile best and Sumer Singh seemed unruffled. I took my opportunity and asked if I could visit the *Sati Sthal*, having come all this way.

The policeman said, 'It is not allowed,' and drove off in another cloud of dust. We looked at each other, and I knew the ice had been broken.

After a brief discussion in Hindi, it was agreed that we should leave and return in a week, after the police presence had been relaxed. Sumer Singh said, 'If you wish to see the *Sati Sthal*, it is not far from here. Just be discreet.' He directed us and we walked not more than five minutes from the house, under the gaze of curious eyes. The tension in the village felt like a monsoon cloud hanging in the air, about to burst.

At the *sthal*, we saw a lone police constable fast asleep on a *charpai* in a tent. The clutter of pots and pans outside indicated rudimentary cooking arrangements around a small *sigri*, a miniature coal-fire cooker. Set in a large open clearing, a tattered, weather-beaten, faded veil hung on an upright *trishul*, symbol of the Hindu trinity. From a distance it looked like the figure of a small woman or a child. The atmosphere was eerie. The silence and desolation got to me, and I felt diminished, unable to move. A woman had been burned alive on this spot and was now the subject of a political wrangle that had nothing to do with her life, her pain, her feelings – or, ultimately, her death. Discarded dried-up coconuts lay scattered around the stone slabs that covered what had been the pyre and the veil on the *trishul* hung limp on a windless day. Prakash took the camera from my bag and said, 'Let's get some proof that we have been here. It will perhaps help you with your publishers in London.' I stood mesmerized while he took a few shots of the images before us, including the sleeping policeman in his tent.

On the way back to the house, he said, 'Now's your opportunity. Say you brought a coconut but couldn't leave it at the *sthal* because of the police presence. Ask to see the last room in the house that Roop Kanwar lived in.' I nodded, still in a daze.

Back on the veranda, Sumer Singh was talking to a neighbour, who was obviously curious about us. As we approached, the man left and Sumer Singh asked me, 'So what did you think?'

'I felt sad,' I replied. 'It all looked so bleak.'

'That's because the government won't let us build a temple,' was his immediate response.

I didn't reply, grateful for the knowledge that I could speak with this man again. We had gained his confidence and that was a start. I knew I couldn't have done it without Prakash.

Once again, Prakash took the initiative. 'Malaji has brought a coconut and would like to place it in what used to be her room – since the police will not allow us to pay any other kind of tribute.' Looking confused, Sumer Singh called out to Usha and asked her to take me upstairs. Prakash's eyes widened but I kept a straight face as I followed Usha into the house. The inner courtyard contained a small sheltered area which constituted the kitchen, but the rest was open to the elements. Expensive-looking brass pots, *kalai*-ed – lined with silver for cooking – stood in neat rows, indicating the comparative wealth of this landowning family. We climbed a set of stone steps up to the terrace on the roof of the house. A single room had been constructed on one side, to the right of the stairs. It was padlocked like the two downstairs. Usha, a very shy young girl who only communicated with me by gesture, unlocked the room and held the door wide open. Coconut in hand, I entered the room and was completely taken aback. It was not at all what I had expected, having seen the shrine behind the barred window downstairs. This was a junk

room, a storage space untouched by sentimentality. A big refrigerator stood in one corner, wrapped in plastic sheeting. The bed,
once covered in red velvet by Roop Kanwar, was piled high with
spare mattresses and cardboard boxes gathering dust. The stone
shelves, painted white with limewash, were mostly bare apart
from some cheap trinkets and what looked like machine tools. I
placed the coconut on one of the shelves and studied the room.
There was no sign of anything remotely personal. It was a
dumping ground. For some inexplicable reason, I thought of the
Hollywood film based on Daphne du Maurier's book, *Rebecca*,
where the husband, who everyone thought had been besotted by
his first wife, actually hated her. The images of contradiction
were to haunt me throughout my adolescence. One memory
triggered another. I was reminded not only of the feeling of
neglect but of anger and hatred as I stood alone in that room.
Usha had disappeared. I remember feeling a chill. It could have
been the sudden lack of sun in an abandoned, musty room,
dampened by the monsoon air, or it could have been past memories. Whatever the reason, the room gave me a chill.

On the way back to Jaipur in the taxi, Prakash told me that
while I was upstairs, Sumer Singh had apologized for the state of
the room. It would not be used until his next son was married,
he said. It would then become the bridal chamber once again. I
told Prakash of my morbid thoughts in the room and he said,
quite calmly and casually, 'Maybe you're right. Sumer Singh did
say that Roop Kanwar had brought nothing but tragedy to the
family.' He went on to describe their brief conversation. Roop
Kanwar's father-in-law felt much anger and bitterness. He felt he
was no longer a free man, that he and his sons were now 'under-
trial prisoners', subjected to police scrutiny. 'He is quite a bitter
person really,' Prakash concluded. 'Not the proud relative of the
Sati Mata of the village. Anyway, that's the impression I got.
Perhaps he was simply trying to recruit my sympathy so that I'd
see him as a victim of circumstance.'

'And do you think he is?' I asked.

'That's what you will have to find out,' he replied laughing.

Then he added, 'One thing I can tell you, he's a very shrewd man. Careful with his words and deeply suspicious of outsiders. Still, I think he liked you – because you kept quiet!'

The plan had been to stay in Jaipur for a few days and visit the village on a regular basis, in order to get to know people. We had checked into the Atithi Guest House, 'A Travellers' Home' said the billboard in brackets, wedged between the railway station and the bus stop. It was a small hotel, popular with foreign tourists, mostly backpackers, because it was cheap, clean and centrally located. A prominent sign behind the reception desk read: 'Boiled Drinking Water & Ice Available On Request.' We ordered something to eat and sat talking late into the evening on the hotel lawn until the mosquitoes forced us back to our rooms, which were protected by finely woven wire mesh.

Faced with the prospect of a one-week wait, I decided to return to Jodhpur with Prakash the next day. He had work to attend to on the farm in Borunda and we had planned to stay just three days in Jaipur. I couldn't afford to camp in a hotel room for a whole week with nothing specific to do. I had no contacts in the city at the time. The sole purpose of the visit had been to visit Deorala, using Jaipur as a base from which to commute.

Back in Jodhpur the next day, I remember feeling confused and exhausted. I hadn't liked the police, but found it hard to dislike Sumer Singh. Was he a murderer? Had he driven his daughter-in-law to her death?

Prakash, casual as ever, said, 'There is much to be gained from temples and shrines, don't become sentimental. Revisit the village. He has opened up to you, so others will also talk.'

'It's all because of you,' I replied. 'I couldn't have done it without you.'

He laughed in his sudden, spontaneous way and said, 'Let's go and visit Jodhpur Fort tomorrow. You will see the imprint of women's hands in concrete, women who actually committed sati voluntarily in the past, privileged women who were married to kings.'

We had travelled back to Jodhpur by bus, as train tickets were impossible to get at the last minute. The road was rough, and the journey had seemed endless. I admired the way Prakash had been able to sleep soundly, sitting upright or leaning his head on the seat in front, despite the endless jolting motion of this 'Luxury Video Bus' with its sound system blaring popular Hindi film songs throughout the journey. I hadn't been able to sleep a wink, and felt too tired and stiff to make any immediate plans. Though disappointed at having to wait a week before speaking to Sumer Singh again, I told Prakash: 'I'll spend the week in Jodhpur and tax Komalda's brain instead!'

'Yes, speak to Dada. He knows practically everything there is to know about Rajasthan. I'll see you tomorrow. After the trip to the Fort I must return to Borunda,' said Prakash as he left. He had warned me not to jump to conclusions after our brief visit to Deorala.

I felt suddenly vulnerable at the prospect of returning to Deorala alone but put it down to feeling tired and being in need of a shower. I would seek Komalda's advice that evening. I had the privilege of being a guest in his home, and occupied a beautiful large U-shaped room, with its own bathroom and kitchen. Komalda had originally built it as his office-cum-study, detached from the rest of the house, in which four generations of the family lived, ranging from his widowed mother to his grandchildren. It was a sprawling traditional household, buzzing with activity and creative energy.

Essentially a musicologist but also renowned for his knowledge of Rajasthani folklore and village lore, Komal Kothari had a reputation that attracted many visitors from various parts of the globe. A *bania* by birth, he came from the Bania caste of Marwari businessmen, a powerful and prominent Rajasthani community which controls much of India's commerce and industry. Completely atypical of his caste, Komalda – or 'Dada' as he was locally known – commanded much respect in villages throughout Rajasthan, having actually lived for months on end in many.

I had first met him together with Prakash and Professor John

Smith in 1991, when we'd all worked together on the *Bookmark* programme. It had been an intense and memorable experience. At the time, Komalda had invited me to revisit Jodhpur and stay with them any time. This was his way with most people he wished to support and encourage. Next to the room I occupied beyond the vegetable garden, was a large shed, home to many a travelling musician. Komalda spent hours with these musicians, determined to keep their traditions and skills alive in the modern world. Since our first meeting, I had met Komalda in London as well, when he had toured Europe with a hand-picked group of local musicians he had nurtured, villagers who had performed to international audiences at places like the Royal Albert Hall and the Commonwealth Institute. He was a mentor to many and, over the years had become mine too.

My head was buzzing with questions I wanted to ask Komalda, as I decided to sleep through a rainy afternoon. Everyone else was doing the same. At around half-past four we would all meet for tea. It was the daily routine, and I found that strangely comforting, being unused to such regularity myself.

When I awoke, it was dark. Aasoo, a young man who worked for the family, was at the door with a cup of coffee in one hand and a lit candle in the other. There had been a power cut. 'Dada is waiting for you and Indiraji asked me to bring you this coffee,' he announced, placing the candle on a table. No one else in the household drank coffee but Indiraji, Komalda's wife, was renowned for her hospitality and the attention she paid to the needs of their constant stream of visitors. Stumbling out of a dead sleep, I realized it was past seven. Grateful for the coffee, I dressed hurriedly and made my way through the vegetable garden, past the musicians' shed, from which the sound of a lone flute filled the night air, evoking images of sand dunes stretching as far as the eye could see. It was the unmistakable sound of the desert, terrain I had travelled in 1991. The main house ahead was dimly lit with candles in each room and a hurricane lamp on the porch to throw some light on the driveway, that people tended to walk up any time of the day or night.

Komalda was surrounded by visitors that evening, among them Prakash's uncle, a well-known Hindi writer. It was not the time for a serious discussion. The men were drinking whisky, and invited me to join them. I was the only woman in the room but that was not unusual. The women of the house rarely participated on such occasions but were not hostile to the fact that I did. They would eat dinner as usual at around eight, and I was free to join them if I wished. Alternatively, I could eat later with the men. When there were no visitors, we all ate together. Indiraji and her two daughters-in-law were excellent cooks, and their table was always a mouth-watering sight. They were strict vegetarians, and the emphasis was always on seasonal vegetables, which Komalda bought personally each morning at the wholesale market. I accompanied him at times, if I was awake and ready to leave by half-past six in the morning. We walked there and back at a leisurely pace while Dada chewed on twigs broken off neem trees on the way, cleaning his teeth with their bitter extract. My grandfather had used the same method; instead of a toothbrush in his bathroom tumbler, there used to be a constant supply of these medicinal twigs.

I looked forward to my outings in the early hours of the morning with Komalda, when the market was bustling with activity – truckloads of vegetables being unloaded, traders spraying them with water in anticipation of the noonday sun, retail vendors driving hard bargains with wholesalers – while Dada selected the freshest and most economically priced vegetables available at that time of year. Everyone seemed to know him, and he often stopped to exchange a few words with someone or other.

Back at the house, the routine was that everyone sat around a table and peeled vegetables, including Komalda; a quiet, pleasant process over cups of tea which ended before breakfast. The food for the day – allowing for a minimum of fifteen people, often more, depending on how many visitors arrived – lay neatly piled on *thali*s by then, ready to be cooked. The two daughters-in-law of the family took turns over lunch and dinner and Indiraji occasionally made something special. They worked together in complete harmony. Yet, within this communal structure, there were three distinct family units and each mother was in charge of her own children's and her husband's needs. I had never once sensed any friction within this traditional structure and found that amazing in itself. Komalda's mother was old and frail, close to ninety, a gentle, religious woman with her own special prayer room, who interacted with the rest of the family according to her mood, remaining unjudgemental like the rest and surprisingly broad-minded on many issues. I enjoyed spending time with her during the day. Neither of us was welcome in the kitchen!

That evening, I ate with the men after we'd all had a couple of whiskies each, a rare occasion, as Komalda hardly ever drank alcohol. I found myself telling Vijay Dandetta, Prakash's uncle, about our trip to Deorala, saying I planned to return the following week. The question of whether sati was voluntary or not became the focus of the conversation. I was speaking of François Bernier's accounts of widow burning in north India during the time of the Mogul Empire when Komalda interjected and said, 'No, no, no, Mala! Widow burning and sati are not the same thing at all.'

'What do you mean?' I asked defiantly, adding, 'If widows are burned alive on their husbands' funeral pyres, what difference does it make what you call the practice?'

'A very big difference,' he said. 'We'll talk tomorrow. I can suggest some books you should look at.'

Knowing how involved he got during the day with various people, I said, 'Shall I go to the market with you tomorrow morning then?'

'Sure,' he replied. 'I'll send Aasoo to your room at six with some coffee and give you a shout on my way out.' His assertion that sati and widow burning could not be equated played on my mind late into the night. I thought he was splitting hairs but, mindful of his knowledge, also realized that was unlikely, but the 'difference' had me completely confused.

CHAPTER ELEVEN

Walking through the wholesale market the next morning, Komalda spoke in a ponderous, somewhat distracted way as he chose vegetables. 'But how can you say sati is not the same as widow burning?' I persisted. 'Look,' he said, 'the tradition of each culture has to be examined historically, within its own environment. Don't jump to conclusions.' This was more or less what Prakash had said to me the day before. He was to pick me up on his motorcycle later on that morning for a visit to the Jodhpur Fort.

My mind began to drift as I took in the sights, sounds and smells around me. The market was alive. The wonderful thing about Komalda was his ability to assess mood-swings in other people. He could see I was in no mood for a history lesson, and lapsed into silence; not a hostile silence, just a quiet understanding. The conversation turned to other, more light-hearted things once he was bargaining with vendors over the price of corn, beautifully encased in their husks, pale green tresses indicating their freshness.

Back at the gate of the house, I said, 'I'm going to the fort with Prakash today – to look at the sati hands on the wall – will you be free later?'

'Sure,' he said, with a warm and gentle smile. 'Before lunch if you like. Are you not coming to the house?'

'Sure,' I said. 'I just need a few minutes to have a wash. See you soon.' Having seen us enter the gate, Aasoo was coming towards us to relieve us of the load of shopping bags, made of jute, which contained the vegetables for the day.

We parted company and fifteen minutes later, everyone was sitting around the dining table, peeling and cutting, removing peas from pods and separating corn from cob. It was too damp and chilly to sit outside on the patio, which we normally did. Suddenly, through the silence that surrounded this early morning ritual, Komalda said, 'Speak to these women,' indicating his wife and daughters-in-law with his eyes. 'Ask them what they think about sati.' Then, turning to his wife, he explained my interest in the Roop Kanwar case. Indiraji looked at me and nodded and I felt she saw in me the 'tourist', a virtual foreigner, probing traditions they understood in their souls.

Later that morning, Prakash turned up on his motorcycle. As we rode through the swirling dust of Jodhpur's streets, I looked around the town and its people, women ornately dressed, however poor they were. The men were equally flamboyant, wearing jewellery and flaunting incredible turbans – ranging in style and colour in a way that was almost mesmerizing. I felt truly ignorant of their culture and tradition. I thought of a book I had bought on my travels, *Rajasthan: Splendour in the Wilderness* by Dom Moraes. It was a coffee-table book which had cost a fortune but had been well worth it. It included spectacular photographs by Gopi Gajwani and an inspiring introduction by the poet-cum-writer, Dom Moraes, whom I had got to know and like over the years, and who also happened to be the first cousin of a close friend of mine in Bombay. Dom opens his introduction to the photographer's work by saying:

[Rajasthan] is a dry country. It is also very old. Though the great lake glimmers like a shield of water in the middle of Udaipur, three-quarters of the land area is covered by the bitter sand and tamarisk of the Thar Desert. If you walk a little way into the sand, you may find fossilised bits of forest, or even seashells. This is indicative of the fact that, perhaps millions of years ago, the desert was a seabed, and that later trees lifted their heads towards the blue sky where now no tree stands. It is said that

Kardam Muni, a saint and the father of another saint, Kapil Muni, used to live on the banks of a huge lake called Karoamsar. It is now called the Kodam Desert, but if legend is true there was once a great deal of water where now there is none, and the river Saraswati, flowing lavishly down from the Himalayas across the plains of Kurukshetra to the sea, was the source of most of it. There is a legend of what happened to the Saraswati. There is a legend about almost everything in Rajasthan. It is a land of legends, a place of princes.

He goes on to explain the legend:

According to this particular legend, Rama was about to attack Lanka to rescue Sita. The god of the sea, however, wouldn't let him cross to the island. So Rama, justly incensed, fitted an arrow to his bow. This arrow was programmed, as it were, to generate great heat: a kind of atomic arrow. The heat would dry up the sea. Threatened by this missile, the god of the sea relented, and told Rama he could cross. But the arrow, once poised on the bowstring, had to be sent somewhere. Rama shot it into the Saraswati basin. The river promptly dried up. Scientific opinion has it that upheavals of rock near Jaisalmer – for the state lies within the seismic belt – caused the Saraswati to change course till it became a tributary of the river Sindh.

No river, no tree, and few people exist in the lion-coloured sands of the Thar. Rajasthan is a land of extremes, not only scorched by the sun in the endless summer but bitterly cold in winter. The gritty sand becomes so hot in summer that it burns the soles of your shoes. The desert wind blows drifts of it across the roads that penetrate this wilderness, and anyone who drives has to spend time making a passage through the drifts. If a car travels fast, as most cars do to get out of this hellhole, the friction of its tyres on the overheated macadam often causes them to explode. Spare tyres and a spade are essential to anyone who is driving in the desert, where few of the sparse local population care to walk abroad in the day.

We had begun to climb the steep hill road that leads to Jodhpur

Fort. Though partly blinded by the sun and wind, I could see the city recede into the distance below, the Thar Desert stretching beyond as we made our way up in silence, engulfed by the roar of the engine. Feeling dwarfed by both the landscape and my own lack of knowledge about Rajasthan in general, I resolved to tape all further discussions with Komalda during what was left of my stay. The breadth of his interest and knowledge of all aspects of Rajasthani life was phenomenal.

Inside the fort, Prakash parked the bike and we joined other visitors struggling up the steep stone slopes that horses once negotiated. A group of American tourists were being told historical facts by their guide, who carried a long stick with which he pointed in various directions. I tried to absorb some of what he was saying but felt far too drained by the climb and the dry heat of the sun. The chill of the early morning air had gone.

A stone panel on the wall leading to an inner shrine was lined with the imprints of small, childlike hands. These were the symbols of sati, embedded in a concrete wall by women who had burned themselves alive within these walls generations and centuries ago. The handprints didn't look real to me. The fact that they had been painted over with a kind of red gloss added to a sense of artificiality rather than evoking any pathos. Prakash assured me they were the actual *nishan* (marks) of actual queens, concubines and their slaves who had voluntarily committed sati on the funeral pyres of Rajput kings and princes in the past.

In other rooms constituting the museum, weapons of war and the changing face of battle dress – ranging from chainmail to plate armour – dominated glass showcases. Rows and rows of swords stood on display as we wandered through the cool stone rooms, relieved to be in the shade once more.

I had expected some form of emotional reaction within myself at the sight of all those women's hands embedded on the wall, the famous sati hands, but they had left me feeling even more disconnected from the story I was trying to research than I had felt the night before. I knew I was inexplicably tired, anxious to get back to the house and talk to Komalda about my conflicting thoughts. I knew Rajasthan's history was full of wild and passionate extremes but surely times were different now? The old, feudal order no longer existed and dreams of courtship and valour seemed like fantasies of the past. Yet the mystique of the place was undeniable. The myths and legends of the past remained firmly entrenched in the Rajput psyche, kept alive by religious rituals, songs and a whole range of performing arts.

Back at the house, we found Komalda surrounded by a group of musicians, including the flute player who had camped overnight in the shed. They were to attend a recording session at the local radio station that evening, which Dada had arranged and which would earn them a small fee, after which they would return to their villages. Prakash and I joined the group, and what struck me was the silence. Hardly anyone spoke. As if reading my mind, Dada said, 'It is only city people who need to make conversation. Here, people are comfortable to just spend time in each other's company.'

Later that evening, Walkman in hand, I made my way to Dada's room. There was much excitement in the house among the children. Aasoo had just killed a snake in the vegetable garden and it was about to be cremated, on a pyre made of two bricks in the driveway. I decided to attend the ceremony and take pictures of the event for the boys, who wanted a record for their school friends. The snake, about an inch in width and over two feet long, lay coiled on a bed of dry grass; *sindoor*, the red powder used for *bindhis*, and turmeric were sprinkled over its black and silver patterned skin. Aasoo and the children posed for photographs and then lit the fire with solemn precision, watching the snake writhe as it burned to death. Snakes are considered sacred within Hindu tradition, and this little ritual was a show of respect. Later I was told that during the rains, snakes often frequented the vegetable garden and the area surrounding my room at the end of it. Few were poisonous, I was assured, but it was advisable to carry a torch and not walk barefoot in the dark. The calm rhythm of the household resumed with little fuss.

Talking with Dada soon after this event, I tried to refocus on the point of my visit, 'What are your feelings about the Deorala sati then?'

Komalda was an avid reader of newspapers and Roop Kanwar's death had stirred quite a political storm in Rajasthan. The tape ran silently on the table between us. After what seemed like a long pause, he said, 'One thing I can say, having read press reports, I don't think she was forced in the way they are saying. Whatever this family is like, however bad they are, I don't think they forced her physically.' I decided to remain silent. After another lengthy pause, he continued, 'But another thing could have happened. At one moment she may have said she had decided to become a sati, and later, if she changed her mind, then people would not have listened. She herself must have gone through a range of conflicting and emotional experiences in such a situation ...' His voice trailed off into silence as he shook his head slowly and gazed at the bedspread absently. It covered a vast, wooden double bed – much like the one on Sumer Singh's veranda in Deorala – on which he and his wife slept. During the day and in the evening, it became a place for all to sit on, cross-legged or otherwise, in the informal atmosphere of their room. Chairs usually surrounded the bed as well, depending on the number of people in the room. The other venue for social gatherings was the covered veranda just outside, but its close proximity to the garden attracted mosquitoes that bred wildly at this time of year, driving people indoors at twilight, when they swarmed towards their victims in alarming formation. The living room was the TV room where the children and other members of the family congregated in the evenings and at night after dinner. Those who came to see Dada converged on his bedroom if he was not outdoors.

Coming out of what seemed to be some deep and concentrated thought, he continued, 'You see, in our community, among the Jains, there is, for example, one particular tradition. When we are very old, or very ill, or something like that and you feel that now you won't survive, then you say, "I will become *Santara*", meaning, "I will not eat or drink anything." When a person decides to do this, there are certain religious rituals and things that are done within the family. The person who has taken *Santara* may feel at the time that he will die within the next few hours. Then suddenly you find two hours and then four hours have passed. Then ten days, then fifteen. Then, one day you will perhaps say, "I am thirsty. I want some water." By this time, you will have twenty or thirty people around you who will start saying, "Don't do this. Don't give up now." Perhaps gently cajoling, at the same time saying, "No, no more food, no more water." Perhaps at the same time stroking your head to give you comfort or strengthen your resolve. This sort of thing may have happened. It may not have happened. It is difficult to surmise in this case.'

There was another long pause, then Komalda continued, 'There can be no doubt about one thing. There's an element of shock here.'

'Shock?' I asked.

'Yes. Shock. There are a lot of things that can result from shock. For instance, some people have been known to die of a heart attack, in a state of shock, having heard bad news.' He went on to tell me a story about two elderly brothers who used to be his neighbours. 'One brother was about to catch a train to somewhere and he suddenly collapsed on the platform. Other passengers who knew him rushed to his home, leaving the train to depart, in order to give his brother the news. They found him sitting on a bench and told him what had happened saying, "Come quickly, come just now. So and so has happened." He just collapsed and died as well. So, you see, all kinds of things can happen in unexpected situations.'

I was beginning to wonder what this had to do with the tradition of sati, which is what I had come to his room to talk about, Walkman and cigarettes in hand. Komalda continued, 'But presently, all said and done – and in any given society this is so – this society is not conducive to the institution of sati.'

'Do you agree with the government then?' I asked. 'They are saying more or less the same thing.'

'The government is tense,' he replied, 'over one single thing. This tradition exists but is against the whole ethos of women. The kinds of abuse that can result out of this are tremendous.'

'In what sense?' I asked.

'In the sense that people will start killing their women.'

'But *that* is the allegation! That many of these satis are killings rather than anything else – they are not "divine" or "spiritual" acts,' I jumped in hastily, relieved that he was not merely supporting tradition. In earlier conversations, I thought he had been doing so, and had reacted emotionally – a serious personal fault – by retreating to my room, disappointed, unable to see the subtlety of his position.

At one time, in a rare show of irritability, Komalda had said, 'The trouble with you is, you just want to take sides! Somebody is right or somebody is wrong. This is not what writing is about!' I had taken offence, felt resentful, retired once more to the solitude of my room thinking he didn't understand women, thinking he didn't understand me! I knew I was frustrated by the fact that I was not getting what I had expected. I wanted to understand but knew I didn't. I wanted clear-cut answers and there seemed to be none.

'As I was telling you the other night,' Komalda continued, 'there is a big difference between the practice of widow burning in West Bengal and sati in Rajasthan.' He spoke slowly and thoughtfully, aware, I suppose, of my confusion. He went on to define the word 'sati'. It comes from the word *sat*, which, he said, I had to understand in both its female and male context. It was not an exclusively female term or concept. Neither did it describe an act. It was a very specifically defined quality in a human being. Generally speaking, it meant goodness, truth and purity. It also had other related meanings in ancient texts such as 'true essence, the principle of being'. The anti-widow-burning movement in Bengal at the turn of the nineteenth century, he added, had been linked to property inheritance laws and the middle-class move to empower women in this respect. Also, many of the women affected came from a background of poverty. In Rajasthan, no such obvious link existed where the practice of sati was concerned. Historically, it had been the practice of the ruling class, of Rajput kings and their queens. It was not common practice, nor was it commonplace. 'In fact,' he said, 'the precise number of women who have died as satis is unknown. Estimates range between one and two per cent, based on a study of sati monuments and stones, but no one really knows about medieval times.'

Komalda and I had several such conversations during the time I was his guest. He suggested books I should read every time something came to mind. I added his suggestions to an ever-growing list – some books were in print, some were not and were now only available in libraries. It seemed like a mammoth and were daunting task. Meanwhile, I started reading what I had. I had the big, coffee-table book on Rajasthan that I had bought in Delhi, *Rajasthan: Splendour in the Wilderness*, with photographs by Gopi Gajwani and an introduction by Dom Moraes. I studied the photographs of people and landscapes, trying to see history in them. I loved the feel of Dom Moraes's prose. Speaking of Rajput tradition and its legendary history of valour and courage, he had written:

The Rajput princes were many, because each started out as the warlord or chief of a clan, somewhat like what happened in Scotland. The old Aryan divisions of duty, which led to the caste system, were very apparent in Rajasthan. Here the Brahmins were priests and scholars, the princes and their followers, who went to battle, were Kshatriyas of the warrior caste. The lesser castes performed the functions assigned to them in the holy books. The princes continually fought one another – there were many blood-feuds as in Afghanistan. It was because of these constant internal battles that the armies of Rajasthan, some of the best in the subcontinent, usually failed to drive back invaders from the north. If two powerful princes had a feud, one would often throw his lot in with the foreign armies in order to defeat the other. It was not until fairly late in history that the princes, perforce, banded together against the Muslims who were stealing their women and destroying their temples, but this was religious warfare, not a question of political intelligence.

Referring to the practice of sati, Dom Moraes had this to say:

There was a certain melancholy about many of these battles. When a Rajput army was besieged in its home fort, outnumbered, and without allies to call on for help, the prince and his warriors would behave like *kamikaze* pilots. Clad in saffron robes to symbolise their imminent death, they would drink the very strong liquor brewed in the palaces, *asha*, throw open the fortress gates, and ride out to kill as many enemies as they could before being killed themselves. While they were in their last battle, their womenfolk, still in the fort, would throw themselves into a large fire where they burned alive. This was called *jauhar* and, except that it was a mass activity, was not dissimilar to the immolation of widows, which was widely practised throughout India till the British stopped it. *Jauhar* was designed to prevent the Muslims capturing the Rajput women, but also had religious overtones – the women, dying with their husbands, would be reunited with them beyond the pyre, or so it was believed.

The Rajput leaders were like European knights; they wore light armour to battle, and carried shields, swords and lances. European knights, of course, did not habitually ride to battle on elephants, but otherwise the scene was the same, the mounted warriors, on elephants or horseback followed by a rabble of crudely armed footsoldiers. The fighting appears to have been done by the book. There were certain traditional manoeuvres carried out, and few innovations. Medieval European cavalry charges were equally suicidal, and the obsolescent concept of tactics hadn't changed by the time the Light Brigade galloped to death in the Crimea in the 19th century. Courage was something the Rajputs had plenty of; imagination was what they lacked, at least on the battlefield, though they displayed plenty of it in their architecture, their arts, and their handicrafts. They built palaces that were amidst the most ornate in history, grimly splendid forts and suave temples; and the delicacy of their miniature painting and textiles seems strange in a warrior race.

I carried these images in my head as I spoke with Dada or wandered through market places, biding my time for the return trip to Deorala. After that, I had decided, I would return to Delhi to see friends and figure out practical plans. I had to use this time well before returning to London.

On the morning before I was to leave for Jaipur on the early morning train, I was chatting with Dada as usual. He seemed quiet and pensive. Suddenly, he said, 'Ask them if she left an *ok*.'

'A what?' I asked.

'An *ok* is a customary observance, based on the *Sati Mata*'s last wish, so to speak. Ask if she left them with an *ok*.' He explained that the observance of such *oks* within the family, indicated true faith in the *Sati Mata* tradition, if indeed her in-laws considered her to be one. That would be an indication of their adherence to faith and ritual.

'What sort of *ok*?' I asked.

'For instance, she may have asked that certain things be prohibited within the family. It could be anything – such as not wearing certain types of clothing or jewellery, or prohibiting the use of *sindoor* (the vermilion powder worn by married women in the parting of their hair, or as a dot on the forehead). There are a whole range of things, mostly affecting the women and children of the household. Mind you, it could also involve changes in the diet for the whole family, such as giving up eating meat. Just ask if she left an *ok*. Ask about that.' I nodded, somewhat confused by what seemed to be a minor point at the time.

CHAPTER TWELVE

Back in Jaipur, I checked into the Atithi Guest House once more. This time, I was allocated a large spacious room on the ground floor with twin beds, a sofa and two chairs around a coffee table and a spotless white-tiled bathroom. The simple blue and green gingham curtains turned the white heat of the afternoon into a cool, bluish light once drawn. I decided to sleep and then organize some form of transport for the next morning. If I left Jaipur by 6 a.m., I thought, I'd be in Deorala before 7.30 and that would be a good time to arrive at the village. People rose early there and I didn't want to make a wasted trip. I had to meet Sumer Singh before he wandered off to another adjoining village, where he had relatives and where, he had told Prakash, he spent much of the day. There were no telephone connections to the village at the time and Prakash's parting shot to me had been, 'Get there soon after dawn so you don't miss him.'

Later that evening, walking around the streets surrounding the guest house, I discovered a taxi rank, a small wooden shed next to a huge banyan tree, around which a circular platform had been constructed in concrete. On it, a group of taxi-drivers sat playing cards. After negotiating a daily rate, a young man called Swapan said he would collect me at 5.30 the next morning. The highway was in a bad state, they told me, the journey would take longer than I had anticipated. I noticed that as soon as I mentioned my destination, they all identified Deorala as 'that sati village' in a matter-of-fact, casual manner, without any definable attitude. Apparently they had ferried others to and from it and regarded it as a tourist spot. I left them to their card game and wandered back to my room, past the pigs that roamed the city unattended, like the cows did in Jodhpur.

Swapan arrived literally at the crack of dawn. As we hit the Agra-Bikaner highway I could see the rising sun on one side and the moon, still high in the sky, on the other. The slogan, 'The sun and moon will remain, as long as Roop Kanwar's name remains' came to mind and I asked Swapan what he thought of the Deorala sati. 'I think the family are guilty of her murder,' he replied without hesitation. He went on to tell me that preserving life was a family duty; that he had an alcoholic brother whom they sometimes locked into a room to prevent his violence against other members of the family and himself. 'They could have locked her up too – until she came to her senses – but they didn't.'

It was a blunt and unexpected response to which all I could say was, 'I see what you mean.' After a while, Swapan told me that he knew the son of the pundit who had presided over the ceremony in 1984. The man owned a *paan* shop in the city. He asked if I wanted to meet him, although, he added, it was unlikely that he would say anything that might compromise his father, who had been charged with 'aiding and abetting'. I realized that I was in the company of someone who had followed the Roop Kanwar story and had a strong opinion. Swapan was not a Rajput but from Uttar Pradesh, often referred to as the 'cow belt', the Hindi-speaking heartland of the country. I said I'd like to meet the pundit. Perhaps he could speak with his friend, or perhaps we could find the pundit in the village?

'No! No!' he replied, shaking his head dramatically, 'Punditji is now totally underground!' The words 'totally underground' were said in English.

'Totally?' I asked. 'Is he dead?'

'No, no,' he said, exasperation in his voice, 'he is no longer available to the public. Only his family know where he is.' So, the priest is on the run, I thought, as we pulled up on the outskirts of the village. Swapan was eager to drive into it, up to the house, but I stopped him, remembering the police jeep that had thrown up all that dust in the lane a week earlier. He wanted to accompany me. It took some persuading to make him stay with the car. He was eager to confront Rajput egos! Much of the casual conversation on the way had reflected his own brand of communal pride, scornful of Rajput values. Any interaction between him and Sumer Singh would have been a disaster from my point of view, so I insisted he wait with the taxi on the approach road to the village.

I found the house easily without having to ask for any directions. It was just past seven and the pathways leading to it were quiet and almost deserted. I felt none of the tension of the earlier visit. Sumer Singh was sitting on the veranda, cross-legged on the wooden bed, talking to an old man. He rose to greet me as I approached and exchanged a few words with the old man, who gave me a curious stare and then departed down the lane. 'I'm so glad to find you at home,' I began in Hindi, 'I got into Jaipur yesterday.' His manner was immediately hospitable, almost gracious, as he offered me some tea, calling out to his daughter, Usha, who was the youngest in the family and seemed to do most of the housework. It was clear that he had agreed to co-operate with me, to 'help me with my project' as Prakash had so diplomatically asked.

He wanted to know a bit about me. How long had I lived in London? Was I married? Did I have children? I answered his questions and asked a few myself. How had he come to be a schoolteacher? Was it a traditional occupation within his family? He said his father had been in the army and he'd wanted to join it too. He hadn't passed the fitness test, so decided to become a schoolteacher instead. Could I speak with other members of his family, including his wife? 'My wife has a mental problem,' he said. 'She has suffered from depression for many years and all that has happened in our family since 1987 has made her worse.' He told me she spoke no Hindi, adding, '*Vo apne mun ke ander ghoomthe rahethi hain* (She wanders around in her own mind).' I asked him if I could use my Walkman to record my conversation with him. 'No problem!' he replied in English, with a faint smile.

Speaking of the events of 4 September 1987, when Roop Kanwar burned alive on his son's funeral pyre, I asked him to describe the day. Interestingly, he began: 'On 19 September that year, I and members of my family were arrested by the police. I had to spend four months in jail – at Neem-ka-Thana.'

'How many people from your family?' I asked.

After what seemed like a long, calculating pause, he replied, 'Seven, yes seven.'

After so many years, I had thought the number of family members arrested would come to mind immediately. The pause puzzled me. 'Including your children?'

'Yes, the children too. My youngest son was only eight years old at the time, attending school. He and his older brother were both arrested when I was, but we were separated and they were sent to a juvenile detention centre in Sikar.'

'It must have been a terrible time for all of you,' I said.

'That it was,' he replied, sadness in his eyes. 'These last few years have been the very worst in our entire lifetime.' Calling out to Usha for more tea, he asked if I wanted to walk around the village, if I wanted to eat something.

I felt he was being evasive but thanked him for his offer saying, 'Perhaps in a little while', trying to bring him back to the original question. What could he tell me about that day, about the 4th of September? I started again:

Q: On the day your daughter-in-law decided to commit sati, were you here in the village?

A: At first I was. As you know, my eldest son died in Sikar in the early hours of that morning. I was with him at the time...

[His voice trailed off as he seemed to be fighting inner emotions.]

Q: So, what happened after you left the hospital?

A: We came back here in a jeep with his body. Many people had gathered around the house – inside, outside, everywhere. I saw my son's body being carried into that room [now the shrine] ... Then ... She was there...

Q: Roop, your daughter-in-law?

A: Yes, yes. She was crying. She was saying, 'I will go with him. I want to go too.' There was much confusion. I couldn't take it any more so I collapsed.

Q: Collapsed?

A: Yes, I collapsed. I 'fainted' as I think you say in English.

Q: I see. It must have been a terrible time ... What happened? What did the doctor say? Was it anything like a stroke?

A: No, I don't know, I just fainted, I just became unconscious. [Again the word 'unconscious' was said in English.]

Q: What else do you remember about that day?

A: Nothing more. That's it ... Dr Magan Lal [sic] who was treating my son, also treated me. He admitted me into hospital.

Q: I've read that you were admitted into the Ajitgarh Hospital. Is that true?

A: No, no, it was the hospital in Sikar, where my son had just died.

Q: Doesn't Deorala have a hospital?

A: Yes, there is one but there was nobody competent there that day, so I was taken to Sikar.

Q: What was going through your mind at the time?

A: My mind? At that time? I can't really say. There was much confusion. I felt I was going mad. She was saying, 'I will go with him, I want to go with him ...' I was trying to calm her down. All of us were – my sons, members of her own family ... but she wouldn't listen...

Q: She has relatives living in this village?

A: Yes, several. They were arrested too. Arjun Singh, her aunt's husband and their son, Anand Singh. Mangej Singh and Bhanwar Singh, and another aunt's husband and son.

I asked if it was possible for me to meet these people and he said they now lived mostly in Jaipur, he had lost contact with them following the events of the last few years. However, he gave me the address and telephone number of Roop Kanwar's eldest brother, who ran the family transport business which ferried cargo between Jaipur and Ranchi, where Roop Kanwar had been born. I said I was thinking of making a trip to Sikar, to talk to the police officers involved in the case. Was there anyone useful I could meet there? He said he'd give me his lawyer's telephone number. Once again, I was beginning to feel confused. On the one hand, he was being open enough and extremely hospitable. On the other, he had the sort of evasive manner that is often hard to fathom.

Returning to the events of that day, I asked, 'You say Roop was crying, close to hysteria. Isn't that normal in a moment of deep grief – in a state of shock?'

A: Yes, there was a lot of grief . . . [his voice trailed into silence]
Q: Looking back on it, do you support the decision she made that day?
A: No. I tried to stop her. I tried to reason with her.
Q: But you just told me events were beyond your control, that you fainted and were admitted to hospital.
A: Yes, yes, I know I said that but I'm talking about before that happened . . . anyway, it is getting late. I must go and say my prayers and have my bath.

I asked if he would still show me around the village. 'Of course,' he replied. 'I will be back as soon as I have had my bath.' He asked if I wanted something to eat, Usha could make a few *roti*s and there was always cooked food in the house. They were 'strict vegetarians', he said in English.

'But I thought Rajputs were traditionally meat eaters!' I said in jest, assuring him that I was not hungry, I was not a 'breakfast person'.

He left saying, 'All right, we will buy some fruit in the market – you must eat something before you leave.'

Sitting on the veranda waiting for him to return, I lit a cigarette. I thought about our conversation and decided I should not push my luck. He had offered to give me important contacts in Jaipur and Sikar and, I told myself, I'd have to be content with that for the time being. I'd ask about the doctor and the priest some other time, I decided, as I passed the time watching the odd donkey or pig wander past on the dusty lane about four feet below the house. This part of the village seemed quiet and more spacious than the other lanes I had walked through. All the houses were made of brick. The hut dwellers, lower-caste people, lived on the outer fringes of the village.

When Sumer Singh returned, dressed in a spotless white *dhoti* and *kurta*, I was listening to the conversation I had just taped. I offered him the headphones, which he took, listening intently to his own voice for a few minutes. As he handed them back to me, I took one last shot at his involvement that day. 'Forgive me,' I said, 'for asking you to relive such painful times, but, since you've told me you were not present at the time of the funeral, who made all the arrangements?'

He shrugged, getting visibly impatient with my line of questioning, and replied, 'The rest of the family did. I was *unconscious*!' He used the English word with such emphasis that I decided to drop the matter. 'You are asking me things I cannot answer because I was not there, I was in hospital.'

'I understand,' I said. 'I'm sorry if I've upset you.'

Regaining his composure he asked, 'You want to see the village market and our temple?'

'Temple?' I asked. 'I thought you had not been allowed to build one.'

'I'm not talking about the Sati Temple, I mean our local, village temple.'

'Sure,' I said, 'I'd like that very much.'

As we walked towards the market, Sumer Singh's attitude was more relaxed. On the way, he exchanged words with several people, who stared at us with curiosity. I heard him say the word 'London' in conversation with others, as he presumably explained my presence. People looked me up and down and nodded. I smiled back. Some returned the smile but mostly people just nodded and watched as we moved on. However, the edge of hostility I had felt on the first visit with Prakash had gone. I was with Mart Saab so I was acceptable. Sumer Singh certainly commanded respect and authority in this village, as far as I could see.

In the small, narrow market street – containing mostly vegetable stalls a *paan-bidi* shop and a grain merchant – Sumer Singh stopped to buy some bananas and apples. I offered to pay but he refused. I asked him about his land. How much did the family own and what did they grow? He looked distracted as he said, 'We have some land, not much. It doesn't yield much. This year the crop has been bad. It's as if we have been cursed. Everything has been ruined. The wheat, the barley, the mustard and the *urhad dal* have all been scorched by the sun and then flooded by the rain. We have suffered a great deal.' I asked if they relied on rainwater alone or had tube wells. He had no tube well, he said, and although he owned about sixty *bhiga*s, which was not much, his plots of land were scattered. I asked to see one of his fields but he said that wasn't possible. 'They are scattered and not close to the village. I have no time today. I must go to Ajitgarh soon on some urgent business.' Again, the word 'urgent' was emphasized in English.

Back at the house, much to my surprise, he invited me inside and directed me towards the stone steps. Handing the fruit to Usha, he followed me up, asking her to wash it all and bring a plate. The room upstairs, which I had been in just a week earlier, was completely transformed. The clutter had been cleared. The enormous bed was now covered with a red velvet bedspread, the one Roop Kanwar must have bought originally, I thought. Next to it, a small, black sofa and a chair covered in rexine had been placed neatly along the edges of a richly pattered red carpet. The open door looked on to the open terrace, where a large and beautiful male peacock strutted at one corner. The refrigerator, covered in plastic sheeting, was still there in a corner beyond the bed. The shelves had been cleared and dusted, the floors swept and the coconut I had placed in the room had disappeared. Somewhat taken aback by the contrast, wondering what to say, I asked if they owned the peacock. No, the village was full of them. They were considered auspicious, so chose their own perches on walls and terraces and were tolerated despite the terrible noise they made from time to time, especially at night! I laughed at the memory of that incredible shriek – more like the howl of wild cats on heat – which I had woken up to in another village at another time some years earlier.

Usha brought the freshly washed fruit on a plate, placing it on the sofa next to me. Not overly keen on fruit, I said, 'Really, I'm not at all hungry, but thank you anyway.'

Sumer Singh snapped at his daughter in Hindi, 'What's wrong with you? Where's the knife?'

She rushed out of the room as I looked at the bananas and apples and said, 'We don't need a knife.' He ignored my remark and left the room in order to shout something down the stairs which I didn't understand. Within minutes, his wife arrived, holding a kitchen knife which she offered to me, blade first. She wore a scruffy nylon sari and a vacant but suspicious look on her face. Her husband muttered something to her as I accepted the knife from her and put it on the plate. Before I could say a word, she had gone. She left as swiftly as she had arrived. It was the only time I caught a glimpse of her.

I watched as Sumer Singh started peeling apples, one after the other, shedding the peel on the floor, as is the way in village culture. This was not a mud or concrete floor that could easily be cleaned, this was a carpeted space. The whole thing struck me as odd and out of character, but I said nothing as I accepted slices of apple, neatly peeled. We ate in silence. I was trying to think of something to say but the image of his wife, who had appeared and disappeared so suddenly, left me speechless and unsettled. I had not met his sons yet. I felt he had had enough of me for the day and I didn't want to antagonize him. I wanted to think the events of the day through and keep the lines of communication open.

'You said you had some urgent work in Ajitgarh,' I said suddenly. 'I came in a taxi from Jaipur. Would you like me to give you a lift on my way back?'

'It is not really on your way,' he replied. 'It would take you about eight kilometres out of the way.' I said I didn't mind. I had hired the taxi on a daily rate and had nothing much to do once back in Jaipur.

Walking back towards where I had left Swapan with the taxi, I asked Sumer Singh if there had been any other satis in the past, in either his family or Roop Kanwar's. He said, 'Not as far as I know.' I asked if his daughter-in-law had left any form of an *ok*. He wasn't sure what I was talking about and when I explained its meaning in terms of a last wish or request, he shook his head and said again, 'Not as far as I know,' adding, 'As I've told you, and the police, and every single journalist I have spoken to, I was not present at the funeral. You can ask anyone.'

We approached the taxi in silence to discover that Swapan had vanished. The car was unlocked, so we got in and Sumer Singh suggested I press the horn a couple of times, which I did. Within about five minutes, Swapan emerged from somewhere behind us, just as Sumer Singh was about to walk off towards the bus stop, not far from where we were. He was getting restless and increasingly impatient in relation to almost any question I now asked. He had spent several hours with me and I realized it had been more than I had expected.

Swapan was full of apologies and explanations and, as if to make up for keeping me waiting, drove in silence, without any sign of his earlier exuberance. I later realized he was merely being cautious – for my sake – not wanting to impose on what he saw as my strategy towards uncovering a murder-mystery, or something along those dramatic lines! I was aware that he was listening carefully to everything Sumer Singh said in passing as we headed for the adjoining village of Ajitgarh. I had decided not to ask any more sensitive questions anyway, so the conversation was casual. Interested in the terrain, I asked about water levels and the quality of the land instead. In order to reach the water level, he said, tube wells had to be drilled to a depth of two hundred metres or more; the land was fertile enough to grow wheat and other cash crops only if this form of irrigation were possible. He was comfortable with such questions, and spoke freely. I decided not to question contradictions either. He had told me he grew wheat on his land, among other things, but had no tube well.

All of a sudden, he pointed down a road we had just passed and said, 'There is a village a few kilometres down that road where they worship a famous *Sati Mata* of this region.'

'When did she commit sati?' I asked.

'She is still alive,' he replied. 'She became a sati about ten years ago, when her husband died. She has not eaten any food, nor drunk any water in all these years and is worshipped by many people.' I was reminded of Komalda's words, when he had emphasized that, in Rajasthan, the concept of sati was not necessarily an act but a quality. Excited by the possibility of meeting a living sati, I asked if we could make a quick detour, just a short visit, before I dropped him off in Ajitgarh. To my surprise, Sumer Singh agreed, and we turned the car around.

We were now headed for the village of Devipura – literally translated as Village of the Goddess – where Jaswant Kumar was said to have lived without food or water for ten years or more since the death of her husband, Ganpath Singh. Because of this, she was addressed as 'Sati Ma' and villagers in the surrounding area sought her blessings. We drove in silence.

A cluster of small stalls, built under the shade of two enormous banyan trees on either side of the narrow, tarmac road, riddled with potholes, constituted the village centre. Beyond the trees stood a small stone temple with about ten steep steps leading up to the shrine, and in the surrounding fields, isolated huts marked the ownership of small landholdings. Apart from the stalls – a tea shop, a barber, a blacksmith and a shoemaker, who was surrounded by old tyres from which he made sandals – there was little else. The traders selling fruit and vegetables had their wares spread out on handcarts, giving the impression that they were passing through on the way to somewhere else. Everyone clung to the shade of the trees.

We pulled up outside the tea shop, which also displayed *bidi*s, brands of cheap cigarettes and even cheaper looking sweets, in a well-worn, dusty glass showcase. Sumer Singh stepped out of the car and spoke to the owner, a handsome young man with gold rings in his ears, who was wearing a tattered singlet and striped shorts. We waited in anticipation, and Swapan whispered conspiratorially, 'This is all humbug – don't believe a word of it!'

'Let's see,' I replied, indicating that he should remain quiet. Sumer Singh returned to say that Sati Ma had left the village at dawn to attend a ceremony at another. What ceremony? Where? No one knew. When was she likely to return? No one was sure. I suggested we take a break in the tea shop, inviting Swapan to join us. Sick at the thought of more tea – which I prefer not to drink unless I'm trying to be polite – I asked for sugarcane juice, having noticed the machine at the back as we entered, huge lengths of cane half crunched in its metal wheels. Mixed with fresh ginger and crushed ice – hammered off a block under jute matting – it was delicious.

Sumer Singh was in his element as we gathered a small crowd of people. Everyone said it was true. Sati Ma had not eaten anything, nor had she touched a drop of water since her husband died. She was a true sati. Where did she live in the village? In the temple. Sumer Singh suggested we go and have a look, even though she wasn't there at the moment. It would give me an idea of how she lived. We finished our drinks, ate a plate of freshly fried *pakora*s and then walked away from the canopy of shade, followed by a few curious onlookers, to climb the steep stone steps to the temple dedicated to the Lord Shiva. An enormous stone lingam, phallic and fertility symbol of the Hindus, stood imposingly in the centre of the shrine. There was nothing else. A narrow passage, no more than three foot wide on either side, led to the rear. I walked around the lingam while the others waited at the entrance, not having taken off their shoes. They were just showing me around, and Sumer Singh was anxious to get to Ajitgarh. At the back, there was a wider open space, completely bare, a room of stone and nothing else. I was told this was where *Sati Mata* lived. She was a *sanyasin*, an ascetic. She had no possessions and slept on the stone floor. Not even a change of clothes, I wondered, and what about in the winter? There didn't seem any point in asking any questions, I could predict the answers. These people were here to convince me that she was everything people said she was. I said I'd like to meet her and would try and return another day.

'Do you have children?' someone from the village asked. I said I didn't. He nodded knowingly and said, 'So that is why you have come! Sati Ma has blessed many women like you and they have all had sons.' Were many such women among her followers? 'But of course. She has given them hope.'

On the way to Ajitgarh, realizing that Sumer Singh had warmed to me, I asked him if I could see him again, after my visit to Sikar. 'You are welcome any time,' he said with a warm smile. I reminded him that he had said he'd put me in touch with his lawyer in Sikar. Without hesitation, he pulled out a bunch of business cards from the breast pocket of his *kurta*, shuffled through them and handed me one. I scribbled down the details of Madan Lal Soni, Advocate of the Rajasthan High Court in my notebook. As Sumer Singh replaced the card in his pocket, I asked, 'Will he agree to see me and speak freely?'

'Don't worry, I will tell him I sent you.' Thanking him profusely for all his time and patience with my project, we dropped him off in Ajitgarh and started the return journey, by now a three-hour drive back to Jaipur.

Trundling back along dust tracks that would eventually link up with the highway, I asked Swapan, 'So, what did you think?'

'*Bakhwas*,' he replied. '*Bilkul bakhwas*! [Rubbish, complete rubbish!]' Then, as if trying to persuade me, he went into a tirade, 'You tell me! Who can live without food and water for eleven years? You can't possibly believe that? An educated person like you! Ask any doctor, ask any normal person. These people are only after making money and they want you to believe the impossible!' I had to reassure him that I didn't believe it; that my purpose was to investigate the story of Roop Kanwar. For that, I said, I needed Sumer Singh's support. Satisfied with the answer, he asked when we were going to Sikar. I had found myself a strange and unexpected ally.

When we pulled up outside the Atithi Guest House, looking at Swapan and the state of the taxi, I realized that I too must be covered in dust. I said I'd think things over and make some plans for the next few days. He said he'd come at around ten the next morning, and refused to take any money, saying, 'Don't worry, I will write everything down and give you a proper receipt. You can pay me tomorrow.' Back in my room, I ordered some ice and a Coke into which I poured a stiff shot of rum before ordering the fifty-rupee *thali*, for 9 p.m., that Prakash and I had sampled the previous week – rice, *puris*, three vegetables, *dal*, pickles and chutney, yoghurt and freshly sliced onions – a feast by any standards, which had to be ordered in advance. The visit to Sikar had now become a must. I had the name and telephone number of the Deputy Inspector General of Police (DIG) in Jaipur through a journalist friend in Delhi, and decided to call him from the reception desk.

It was late evening by the time I'd had a shower and washed the day's dust out of my hair. The DIG was not in his office, but I managed to speak to his secretary, explaining that I wanted a brief meeting with DIG Sahib urgently. I said I was a journalist. He gave me an appointment for 4.30 p.m. the next day. Glad to have the morning free, I thought of the events of the day, my mind swimming with images of contradiction but also filled with a sense of relief. I was getting somewhere, one thing was beginning to lead to another.

The next morning, when Swapan turned up, I invited him in and offered him some tea. We talked a while and decided to leave for Sikar the next day, whether the DIG was helpful or not. He reminded me that we had other contacts. I agreed. Meeting Sumer Singh's lawyer was worth a trip in itself. Meanwhile, since it was a 'free day', as he put it, he would try and track down the pundit's son at his *paan* shop. Perhaps he could persuade him to talk to me. They played cards together sometimes. I thanked him and decided to take a cycle-rickshaw to Ajmeri Gate, the city's shopping centre, from where a maze of small lanes lead to all manner of stalls and shops, through huge archways of pink stone.

Wandering around market streets that day, buying glass bangles, Jaipur pottery in blues and greens and chatting with people along the way, I could see an inherent elegance in Rajput manners, a reflection of the artistry that existed in their culture.

Later that afternoon, I set out to keep my appointment with the DIG of police, Omedra Bharadwaj. He was in charge of the crime branch, and turned out to be surprisingly youthful – in his mid-forties – and extremely helpful. Having heard me out, he picked up the telephone on his desk and spoke to a few people in Sikar. He suggested I see Manoj Lal, the superintendent of police in Sikar, who would 'guide' me and put me in touch with others. Without asking, he also arranged for me to stay overnight at Circuit House, government-subsidized accommodation for government officials, occasional journalists and other guests of government officials. I would not find a 'suitable hotel in Sikar', he said with a smile. It was far more than I had expected.

Bharadwaj spoke of the Roop Kanwar 'murder case' and the connection between crime and politics. 'Sometimes it suits the state not to prosecute in the wider interests of the community,' he said. He thought it would be 'a difficult case to prove because it was not a conventional murder'. People in the area, he said, were steeped in tradition, rituals and religion. In his view, the police seemed to have a case against the doctor, Magan Singh, who had been struck off the medical register. 'Even that,' he added, 'will probably end in reinstatement as eight years have now passed and the doctor has appealed against the decision.'

'Where is the doctor now?' I asked.

'According to our records, still in Deorala. But it was not a condition of his bail that he remain there, so he could be any-where. Deorala is still his official place of residence.'

I took my leave, thanking Bharadwaj for all his help and the time he had given me. His phones had rung constantly throughout our conversation and I got the impression that he was an extremely busy man, although he seemed quite relaxed, open-minded and easy to talk to.

Pleased with the day's results, I passed by the taxi rank. Swapan was not among those playing cards under the tree. I left a message saying we might have to stay in Sikar overnight and asked if that would be a problem. 'No problem,' said his boss. 'He will come prepared.'

CHAPTER THIRTEEN

We set off early the next morning. Swapan informed me he had spoken to the pundit's son, who was reluctant to speak about the affair. In any case, he hadn't been there and his father would have nothing to do with 'the press'. I thanked Swapan for trying and said it didn't really matter. He was pleasant company and shrewder than I had first thought. He told me about himself. He was twenty-eight, married and had a son of four. His family lived in his ancestral village in Uttar Pradesh, and he saw them about once a year. He couldn't afford to bring them to Jaipur because rents were high, but he sent money home every month. He himself shared dormitory-like accommodation with other taxi-drivers who worked in the city.

Sikar turned out to be quite a large town, crowded and noisy, congested with traffic, the air thick with diesel fumes. We went straight to police headquarters, and I asked to see the 'SP Sahib'.

Manoj Lal, a thoughtful-looking young officer in his thirties, said he had been expecting me. He had made arrangements for me to stay at Circuit House, 'As Mr Bharadwaj has requested. Unfortunately,' he said, 'they were unable to provide lunch at short notice, but you will get dinner there tonight.' Having greeted him with a *namaste* as I'd entered his office, I'd hardly said a word apart from introducing myself. Taken aback by this he pointed me towards a chair across his enormous desk, on which four or five different telephones were arranged neatly on one side. 'I have to leave Sikar in a few minutes. There has been an incident in a nearby village last night. One man has been killed in some feud between two families, and I must go in order to investigate the circumstances, perhaps make some arrests.' He looked as if he was in a great hurry. Again, before I could say anything, he continued, 'I have arranged for you to have lunch at a local hotel, after which my driver will take you to Circuit House.' Lunch was the last thing on my mind but I didn't want to appear ungrateful in the face of such 'five-star treatment', as Swapan put it later.

Disappointed that I would not, it seemed, have the opportunity to speak with him at any length, I said, 'This is all very kind of you but I had hoped to discuss the Deorala sati case, ask for your opinions and so on.'

'I know of your interest in this matter,' he replied with a reassuring smile. 'I myself have not been too involved in this case. The matter is now in the hands of the courts and the Public Prosecutor. However, I have arranged for Ram Rathi, who is now an Assistant Sub-Inspector here in Sikar, to meet you at Circuit House at 4 p.m. He was the first policeman on the scene in 1987. He is also a key prosecution witness. At the present time he is on leave but I have sent word to his village.' Overwhelmed by now, I expressed my gratitude as best I could. Lal merely nodded, pointing to the tea that had just arrived, and got on to the telephone. Swapan was summoned and instructed to take the car to Circuit House. A police driver would take me to the hotel for lunch and then drop me there. All these matters were dealt with in the form of quick instructions. I sat back and allowed him to organize my day, trying to finish my milky tea.

The driver arrived in a crisp khaki uniform and saluted at the door. More instructions and a few minutes later, I was being driven through crowded streets at breakneck speed in a police jeep. I tried to make conversation with the driver, a very stiff young man who kept his eyes fixed firmly on the road ahead, his elbow on the horn. He's probably been trained to drive aggressively, I thought, as I watched people scatter before us. There were so many near misses – in congested lanes, at major crossroads, around sharp bends – but I remained silent, aware of his authority as a policeman. Besides, I could tell he was not comfortable in my company, probably not used to driving women around.

Lunch was a bizarre affair. The 'hotel' turned out to be a crowded eating-house. The driver took me up a narrow wooden staircase and introduced me to the proprietor, a tubby middle-aged man who seemed rushed off his feet as he directed me to a table. I turned to the driver but he had vanished back down the stairs. As I sat down, I realized I was the only woman in the place and the only one sitting alone at a table. The place was packed. The food was good but I had not felt so self-conscious and uncomfortable in a long time. My entrance accompanied by the uniformed driver had not helped. All eyes turned to weigh up the situation and I didn't know which way to look. I ordered a chicken curry and two *chapatis*, and somehow managed to eat most of it under the gaze of the men at several surrounding tables. Fortunately, the service was fast and the food exceptionally good. When I asked for the bill, the proprietor merely said, '*Aisi kya bath hai*! [What sort of talk is that!]' and walked away. It was not the sort of place where people leave tips – besides he was the owner – so I left, thanking him on the way, grateful to be back in the jeep.

I felt even more grateful for my room in Circuit House, a large sprawling bungalow with covered verandas, surrounded by a well-maintained lawn, bordered by flower beds. All I had to do was wait for Ram Rathi to turn up. Swapan said he had been given sleeping space too, behind the building where the staff had their quarters, but said he preferred to sleep in his taxi. He was used to 'night-halts'. I had a spacious room with a big double bed and a mosquito net. The *jahli* on the windows kept the insects out but let the light in. I must have dozed off and then fallen into a deep sleep, lulled by the hum of the fan and the twittering of birds outside.

I woke with a start, looking at my watch. It was exactly 4 p.m. and someone was banging on the wooden door. I had bolted it, as it had kept swinging open on loose hinges. 'Rathi!' I realized, jumping out of bed.

An old man stood at the door. 'There is a man on a bicycle here to see you. I told him you were resting. Shall I tell him to come back later?'

'No, no!' I said. 'Please send him in.'

'In here?' He looked taken aback.

'Yes, in here,' I repeated. I explained that I was a journalist and this man was a policeman I wanted to interview.

His expression turned to understanding as he nodded and asked, 'Shall I bring some tea?'

'Please,' I replied.

'Shall I leave this door open?'

'Yes,' I said, still struggling to wake up properly. I realized the old man was merely being protective, and thanked him for waking me up. He must have thought I was some government official's wife or relative and that it was inappropriate to call a man to my bedroom. As he shuffled off down the corridor, I straightened the bed, straightened my hair and waited for Ram Rathi.

Sporting a dramatic moustache, typical of the region, Ram Rathi was wearing khaki trousers and a bush shirt. A bicycle clip was still fastened to his right leg. I could tell almost at once that he was an excitable, intense sort of person. His dark eyes held me in a fixed gaze. I thanked him for coming at such short notice. 'SP *sahib ka hukum tha*. [It was at SP Sahib's request].'

How far was his village? Had it taken him very long? He brushed my questions aside, eager to tell his story and come to the point. I asked if I could tape my conversation with him.

'No, no!' he responded immediately, somewhat alarmed. 'What I am going to tell you is not part of the official record but SP Sahib has said I can speak freely, since you are only writing a book – for your own purposes.'

'Yes,' I said, 'I want to write a book.'

'When will it be published?' he wanted to know.

'I don't know,' I replied. 'I haven't started writing it yet. I will have to try and find a publisher when I get back to London, where I live.'

'I hope you succeed,' he replied, and then, after a thoughtful pause, 'Have you written a book before?'

'Yes,' I said.

'That's OK then,' was his reply.

The old man had returned with a tea tray. I asked if they had any coffee. He looked puzzled so I asked him to bring some hot water in another teapot. He looked even more puzzled but shuffled off down the corridor again, making sure the door was left wide open. Rathi poured himself a cup of tea and said, 'Coffee is a south Indian thing. Not many people know what it is here.'

'I know,' I said, 'but I carry a small bottle in my bag.' He nodded, annoyed by these petty interruptions. 'So, tell me ...' I said, 'You were the first policeman to arrive in Deorala that day?'

'Yes,' he said with pride in his voice.

The story he told me, which he would not let me record on tape, is as follows. He had gone to Deorala that day on his bicycle. What he saw was the remains of the pyre. There was nothing much he could do but report the matter to his superior officers. After the police investigation into the affair began, he became personally interested, and visited the village several times in order to glean facts. He had spoken to several people in the village, rich and poor alike. After all these conversations with local people, his theory was that Roop Kanwar had been 'encouraged' to commit suicide. She had not loved her husband; in fact she had been having an affair with her childhood sweetheart from Ranchi. Her parents had been appalled when they found out, and told her to return to her husband. She had not wanted to leave Jaipur, where she had been reunited with her lover who had moved there from Ranchi. She became pregnant as a result of this affair; afraid to confront her parents, she returned to Deorala and told her husband that she was pregnant, hoping he would accept her back, and the child as his own, since he too had to prove his 'manhood'. Their marriage, it was said in the village, had never been consummated because Maal Singh, like his mother, had 'mental problems'. On hearing all this, Maal Singh – so village gossip said – tried to kill himself by swallowing a large quantity of chemical fertilizer, which they used in their fields and stored in the house. He became desperately ill, and in order to hush up the suicide attempt, his father got his friend and neighbour, Dr Magan Singh, to rush him to Sikar hospital. Dr Singh had contacts there, and could arrange quick admission. When Maal Singh died in the early hours of 4 September 1987, they rushed his body back to the village for an immediate cremation so that an autopsy would not be carried out on him in the hospital. The rest was common knowledge.

I stared at Rathi, amazed. His version of events sounded like the plot of a Hindi movie, and his highly dramatic tone of voice as he narrated the story, tapping the table with a teaspoon whenever he wanted to emphasize a point, added to this feeling. When he had finished listing his catalogue of events, told in staccato, he sat in silence, tapping the spoon rhythmically, as if asking, '*Now* what do you have to say?'

Trying to look unfazed, I said, 'If this is what happened, why haven't you made a statement to this effect?'

'It would not stand up in court. It would be hearsay evidence.'

He was about to begin explaining what that meant but I said I understood, I told him I'd worked in the law too at one time, in London, with defence solicitors who defended the rights of black people and so on. I realized I was beginning to talk like him in quick, staccato fashion.

If what Rathi said was true, it explained a lot of things. 'So, then,' I asked. 'Do you think Roop Kanwar was murdered?'

'I have already told you, I think she was encouraged to commit suicide.'

'But then,' I persisted, 'can't you make a statement to that effect?'

'It is purely *hearsay* [his emphasis] in the courts. No witness will come forward.'

'Why?' I asked.

'Because the Rajputs are powerful in that village and low-caste people cannot afford to cross them. No one will come as a witness.'

'What do low-caste people have to do with it?'

'They have swept their floors. They have seen and heard things – but they are afraid to speak out against the majority.'

After Rathi left, I sat wondering if the truth lay in his story. It was perfectly logical. It also fitted in with what Komalda had said in Jodhpur about the element of shock and what people are driven to do in such circumstances. I sifted through my notebook, found the home and office telephone numbers of Sumer Singh's lawyer, Madan Lal Soni and decided to call him. He was the only other contact I had in Sikar. There were no telephones in the room so I walked through Circuit House for the first time, looking for the reception desk. The place was silent; I seemed to be the only occupant. Outside, the crows were making a huge racket, fighting for tree space in the gathering dusk.

I found what looked like the reception desk, a table and chair on a veranda at the entrance of the building. There was a telephone on the desk but it was firmly locked with a small brass padlock. I wandered around to the back of the building, where I found Swapan in the kitchen chatting to the old man. As far as I could see, only the kitchen and my room had lights on, the rest of the building was dark. As I entered through the *jahli* door, they both looked surprised. 'Why didn't you ring the bell?' asked the old man.

'I didn't know there was a bell,' I replied.

'Under the fan switch,' he said, turning back to something simmering on a gas stove.

'I wanted to make a phonecall,' I said. 'Is that possible?'

'Everything in life is possible,' he replied, and turned off the fire, indicating that I should follow him. As we walked into the darkened building, he switched lights on as we made our way to the front veranda. We walked through a colonial-style dining room with a huge table that probably seated twenty or more, then through the lounge which was also vast, with two enormous sofas and several armchairs. There was no one else around.

He unlocked the telephone and stood at a discreet distance, waiting to lock it again. I rang Madan Lal Soni's residential line, and was told by a servant that sahib was still in the office. It was well past 7 p.m. I called the office, and the lawyer answered the phone. I introduced myself and asked if Sumer Singh had called him. He hadn't. Having heard me out, he said, 'I shall be here till 9 p.m. You can come now or we can meet after 4 p.m. tomorrow. I am in court all day.' He spoke in perfect English. I said I'd come now because I had nothing else to do in Sikar and was anxious to return to Jaipur.

'Sure,' he said, and I realized so many people used that word in Rajasthan. Even though it had sounded so American to me at first, I had begun to use the expression too.

Following the old man back to the kitchen, I told Swapan we were going somewhere, showing him the address in my notebook. He nodded and said he'd meet me at the car which was parked outside my room, something I hadn't noticed. The old man lifted the lid of the pot and said, 'Chicken curry!' There was a massive amount.

'How many people are staying here?' I asked.

'Only you – this is for all of us. Not many people come here so it gives me pleasure to cook.' I thanked him, tasted the curry and made my way back to my room, assuring him that we would be back by nine.

Madan Lal Soni was a large, expansive sort of man who said little. I tried to gain his confidence by saying I had spent time with his client, that Sumer Singh had suggested I see him and so on. He heard me out and then said, 'You see this is an easy case for me because I have nothing to do!'

'What do you mean?' I asked.

'The simple fact of the matter is,' he said without any hesitation, 'the state have to prove their case and they will not be able to do so.'

'Why do you say that?' I asked.

'Because they will find it difficult to get reliable witnesses.'

This was what Ram Rathi had said. I asked him about his own stance on the matter. Did he agree with the practice of sati? 'That is a loaded question,' he said with a slight smile. 'I am a lawyer. I am paid to defend my clients. I have defended other such people who see themselves as "defenders of the faith", these people truly believe that they are justified in what they do. They pay me. I represent them and, as I've told you, this case will collapse of its own accord.' I didn't know whether to be annoyed by his smugness or to just accept the reality of the situation and appreciate his honesty. I decided to do the latter and left, thanking him for his time.

Back at Circuit House, after a dinner of chicken curry, rice and *chapati*s, I looked at a map of Rajasthan and realized that Jhunjhunu was not far from where we were. Jhunjhunu was where the famous Rani Sati temple had been constructed in memory of a seven-hundred-year-old legend. Built relatively recently for Dadi Narayani Devi, who is said to have jumped into the pyre of her husband, Tandhan Das, it had played an important political part in the saga that had unfolded after the death of Roop Kanwar. Narayani Devi had been of the Bania caste – the same caste as Komalda and his family – and was said to have been seventeen at the time of her death. Paid for and controlled by Marwari businessmen, the temple had been the rallying centre for the pro-sati lobby in September 1988, the first anniversary of Roop Kanwar's immolation. We would go there tomorrow, I decided, before returning to Jaipur. According to the road map it was easily accessible, although further north and in the opposite direction. Having agreed to daily rates, I'd have to pay for the taxi in any case, I thought as I lay in bed under the mosquito net, listening to dogs barking somewhere in the compound.

Before leaving the next morning, having paid a minimal amount for my stay, I rang Manoj Lal to thank him for his assistance. I told him of my meeting with Madan Lal Soni, and could hear him chuckle over the phone. 'He's as sharp as a fox – a very competent lawyer, with quite a reputation in this area. I wonder how much Sumer Singh is paying him.' I said I hadn't asked. 'He wouldn't have told you anyway,' he said.

'Do you think he's right? That the state will fail to prove its case?' I asked.

'It's more than likely,' he replied. Then, after a slight pause, 'In my opinion, I think these women's groups who have brought about these prosecutions acted in haste. They should have gone for the lesser charge of aiding and abetting suicide. That would have been easier to prove and the punishment for that could have been ten years.' I said I saw what he meant.

Jhunjhunu was like a ghost town. Stray dogs lay on the roads, listless in the heat, and the temple complex looked deserted. We parked next to a couple of jeeps and I went through the entrance, which led into an enormous courtyard protected by huge iron gates, much like a prison. Just before it on the right was an office in which a man was working on an accounts ledger, tapping away at a desk calculator. As I entered, he looked up and said, 'The temple is closed. It will open only for the evening *arti* at 7 p.m.'

I said I was a journalist and had come all the way from Jaipur by taxi. Could I look around the complex?

He shook his head and said, 'You have come at the wrong time.' I tried talking to him about the temple, its management and its trustees, but he got increasingly impatient and finally said, 'Look, Madam, I am merely the accountant. I cannot give you any information. If you wish to attend the *arti* this evening, you may return at 7 p.m.' I asked if there was anyone else around whom I could speak to. Reluctantly, he wandered off to enquire but returned within a few minutes to say there wasn't. On my way out, I stood a while looking into the vast rectangular courtyard.

The accountant said, 'This was built in order to accommodate pilgrims during major festivals.' He pointed to the upper balcony, where rows of blue wooden doors indicated individual rooms, which he told me were always fully booked in the festival season. I had never seen a temple before that was part hotel. There was an unmistakable feel of commercialism to the place and, years later, reading Sakuntala Narasimhan's book, *Sati: A Study of Widow Burning in India*, that feeling was confirmed. Narasimhan writes:

> This temple is reported to have assets estimated at seventy-seven lakh rupees and an annual income of around twenty lakh rupees. The day of its yearly fair used to be a state holiday, with some four lakh people turning up to worship at the shrine; even the government would put up stalls at this annual event. The temple complex, spread over thirty acres, boasts no less than 350 rooms for the use of visitors. The state governor who signed the ordinance banning the glorification of sati on 1 October 1987 following the Roop Kanwar immolation, was himself the chief guest at this fair the year before.

I left thinking it had been a completely wasted trip, but consoled myself with the knowledge that I had at least got a sense of the place, accountant and all.

Back in Jaipur, I decided to try and find Roop Kanwar's eldest brother, Narayan Singh, before revisiting Deorala. The telephone number Sumer Singh had given me appeared to be out of order but I had the address of the Saraswati Carrier Company in Transport Nagar. I set out the next morning in a scooter-rickshaw, having refused Swapan's offer of a local rate for the return trip in his taxi, something I was to regret.

The scooter driver was a surly young man, and Transport Nagar was a maze of sludgy lanes, made worse by a sudden burst of rain. As we lurched through deep potholes, mud mixed with black engine oil began to spray my clothes. It took almost an hour to find the place, after asking scores of people for directions and zigzagging through endless lanes full of parked trucks and an amazing number of pigs wandering around, nose down, covered in black grease. When we finally found the place, the scooter driver refused to wait. I offered to pay him extra and he promptly asked for a hundred rupees 'waiting time'. Annoyed by his attitude and the rip-off price, I refused. A huge wrangle over the one-way fare followed, and I was aware that what I finally paid was more than Swapan would have asked for the taxi. Cursing myself for this foolish attempt at an economy drive, I climbed a set of rickety wooden stairs, my clothes splattered with oil and mud.

The room upstairs was surprisingly spacious but quite bare apart from two large desks and a telephone. There were three men in the room, one on the phone sitting on the only chair in the room, the other two perched on the desk before him. They looked me up and down without saying a word. I said I was looking for Narayan Singh. One of them pointed to the man on the phone, who ignored me completely. I stood near the desk and started introducing myself as he put the phone down, saying Sumer Singh had given me his address. He looked unimpressed and merely glared back at me with an unreadable look. Nobody moved and nobody said a word. I said I was doing some research for a book I wanted to write and wondered if he could give me a few moments of his time. I hadn't mentioned his sister's name but his response was immediate: 'I know nothing about all that. I was in another place four hundred miles away at the time.'

Somewhat taken aback by the bluntness of his manner, I asked, 'But were you not shocked when you heard of your sister's sudden death?'

'Not really,' he said, 'she was always religious-minded, even as a child.'

'In what way?' I asked, thinking this might be an opening.

'She never played with dolls as other girls do, she collected *murthis* [religious icons] and spent hours with them instead.'

What a strange response, I thought, looking at this pot-bellied, *paan*-chewing, thoroughly unattractive man who looked nothing like his sister. 'So, in your view, there was nothing strange about the circumstances of her death at such a young age?' I asked, still standing in front of the men seated on and around the desk.

'No. It was her wish.'

'How do you know it was her wish if you were not there?'

'I have been told it was.'

'By her in-laws?'

'Yes.'

'And you believe them?'

'Yes.'

'Why were your parents not informed of her decision to commit sati?'

'They were informed but the message didn't reach them on time. The car broke down.'

'How did your mother react when she heard the news?'

'I don't know. I wasn't in Jaipur at the time.'

'But surely you asked her later?'

'There was nothing to ask. We have all accepted what happened.'

'Would it be possible for me to meet your mother?'

'She is visiting relatives. She's not in Jaipur just now.'

'When will she return?'

'I don't know. She didn't say.'

He picked up the phone and started dialling a number. The other two men remained silent, staring at me expressionlessly in a way that was almost intimidating.

Knowing that I was getting nowhere, I tried once more as Narayan Singh replaced the receiver. 'I can see you are busy. Can I speak with you later – perhaps on the phone?'

'Yes, yes, I have a lot to do today. One of our trucks has broken down. I must get it fixed.'

I asked for his telephone number and he scribbled it down on a scrap of paper, thrusting it towards me across the table with an air of dismissal as he turned to talk to one of the men in Rajasthani. It was definitely time to leave. I said something about calling him later but he took little notice of me, apart from a quick nod and a sideway glance.

Back in the sludgy lane, with no means of transport in sight, I walked for what seemed like ages to find an exit to the main road. The ground under my feet felt slippery and I was forced to walk cautiously, at a snail's pace, feeling self-conscious and vulnerable, silently cursing this swill-hole of a place as I passed leering truck drivers who must have thought I was quite odd, wandering through this world of men. There was not a single woman in sight. To make matters worse, my *chapal*s were soggy and heavy with mud. Eventually, I took them off and walked barefoot through the filth, carrying my ruined sandals in my hand. The knowledge that I was probably walking in pig dung made me feel even worse.

Back in my hotel room, after I'd had a shower, soaked my clothes and scrubbed my *chapal*s clean, I remember lying on the bed for ages, staring at the ceiling, feeling the emptiness of depression. Roop Kanwar's suicide had been readily accepted by her family. In fact, her brother seemed to have been completely unmoved by it. Was that because of the other two men being present? I decided to give it one more try. The number he had scribbled was different from the one Sumer Singh had given me. That day, however, I felt I had nothing to say to him and decided to leave it for another time. I was feeling so negative and despondent myself that I thought it best to make no immediate move.

Another day passed without much activity. The following morning, Swapan turned up at ten to ask what my plans for the day were. I said I was feeling ill, which I was, and asked him to check for messages at the taxi rank later that evening. If I felt better, I would walk there to leave a message. He handed me a card with a telephone number saying, 'Just phone, you don't have to walk.' The taxi rank was literally round the corner from the hotel.

Touched by the concern in his eyes, I felt as if I was about to burst into tears, so turned away and said, 'I need to have a bath and make a few phonecalls, I'll let you know about tomorrow.' He left asking if there was anything I needed. I thanked him and said I was fine.

By the evening, I had managed to pick myself up emotionally and walked over to the taxi rank. Swapan was not there. I left a message and returned to my room, wondering whether to call Roop Kanwar's brother, whom I had taken a great dislike to by this time. Wrong timing, I told myself again, and decided against it. I made a few notes and shifted my thoughts to the next day's visit to Deorala. Once again, it had to be an early start.

Swapan turned up at 6 a.m. exuding energy and optimism. The city was empty of all traffic and looked magical in the light of dawn, the pink sky reflecting light off Jaipur's famous pink-stone buildings. By now, Swapan and I had accepted each other's smoking habits. He preferred *bidi*s but would not refuse a cigarette if offered one. He had tried to persuade me that *bidi*s were a better smoke. I told him they made me cough, although I liked the smell of raw tobacco leaf.

As we travelled through the dawn, smoking in silence, the scene changed rapidly on the Agra-Bikaner highway. Within the last few days, long stretches of the road had been repaired and freshly tarred, encouraging traffic to speed. Stray dogs had been the first casualties. We passed several carcasses – dogs crushed on the Tarmac – crows hovering, feasting on their guts; a revolting, stomach-churning sight which I tried to avoid by fixing my gaze on the wheatfields flashing past the open window. Perhaps the dogs were confused by the sudden change of pace. Only days earlier, we had trundled along over countless potholes and now the landscape was whizzing past.

As we approached Deorala, just after 7.30, Swapan said, 'You go and see Mart Saab, I'll try and speak to others in the village.'

'Be careful what you say,' I replied. 'Word travels fast in these places.'

'I know,' he said. 'Don't worry, the kind of people I will speak to will not be on terms of friendship with Mart Saab! They live on the other side of the village and use another well.'

Even today, in villages all over the country, low-caste people cannot draw water from upper-caste wells. Swapan was referring to a part of the village I had not been to in the company of Sumer Singh. Being a Rajput landowner, he lived on the prosperous,

developed side, where most people had double-storeyed houses
made of brick and cement, with electricity and running water.

Swapan and I parted company, leaving the taxi on the approach
road, in the same spot as before, under a neem tree. I would press
the horn when I returned; a sound that cut through voices and
bird calls, easily heard and instantly identifiable.

It was a Sunday morning, and all was quiet as I made my way
to the house, not far from the *Sati Sthal* which I had seen only
once with Prakash. The last tribute to Roop Kanwar there was
a faded, weather-beaten veil draped on a *trishul*, producing the
eerie effect of a small female figure standing erect, head covered.
The image had haunted me, and I didn't particularly want to
revisit the spot but decided I should – perhaps I could speak with
the lone policeman on duty who lived in the tent. Did the place
still hold any magic for villagers after all these years? I needed to
know. Walking slowly, savouring the early morning atmosphere,
I suddenly became aware of the strains of an old Hindi film song
coming from a radio somewhere. It was from the film *Anarkali*,
sung to the lilt of a waltz:

Yeh zindagi usiki hai
Jo kisi ka ho gaya
Pyar hi mein kho gaya
Yeh zindagi usiki hai...

[This life belongs only to those/Those who have given themselves
to someone/Those who have lost themselves in love/This life
belongs to them alone...]

Following in the footsteps of Hollywood, the Bollywood film
industry has had an enormous impact on the Indian public psyche
and romantic love is every woman's dream of emancipation in a
culture which encourages the sacrifice of women and the power
of men. Had Roop Kanwar killed herself for love or out of
despair? Had she been given a choice? In the film, Anarkali,
professional dancer and concubine to the Mogul emperor Akbar,
in sixteenth-century India, falls in love with Prince Salim, Akbar's
third son. Her love is reciprocated. It soon becomes clear that

during public performances, Anarkali is dancing for Salim. Enraged by the affair, Akbar orders her to stop seeing his son. The affair persists. Anarkali's public performances become more and more outrageous as time passes. Akbar is livid, and sentences Anarkali to death. Anarkali dances her last dance on broken glass before she prepares for her death. Legend has it that she was buried alive, bricked up behind one of the palace walls and left to suffocate to death.

The film was a big hit in the 1950s but the music has survived way beyond, sung by Lata Mangeshkar. Prince Salim, they say, fell into a deep depression that was to last for the rest of his life. His half-brother, Jehangir, succeeded his father as emperor. Born of another woman, the second wife, neither Salim nor his brother Danyal had any claim to the throne. In Lahore, now in Pakistan, an entire section of the city is named after Anarkali, and the song remains a national favourite. But whom had Roop Kanwar loved? Was it her husband or her forbidden lover from Ranchi? No wonder that Swapan had got interested in the story. His name meant 'dream' and he was certainly a bit of a dreamer, very much a product of the pop culture of Hindi movies. I wondered how he would fare at the other end of the village as I diverted my route in order to pass by the *Sati Sthal*.

I had been told by Sumer Singh that the bulk of the police force had left the village after Roop Kanwar's death anniversary had passed without incident that year, but a lone police constable remained on guard duty. Apparently, the police tent had been a permanent fixture since 1989.

The lone policeman was boiling water for his morning tea. Not yet fully dressed, fanning the coal fire, he looked like any other villager in a *lungi* and vest. An unassuming young man, he was quite happy to talk, probably glad of the company. He was based in Sikar, he said, and doing a three-week shift on guard duty. He was looking forward to normal duties when his replacement arrived in two days. It was a boring job and the site was perpetually deserted. I asked if anyone from the village ever came to pay any kind of tribute. He looked at me with a cynical smile,

pointing to a pile of garbage along the far edge. 'Yes, they come
to leave rubbish! This used to be a dumping ground but now it
has shifted to that spot.' I said I found this lack of interest strange
and the police presence even stranger, given the circumstances he
described. 'It is all political, Didi,' he said in a weary voice. 'We
are here to prevent any construction on this site, that is all.'

'How could you prevent such a move on your own?' I asked.
'Just being here prevents it, because I only have to report to SP
Sahib in Sikar if anything unusual happens, then he will send
others – but nothing has happened in years.' He said he hated
these three-week shifts. Days could pass without any conversation, social interaction or incident. 'We are trying to persuade the SP to introduce one-week shifts.' I asked if I could take
a picture of him but he declined, shaking his head vigorously. I
thanked him for talking to me, having refused his offer of tea,
and made my way to Sumer Singh's house.

CHAPTER FOURTEEN

Sumer Singh was in an impatient mood that day, but remained polite. Usually he warmed up slowly to conversations, starting in a monosyllabic manner. Today he came straight to the point. 'Look, I have told you all I know, what else do you want? I really have a lot to do today.' I told him I'd been to Sikar and spoken briefly with his lawyer. 'And what did you think after that?' he asked sharply.

'He's a very intelligent man,' I replied cautiously. 'I hear he has a high reputation in this area.'

'Who did you hear that from?' he asked, genuinely curious.

'From the police,' I said with a laugh. 'The SP in Sikar, Manoj Lal.'

'You met him ... the SP?'

'Yes,' I said. 'There had been some killing in some village – a family feud apparently – and he was very busy. I spent hardly fifteen minutes with him. Anyway he said he was not involved in this particular case; that it was in the hands of the lawyers and State Prosecutor now.' All this was true, but I decided to say nothing of my meeting with Rathi at Circuit House.

Somewhat more relaxed, Sumer Singh sat in silence for a while. I said nothing. He had asked Usha to bring some tea and biscuits, so I was not being asked to leave just yet. After a few minutes, I asked if he had any photographs of Roop Kanwar and Maal Singh at their wedding, saying I had of course seen some in the press. He nodded, and when Usha arrived with a small metal tray, he told her to get the wedding album.

Looking slowly through the large, ornate album, covered in silver paper, questions came easily, questions that generated no hostility. Sumer Singh appreciated my interest in each picture. Both the bride and groom looked extremely handsome. 'Who is this?' I asked. 'And that?' pointing to unknown faces in group photographs. I began to notice the difference in attire between his family and hers. Hers were definitely city people, dressed to the hilt in gold brocade saris, the men in suits. Maal Singh's family, on the other hand, wore simpler and more traditional clothes. Roop Kanwar looked resplendent in red and gold. The make-up, under the traditional Hindu wedding decoration of the face and eyes, was modern in a Max Faxtor sort of way; foundation, eyeshadow and red lipstick. In all the group pictures, Sumer Singh's wife had her face covered with a veil. Roop Kanwar's head was covered but her face was clearly visible in every shot: dark, vibrant eyes surrounded by thick lashes, a slight smile. Maal Singh had the chiselled features one sees in miniature paintings of the Rajput school. He had a proud but soft expression on his face. Dressed in traditional white cotton, covered in garlands with a large red *tilak* streaked across his forehead, an elaborate turban on his head, he had classical features and the same dark, intense eyes as his bride. Turbans are a hallmark of Rajput culture and even the men in suits wore them, but they stood out from the other half of the wedding party that had travelled from Deorala to Jaipur. As is customary throughout India, the girl's family had arranged and financed the wedding. As I studied the photographs, I asked the odd question.

'Where did all this take place?'

'In a hall in Jaipur which her family had rented.'

'Was it a happy occasion?'

'But of course! Who would not be happy to see their children married?'

'How long had they known each other?'

'From childhood.'

'Really?' I had read that it had been a sudden marriage.

'Yes, since they were both very young. Our families have

known each other for many years. As I told you, several members of her family used to live in this village.'

'So, from what age did they know each other?'

'Their marriage was arranged when she was about five or six and he must have been about nine or ten.'

'Was there an official ceremony at that time?'

'The agreement was finalized in 1981 and they got married on 17 January 1987.'

Turning the pages of the album, I suddenly came across a picture of two teenage girls, Roop Kanwar and her elder sister, taken on the streets of Jaipur.

'When was this taken?' I asked.

'Oh, that's nothing ... just a childish picture taken outside a cinema house, somewhere in Jaipur ... she was very fond of her sister who could not attend the wedding ... so she put that one in the album.' I studied the photograph with interest despite his remark. I knew from the gesture of his hand that he wanted me to turn the page. There they were, two young teenagers in a city, posing for the camera with fun and laughter in their faces, wearing heart-shaped, Lolita-style sunglasses made of cheap, bright pink plastic. I'm sure neither of them had heard of Nabokov's novel – nor could they have seen the film in which James Mason played Humbert Humbert, Lolita's besotted step-father – but somehow the image had become global, and American culture had seeped into every nook and cranny of the modern world. That photograph provoked many questions:

'I hear she was very much a city girl – this picture reflects it – did that cause any contradiction in your family after their marriage?'

'No, not really. She spent a lot of time with her own family in Jaipur.'

'Didn't you think that strange? If she had just been married, shouldn't she have been here with her husband?'

'She was. But she felt a little homesick, so came and went from Jaipur. We didn't stop her. It is normal for new brides to take time to adjust to their new home, to another family.'

'What did your son feel?'

'He accepted it. He was studying for his exams at the time.'

'So when did she return to this house? I mean how long before your son became ill?'

'She had been here for about three or four days, having returned from Jaipur with presents for all of us ... mostly little things for the house ... then my son became ill ...' His voice trailed off. I wondered if he knew about the situation Ram Rathi had described, but didn't dare ask. It would have sounded like sacrilege at that moment.

Having gone through the album, Sumer Singh said, 'Look, I really have no time to talk any more today. I have to get to Ajitgarh to negotiate a price for the grain we have left after this terrible weather we've had this year.'

'Who will you be seeing?' I asked out of curiosity.

'A grain merchant whom I have dealt with over the years.'

I thanked him for his time, and asked if he could suggest anyone else I could visit in the village. After all, I'd hired the taxi for the day and didn't want to return to Jaipur just yet. I'd have to pay for the whole day in any case.

He thought a while and then said, 'If you come tomorrow, I'll take you to see Roop's *bua* [aunt]. She lives on the other side of the village.

'Could I not go there now, if you tell me how to get there?'

'I don't think she'll be there at this time,' he said. 'Come tomorrow evening after 6 p.m. and I'll take you there myself. Just now, I have to go and have a bath, say my prayers and then get to Ajitgarh. You have come on a difficult day for me.' I said I understood, thanked him for his time and said I'd see him the next evening.

Back in the taxi, I pressed the horn and waited. I lit a cigarette, thinking of the pictures in the wedding album. Roop Kanwar had definitely been quite different from the family she had married into. There was so much more I had wanted to ask, but I had to remain sensitive to Sumer Singh's moods. I suddenly started feeling guilty. He had been more open with me than I'd ever imagined he would be. Was I really going to write against him? Yet, from all I'd heard, the death of Roop Kanwar had to be understood, if only to do justice to her life. I felt very far away from the truth. Rathi had thrown new and dramatic light on the situation but, I reminded myself, he was excitable and over-dramatic, unlike Sumer Singh. What was the truth? Lost in these meandering thoughts, I suddenly realized that over half an hour had passed. Where was Swapan? I pressed the horn again, twice on a longer hold.

This time it worked. He appeared in less than ten minutes, running. 'What happened?' he asked.

'Nothing,' I said. 'Mart Saab had some business to attend to so I looked at the wedding pictures . . . that's all.'

'Oh!' he said, thinking I'd had a disappointing day. On the way back to Jaipur I asked if he had met anyone interesting.

'They are reluctant to talk,' he said. 'This has been a bad year for them. They have appealed to the village *panchayat* for help regarding many things this year, including the supply of water. Sumer Singh is a prominent member of the *panchayat* and perhaps this is the reason they are not willing to speak against him.'

'Did you ask them anything at all about the day Roop Kanwar died?'

'Yes,' he replied. 'I asked if she had been in love with her husband.'

'And what did they say?'

'That there had been a lot of crying and shouting inside the house that day.'

'So you met no one I can talk to then?'

He thought for a while and then said, 'I met one woman with a small child who may be prepared to speak to you, but I heard the horn so I came running. I know where she lives though.' I said maybe we could go back the next day, as I'd arranged to meet Roop Kanwar's *bua*, her father's sister, who lived at the ashram.

*

When I got to Sumer Singh's house just before six the next evening, he was not there. He had left the village on some urgent business and was not back. The young man who gave me the message was Pushpinder Singh, Maal Singh's younger brother, the one accused of lighting the funeral pyre. I asked if I could wait. He invited me to sit on the wooden platform and turned on the veranda light. Before I could say a word, he had disappeared into the house. I waited, feeling self-conscious sitting cross-legged on that platform-like bed under the naked bulb, lit up for all to see in the gathering dusk. Apart from that, the bulb was attracting moths and insects that buzzed around above my head. After a few minutes of this, I got up and switched the light off. Settling back on the bed, leaning against the wall in a more comfortable position, I waited in the semi-darkness watching the sky turn indigo, casting purple shadows as rain clouds gathered. It was a still, airless evening and I could hear no sound of activity in the house. After a while, as it began to drizzle, the comforting smell of damp earth rose from the lane in front of the house. Soon there were flashes of lightning and the sound of distant thunder. Having decided to wait it out, I must have drifted into my own thoughts, lulled by the tranquillity of this silent veranda engulfed by the sound of rain. It wasn't a bad place to live, I thought, a peaceful-sounding household, comfortable and spacious. That room upstairs would have provided privacy to the newly-wed couple, a rare thing in village culture. Yet Roop Kanwar had spent a very short time in this house – just a few days after her marriage and a few days before her death.

A voice from behind startled me. It was Pushpinder, asking why I was sitting in the dark. Had the light fused, he asked, trying the switch. Under the sudden glare of light, I felt disoriented, and blinked up at him. Maybe he thought I'd fallen asleep. Apologetic in his manner, he said he had no idea when his father would return. It was a polite way of telling me there was no point in waiting. He was a handsome young man, probably in his early twenties, I remember thinking. He resembled his dead brother, even without the turban. He had short-cropped, jet-black hair, with the same dark, intense eyes, rimmed by thick lashes. I explained that I was in a quandary. If I returned to Jaipur in my hired taxi, it would be a wasted – and expensive – trip. Could he not take me to Roop's *bua*? I explained that I had planned to leave for Delhi the next day, and was unlikely to return to the village for a while.

'Where is your taxi?' he asked. I pointed in the general direction. 'Give me a minute,' he said, disappearing into the house. The rain had stopped but he returned with an umbrella, saying he would explain the way to my taxi-driver.

We walked in silence for a while, through slush and mud, picking our way over puddles in the dimly lit lanes. I realized this would be my only opportunity to talk to Pushpinder. I had planned to catch the Deluxe Bus that left for Delhi at noon the next day, from just outside the Atithi Guest House. Funds were running low and these day-long taxi journeys had taken chunks out of my shoestring budget. I decided to take my chance:

'You were the one who lit the funeral pyre, weren't you?' I asked as gently as possible.

'No, I didn't,' he replied immediately.

'But you were there?'

'Yes, I was there but I couldn't see very much – there were many people there that day.'

'So what did you do? How did you participate?'

'I just sat down on the ground near the pyre. I couldn't see very much.'

'Then who lit the pyre?'

'I don't know.'

He was clearly uncomfortable, and quickened his pace to stride ahead, leading the way. As the taxi came into sight, I asked if he would be kind enough to accompany me to the ashram. After all, I was a stranger to Roop's family and it was his father who had suggested I meet her. He seemed reluctant, saying he had things to attend to. I said the driver could bring him back once he'd introduced me. Reluctantly, he agreed. He seemed to be a thoughtful young man, with the same quiet manner of his father.

Swapan was fast asleep on the front seat. I'd told him to wait in the car, expecting to find Sumer Singh at the appointed hour, but it was close to eight by now.

We circuited the outer fringe of the village and eventually turned into another approach road, leading to the ashram, which stood opposite a neat row of small, low-lying buildings. As we pulled up outside, Pushpinder got out of the car, asking me to wait. He returned a few minutes later and said, 'She is about to perform the evening *arti* but will meet you after that.' He seemed in a hurry to get back so Swapan turned the car around while we exchanged a few words. I thanked him and said I was sorry to have missed his father but would return again another time, when I'd made some progress with the book I wanted to write. He waved from the window, a smile on his face for the first time, as I turned to enter the ashram.

Roop Kanwar's aunt was a brisk, volatile person. She looked me up and down and then said, 'You can wait in there, if you like, it's dry inside.' The open courtyard of the ashram, with a huge brass bell hanging in front of an old stone statue of a deity, was in darkness apart from a kerosene lamp that stood at the entrance of the room she had indicated. I watched her from the open doorway as she lit *dia*s – their candle-like flames illuminating the face of stone I could not distinguish from a distance – placing them around the base following a circular movement of the arm across the face of the god. Shiva? Vishnu? I wasn't sure. There was not a single other person in the ashram, but the concentrated energy of her ritual could have been performed before hundreds. I watched, completely mesmerized by the lighting, and then by the sound of her voice, which sang the *arti* at a pitch that rose and travelled through the night. She was not singing for herself. Perhaps others in the village heard this daily evening prayer, like people in an English village hear church bells on Sunday. Three resounding hits on the heavy brass bell completed the ceremony. She stood still, hands folded for a few seconds, then turned and walked briskly towards me. 'Sit inside. The stones out here are wet.'

I looked into the room for the first time, seeing a polished stone floor, gleaming in the light of the lantern. It felt cool to the touch. She picked up a couple of gunny sacks and handed me one, saying, 'Sit on that.' Arranging herself on another, cross-legged, she asked, 'What is it you want to know from me?' I began explaining, speaking of my meetings with Sumer Singh. She listened in silence, looking unimpressed, almost hostile. Then I told her I wanted to write a book about women in India; about what it meant to be a widow – about what it meant to live without a man in this society.

'I see,' she said. I was wondering whether I was getting through at all, although we were both speaking in Hindi. There was a brief silence and I looked around the room: simple, frugal, spotlessly clean. Then suddenly, she started speaking: 'I was widowed myself at the age of sixteen. My husband died in 1945. He was in the army. He went off one day and never came back – just like that. He must have been killed in action. No one ever found out for sure. His body was never found. I lived in the hope of seeing him again but then, as the years passed, I got used to being alone. In a way, I drifted into widowhood, it didn't happen overnight...'

'And what has life been like for you since then?'

'Fine ... I am content with my life ... I'm happy ... the army sends me money every month.'

'How much?'

'Enough. I have no complaints ... At first, after my husband disappeared, I lived with members of my family in Ranchi but now, I prefer to live closer to God.'

'Do you live here alone?'

'Some members of my family live across the road – they come and go from Jaipur and Ranchi. I look after the ashram and live here, in this room. It is quite adequate. I cook my meals at the back. Would you like to eat something?'

I said I was not at all hungry, thanked her for her time and hospitality and then asked what she thought about the sati in her family.

'Think? What is there to think? Both of them have gone. That's all. Life here goes on. It's not as if she was forced to commit sati. I saw her on that day, on the fourth. She was in a gay mood. She went laughing!' I found this hard to believe. Even Sumer Singh had not claimed that state of mind in relation to his daughter-in-law. He had said she was crying and emotionally overwrought. Before I could contradict this image, she started on a vehement tirade against all journalists – 'paper-wallahs' – and politicians alike: 'I am only talking to you because you are writing a book. If you were working for a newspaper, I would have refused to talk to you. It's all that Rajiv Gandhi's fault. He is responsible for all the ills of this village. He sent police to arrest members of our family. Anyway, what could he possibly understand about our traditions and customs? He married a foreigner and became like one himself. He believed the lies of the journalists ...' Her anger and indignation were obviously heartfelt.

I tried getting back to the day of the funeral, but she said she had not been there. All she knew was that it was a voluntary act, committed out of spiritual commitment, without any pain or suffering. It had been her destiny and she had accepted it willingly, having heard the voice of God from within.

As the widow was starting on a new warpath against journalists and 'intruders' from the city, I decided it was time to wind down the conversation. I had heard the sound of the returning taxi some time earlier, and realized it was getting late. Besides, following the rain, mosquitoes had come out in force and I was being bitten on every uncovered part of my arms and feet. As far as Roop Kanwar's death went, she was giving me no more than the official family line. She could see no tragedy in the situation. Strange, I thought, as I thanked her and took my leave. She accompanied me to the taxi, looked in to give Swapan a wordless stare and said, 'Don't let these paper-wallahs in Jaipur fool you.' I said I wouldn't.

As we drove off, I asked Swapan if we could visit the young woman he had mentioned. I would not be returning to the village for a while. He looked dubious but said, 'If you like,' with a shrug. Bored with this trip, he was probably anxious to get back to Jaipur. Still, we stopped for what turned out to be no more than a few minutes. He led me to a thatched hut in a much poorer part of the village. Men sat outside on a *charpai*, smoking a hookah which was being passed around. Swapan hung back, almost embarrassed, as they all turned to look at us approaching. I spoke to the group as a whole, not sure whom to address. Could I speak to the young woman of the house who had a child? Why? Because I was writing a book about women and wanted to talk to her about it. The grilling started: Where had I come from? Why Deorala? As soon as I mentioned Roop Kanwar's name, an old man stood up and said, with great authority, 'I suggest you leave right now! We have nothing to say to you. Let the Rajputs and their women do what they want. We want nothing to do with this affair. There is too much bad blood in the village.'

Exhausted by the events of the day, I realized that it was true, the village had closed ranks. People like me represented an unwanted intrusion. I said something like, 'All right, if that's the way you feel ...' and turned to leave.

Another man, much younger – perhaps the woman's husband – spoke more gently. 'The problem is, Bibiji, we are poor farmers. It is not our business. There are rich and powerful people in this village who are involved with the police on this matter. It has nothing to do with us and we cannot help you in any way. *Maaf Karna*! [Forgive us – said in the dismissive way one might use to a beggar at a traffic light.]'

I said, 'I understand,' and walked away.

Swapan was seething. 'You see, they are afraid to talk! That's why nothing ever changes in these villages.' I said they had a point. We came and went but they lived in that environment and faced the consequences of village politics after such visits. 'I suppose you're right,' he replied in a sulky voice. 'I still say, these people have no guts!'

On the way back to Jaipur, Swapan drove like a lunatic. We seemed to be heading straight for the oncoming headlights of trucks, buses and jeeps, narrowly missing bullock-carts travelling in the dark. The night chill that came from the western desert had begun to descend, and as I thought of what the widow had said, I realized that women themselves perpetuate, accept and encourage traditions of the past, finding strength in their ability to accept whatever life has to offer in a world that is ruled by people other than themselves. At one point she had said, 'If you expect nothing, you will never be disappointed! I want nothing more than God has given.' This was, more or less, what Komalda's wife had said to me in Jodhpur when I'd asked what she felt about the tradition of sati.

'It is my duty to serve my husband and live by his wishes,' she had said one day in the kitchen, somewhat impatient with my questions. 'If God gives me the gift of *sat* when the time comes, I will gladly follow him in death as I have in life.' The tradition of self-sacrifice among women was an inspiration to her way of thinking. It was the way all decent women should live, she had said, eyeing me with pity, knowing that I was no longer married.

Back at the hotel, packing to leave for Delhi the next day, I suddenly realized that I had not called Roop Kanwar's brother back after that first depressing interaction. It was late but I decided to take a chance. He answered the phone, his voice slurred, his manner jovial, in complete contrast to the way he had spoken before. 'Yes, yes, of course I remember you,' he said, cutting me short mid-sentence.

'I'm leaving for Delhi tomorrow,' I explained. 'I wondered if I could perhaps meet you again before I leave.'

'Certainly!' he responded, inviting me to go over right then. It was past 11 p.m. I said I was tired, that I had just returned from Deorala and asked if I could see him in the morning.

'No, no, morning time I am very busy. Now I am relaxing with friends. If you come now, I will show you something.'

'What?' I asked, realizing that he was quite drunk and speaking to impress an audience. I could hear laughter in the background.

'First you come, then you see!' he replied, followed by more background laughter. I said it was late. Could I ask him a few questions? 'Questions, questions, that's all you people are after.'

'No,' I said, 'I'm looking for answers.'

'The answer is simple. She is dead and we are alive. She wanted it that way and life goes on, why do you not come here and enjoy yourself. I will give you Scotch whisky!'

'I don't drink,' I lied, having decided there was no way I wanted to visit this man in his home wherever it was, at this late hour.

'Very good, very good,' he replied, and hung up. I didn't call back.

CHAPTER FIFTEEN

As the bus from Jaipur entered the outskirts of Delhi, crawling along a packed dual carriageway during the evening rush hour, I passed the time by reading the billboards lining the highway. There were advertisements for films and other commercial products as well as government-sponsored hoardings cautioning against drug addiction, drink-driving and Aids. Some things in particular caught my eye from the slow-moving bus. A marriage bureau: 'Consult The Stars – Find Your Romeo – Find Your Juliet!' It struck me as extremely funny at the time, advertising Shakespeare, a doomed love affair and astrology all at once. Shakespeare was obviously popular with copywriters. Further on, an advertisement for women's underwear pictured floating in the wind like kites read: 'Juliet Bras, Panties & Nightdresses of *Romantic* Quality.' Then came something that shocked, an advertisement for an abortion clinic: 'Pay Rupees 500 now or 50,000 in eighteen years!' Under this were stick-figures of a woman in a sari with a row of little girls in frocks, and the whole was 'Approved by Govt of India Family Planning Board'. I searched for a pen to note down the telephone number, but the traffic lights changed and the bus moved on. The message on the billboard was clear: linking the girl child with dowry, encouraging female infanticide.

That night in Delhi, I was telling the old friend with whom I was staying about my time in Rajasthan and discussing the position of women in the state. She said, 'I've saved some press-clippings for you. The situation here in Delhi is beyond belief!

When we have murderers, crooks and thieves among politicians, what can we possibly expect from society as a whole?' She spoke of the much talked about 'Tandoor Murder Case', as it had become popularly known. We moved on to personal conversation, but later that night, relieved to be among close friends again, energized by various thoughts that kept me awake, I took out the clippings she'd handed me in a large brown envelope, spreading them out before me on the bed. I started reading about the 'Tandoor Murder Case' she had referred to. A lengthy, full-page article headed 'All India Racket Club', written by Srinjoy Chowdhury and published in the *Calcutta Telegraph* on 16 July 1995 began:

> Only Dr Hannibal Lecter would have approved of Sushil Sharma, the Youth Congress leader accused of murdering his wife, Naima Sahni.
>
> With idealism giving way to avarice in the last few decades, politics has become the scoundrel's last refuge. Betrayed voters have turned cynical, expecting nothing but the worst from their leaders. But even a scoundrel's 'worst' would not include shooting his wife, chopping up the body, and roasting the dismembered parts in a tandoor. And that too, in one of the capital's government owned restaurants.

It was grotesque. Other articles said that a passing policeman, alerted by the unusual stench of burning human flesh, said that on closer examination of the clay oven, he realized that what it contained was 'not edible'. Later, under forensic examination, they turned out to be the body parts of a woman, of Naima Sahni. The thrust of the *Calcutta Telegraph* piece was the criminalization of Indian politics:

> Sharma, the alleged perpetrator of the murder, belonged to the criminalised elements of the Delhi Youth Congress and mayhem, if not murder, is perhaps part of a day's work in most youth organisations affiliated to political parties. For, youth power has become a euphemism for strong-arm tactics and intimidation. If

truck-loads of people have to be brought to a rally, if the leader requires 'support' during an inner-party power-struggle or if booths have to be captured during elections, the youth leader will provide the necessary services. And for his efforts, the fixer or muscleman is suitably rewarded.

Protected by his godfather, usually a leading politician, the criminalised youth leader has ample opportunities to make money. Apart from regular handouts by the godfather, comes protection money from shop keepers and businessmen, a percentage from deals he has helped to conclude (usually permits or licences from the government or transfers and postings of minor officials) and also 'freelance' work that may include ferrying drugs or procuring women.

In Delhi, Youth Congress leaders help women students from Fiji and Bangladesh who have visa problems, says Jaya Jaitley of the Samata Party. 'In return, they have to "visit" senior politicians.'

Lying in bed that night, I thought of the articles I had just read, and what my friend had been saying. It was true. Speaking to almost anyone in India these days about politics or politicians, the immediate response I received was cynical. They were all 'crooks', corruption was rife. Rich and poor expressed similar views. Idealism had died a quiet death since the Emergency declared by Indira Gandhi in the early seventies, since her son Sanjay Gandhi had institutionalized violence and corruption within the Youth Congress he founded, with the support of his mother, in order to protect her interests. Sushil Sharma, the 'Tandoor Murderer', was a product of this new political culture. Gone were the days of any moral commitment to the electorate.

At one point in his article, Srinjoy Chowdhury quotes the Union Transport Minister and former youth leader Jagdish Tytler as saying: 'You cannot condemn the Youth Congress because of Sushil Sharma's follies ... This murder has only given our rivals an opportunity to malign us. There are enough criminals in other parties.' 'Follies?' I thought. A Cabinet Minister of the ruling

Congress Party considered such an act mere folly? How cynical could any government get? The harsh reality of being in Delhi hit home. This was the capital, the seat of political power, where corruption and violence had become accepted as a way of life, the city with the highest number of dowry deaths in the country.

Against this backdrop of the 'Tandoor Murder Case', the widespread violence against women came under scrutiny once more, and several articles began to appear in both the national and regional press, many of them written by women. Madhu Kishwar, editor of the woman's magazine *Manushi* and a well-known feminist figure in the country – much like Germaine Greer is to the West – argued that the term 'dowry death' was misleading. In an essay, published as an open letter to the press, she had written:

> I personally am not comfortable with the term dowry death. I think the term oversimplifies the problem. I would call it wife murder, under the broad category of domestic violence. Dowry deaths are mostly crimes of passion, rooted in family power tussles rather than pure and simple acts of greed as the term dowry death implies.
>
> What I have discovered by listening to the accounts of the families, who approached us for legal aid after their daughters had been murdered, and from women who faced life-threatening violence in their marital homes, is that the crime is never as simple as it is made out to be in the police records or in press reports.
>
> Reporters or the police attribute a murder to the demand for a scooter, and this just does not make any economic sense to me. In this day and age, it's cheaper to buy a scooter because a family would end up paying much more in bribes to the police and in court expenses if they murdered their daughter-in-law! There are a number of cases where the husband argues that he beat up or killed his wife as she had not cooked a proper meal. We treat these arguments as excuses for violence, not causes. Then isn't

dowry too an excuse for violence and not the immediate cause?

She went on to argue that inheritance laws were the root of the problem and ended her letter laying the blame squarely on parents:

Why do women in India suffer violence and die? It's because most women have no independent incomes and have nowhere to go if they are ill-treated by their husbands or in-laws. Their parental home does not offer them shelter or an escape route, since their parents don't consider them to be members of the family after marriage. And our society lets the parents get away with crippling their daughters by condemning them to lifelong dependence. The strength that the parents give their daughter is the strength she carries to her in-laws' house.

Kishwar's essay created a furore within the women's movement, revealing rifts that had festered for years. The activists, many of whom I met during that time, many of whom had campaigned long and hard for changes in the laws governing the killing of women, many of whom had demonstrated in order to highlight circumstances surrounding particular deaths, condemned this approach. It was a 'chicken and egg' argument, they said, deflecting from the essential fight against the dowry system which, in turn, led to female infanticide. I tended to agree with them, although I could see a certain rationale in Madhu Kishwar's argument when she said, in her open letter to the press:

I have found that many cases of violence against women are registered as dowry deaths because the police will not take the complaints seriously if the families were to list other forms of harassment. In many cases a battered woman is advised to register a case of dowry demand even when no such demand exists. This, because a complaint of domestic violence due to dowry is more socially acceptable. In this process we are oversimplifying the issue of violence against women. The crime is no less if a woman is beaten and killed over issues other than dowry. Then why are we belittling all other forms of harassment?

Taken as a whole, however, Kishwar's arguments failed to impress many women activists, who were bent on using and reforming the legal process. What made matters worse – given public, and, in particular, women's hostility towards the police – was that the same page of the newspaper contained an article by Yasmin Hazarika, Deputy Commissioner of Police, chief of Delhi's Crime (Women's) Cell, supporting Kishwar's argument. An extract in bold print from Hazarika's article read: 'The girl's parents are responsible for cases of domestic violence against women because they often choose not to support her emotionally or financially.' Hazarika ended her piece by saying:

> The girls should not take beating as a deserved punishment and they should not put up with it. If violence is recurrent and shows no signs of letting up, then they should stop hoping for a change and do something to save themselves.

Taken individually, all these statements were valid, but they did little to strengthen the women's movement as a whole, and gave the police further reason to doubt the veracity of the victim's situation.

Other women responded to Kishwar's essay. Sheela Reddy, writing for the *Telegraph*, a national daily published in Calcutta, had this to say:

> It was Madhu Kishwar, India's most well-known champion of women's rights, who first publicly declared that dowry per se was not a social atrocity against women. Naturally, her essay, published in a widely-read English weekly, created consternation among women activists, who have spent nearly two decades fighting against dowry and were instrumental in enacting legislation that makes the giving and taking of dowry a criminal offence.

She goes on to quote a New York-based history professor, Veena Talwar Oldenburg:

> According to Oldenburg, dowry began as a safety net for women,

giving a bride status in her new home and giving her something of her own which she could pawn to tide over a family crisis. But 'the safety became a noose'...

Reddy also interviews the spokeswoman for an organization called *Saheli* (Female Friend), Kalpana Mehta, who points out:

> ... that the practice of extorting dowry is growing even in communities that did not have such a tradition a decade or two ago.
>
> In one study *Saheli* did recently, for instance, an overwhelming 97 percent of families in Haryana admitted paying dowry. 'And this in a state where families used to pay bride price up to a decade ago,' says Mehta. *Saheli* found that cash payments of dowry had almost doubled, and had become a sort of 'down payment' while consumer durables became recurring demands in the husband's family.
>
> Moreover, the dowry paid by the bride's family is almost invariably above the family's means, says Mehta. 'In upper middle class families, they may demand car and cash, while in lower middle class families the demands are usually two-wheelers, TV sets, two-in-ones,' she says, for which families have to dig into their savings or borrow from provident funds. It certainly is not a share of assets the family already possesses. Nor is the dowry the exclusive property of the bride; even her gold is used to marry off a sister-in-law.
>
> The campaign against dowry was certainly no mistake, feels Mehta. Referring to the whole-hearted manner in which women's groups pitched into the struggle at the very inception of the current women's movement which has grown into a considerable pressure group in today's society: 'It averted suicides and empowered women to resist exploitation,' says Mehta.

All the women I spoke to at the time agreed that the number of dowry deaths recorded had soared in recent years: from 1,912 cases in 1987 to 5,157 cases in 1991, according to a report by the National Crime Records Bureau. This was an alarming increase of 169.7% in just four years. Many women activists from various organizations, including lawyers, felt this increase could be due to the fact that more cases were being reported because of the increased publicity and the growing movement of protest by women's groups throughout the country. Reported incidents of domestic violence, rape and sexual harassment had also increased dramatically. Given these factors, the statistics cannot be entirely reliable. One of the many graphs and charts that appeared in print is reproduced below, from the *Telegraph*:

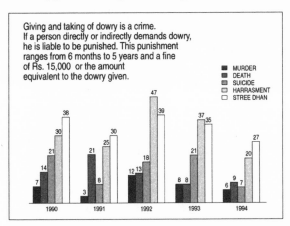

Practically every single day, newspapers carried reports of violence against women. My journalist friend, Praful, with whom I had stayed in 1987, still lived in Nizamuddin and had a virtual library of newspapers and press-clippings which he allowed me access to. I spent hours at his place gathering information. The volume of case histories made depressing reading. An article from the *Times of India* dated 14 July 1995 contained gruesome details that made the stomach churn:

> Sangita Debnath is a woman with a mission. 'I won't let him marry for a second time after what he did to my daughter,' she declares about Gautam Hajra, her son-in-law.
>
> Her daughter Sonia was only 20 years old when she died under unnatural circumstances on May 15 this year, within 11 months of her marriage. Gautam's family claims that Sonia committed suicide by hanging herself when nobody was at home. However,

her mother says she has reasons not to believe this story.

'Sonia's tongue and eyes were not protruding as they should have if she had hanged herself. The post mortem report clearly mentions that Sonia died due to "hanging associated with Baygon [a brand of insecticide] poisoning". A severe head injury is also mentioned in the report. Now, if she wanted to kill herself, why would she try all three together?' asks a disturbed Ms Debnath.

'The three methods used show that Gautam first tried to give her Baygon. When she refused, he hit her with some heavy thing and then hung her up to create a picture of suicide,' Sonia's mother says. Ms Debnath runs a beauty parlour in Goregaon [a district of Bombay]. Her husband is working in the Gulf.

'As I live alone here with my young children, Sonia's in-laws must have thought I would not do anything like lodge a complaint or register a case. But I will not leave any stone unturned,' she says. 'Not even five months have passed since Sonia's death and Gautam is already looking for another wife...'

Sangita Debnath goes on to explain that Gautam's father, Pareshnath Hajra, chose Sonia as his daughter-in-law three years before the wedding. Her family agreed to give Rs10,000 in cash and ten *tola*s of gold to the Hajras. But Mr Hajra went to Sonia's house the next day and demanded Rs25,000 in cash and twenty-five *tola*s of gold. He finally relented and agreed to accept anything the Debnaths gave. Accompanying the article is a wedding photograph, Gautam looking grim, Sonia frightened, her fixed stare at the camera like a cry for help.

In another incredible story from the Calcutta *Telegraph* on 22 July 1995, a man was reported to have forced his wife to have sex with his friends because she had brought 'inadequate dowry'. There was a sickening catalogue of murder and political mayhem right across the country, cutting across communities rich and poor, Hindu and Muslim.

The *Telegraph* had also reported an earlier case in Calcutta on 7 April 1995 in which a woman, whose in-laws claimed she had burned herself to death, was found to have been throttled before being set on fire. Her tongue was protruding, untouched by the flames. A group of women owing allegiance to a Naxalite faction torched the in-laws' house in the Bhawanipore area of Calcutta after the father-in-law suspected of the girl's murder was released on bail the same day:

> This sparked off the riot in the area. A number of women activists had arrived at the dead girl's house ... the activists and local residents rushed to the house of Sharmistha's in-laws. They pulled off the tube from an LPG cylinder in the kitchen, turned on the gas and threw a burning matchstick.
>
> The fire engulfed two rooms at 5A Nandan Road, and spread to the adjoining flat. The fire brigade was summoned but the blaze gutted four rooms in the building.
>
> The police claim that the attack on 5A Nandan Road was led by members of Pragatishil Mahila Samity, an Indian People's Front women's forum, on the basis of posters pasted on the walls of the building.

A neighbour said:

> We have seen this girl grow up before our eyes. And there we were standing in front of her charred body, the heart-rending cries of her parents [who lived next door] filled the air and then someone tells us that one of her killers is free and that three others are absconding ... What else can people expect ... We suspected something was wrong because only half an hour before the incident on March 31, Sharmistha ran out of her house once and screamed, 'They'll kill me, they're planning to burn me alive.' All of us ran to her aid and demanded that the door be opened but by the time they opened up, we could do very little to save her.
>
> 'We rushed her to SSKM hospital where they admitted her with 70 per cent burns,' said Gautam Mitra, who lives in the neighbourhood. 'She died today at 6am in the morning,' he said.

The report concluded:

There have been no arrests so far, police authorities said, but two women from the Samity were taken to the police station for questioning. The police also said, 'We realise this is a sentimental issue but burning down a house is no solution, we should have been informed about the woman being tortured long ago.'

So it went on, case history after case history, enough to fill a book in itself.

Among the women I met during that time, I managed to catch up with an old friend of mine, Brinda Das as she was when we first met in school, now Brinda Karat, a well-known activist of the Communist Party of India (Marxist), or CPI(M), and Secretary of the All India Women's Democratic Movement, a non-party organization that campaigns for women's rights at a national level. We had shared many experiences both in India and in London during the 1960s, before she returned to join the CPI(M) in Calcutta. She now lived in Delhi and we met as often as her busy schedule allowed. One night, after dinner at her sister's place, we talked late into the night. She was active on several fronts and the All India Women's Democratic Movement had supported the women's groups in Jaipur who had protested and demonstrated after Roop Kanwar's death in 1987, petitioning the courts and demanding the arrest of those responsible. She said she would give me copies of the legal documents being considered by the courts if I met her in her office the next day.

I told Brinda that I intended to visit Brindavan – the old name for Vrindavan, known as 'the town of widows' – and asked if she had ever been there. She said she hadn't but felt she should, saying, 'The position of widows in India is so central to the whole movement – for women, for any revolutionary change in this society.' I said I couldn't agree more and asked if she wanted to come with me when I went. She had a tight work schedule and said she could only get away for a couple of days, at most. I said that was fine. I could always stay on longer, if necessary. Leaving her sister's house in a taxi at well past 2 a.m., I said I'd meet her in the office later that day to pick up the papers and finalize travel plans, after which I could queue for tickets at the station. She made a note of the taxi number – a customary precaution in the city after dark.

Taking taxis at night in Delhi can be quite an intimidating experience for women. There are always two men in the front. When asked, they explained that this is for their own safety in the aftermath of the Delhi riots following Indira Gandhi's assassination by one of her Sikh security guards. Sikhs had been targeted in the riots that followed and thousands had died terrible deaths. Many had been set alight, hands tied behind their backs, burning tyres placed round their necks. A large percentage of taxi-drivers in Delhi are Sikhs and I could understand their caution, but nevertheless, the feeling of being with two men in a fast-moving car late at night made me uneasy. I asked why the meter was not turned on. 'It doesn't work,' was the curt reply. This was another common occurrence, inevitably leading to arguments over the fare.

Delhi had changed and expanded so much since I'd last lived in the city for any length of time, and I realized I didn't have a clue as to where we were headed. The roads were deserted and the journey seemed to take ages. Predictably, a heated argument flared up over the fare when we finally arrived at Golf Links, where I was staying with my friend Rupa. There was a night-watchman there, asleep in his wooden booth just inside the gate. Hearing the argument, he came to my rescue, but the aggression of the two men made me give in, fearful for the watchman's safety if I paid any less and disappeared into the darkened house. Delhi was definitely a far more aggressive city than Bombay in many ways, I thought as I climbed the wooden stairs to my room barefoot, so as not to disturb anyone. What should have been a forty-minute journey had taken an hour and a half on open, empty roads! I decided I needed to get a map of the city in order to avoid such situations in the future, grateful to be safely back in my room.

Chapter Sixteen

Early the next morning, I woke to the sound of religious chants and the tinkling of a brass bell coming from the puja room that adjoined the one I was in. Panditji, the family priest, came on certain days to perform rites for the well-being of the household. There was no other ritual and no one else was expected to participate. I lay in bed listening to the sound of his voice accompanied by the bell, as it came through the dividing wall in the silence of the morning. It must carry right through the house, I thought, all the way down the stairs to the kitchen, to Rupa's room, even right into the garden, where the *mali* was probably already planning his day's work.

A warm, comfortable feeling filled my being. I had many fond memories of times spent in this house, which went back to some time in the 1950s when I'd first met Rupa. We'd played *holi* in the garden as children and been ticked off by the adults for riotous behaviour. The servants who worked for Rupa's family were now old-timers and also remembered those days. Alam Singh, who more or less ran the household now, would soon come in with my cup of coffee. He thought that sleeping beyond 8 a.m. was a sign of degenerate behaviour. In many ways, he still treated me as a child whenever I stayed there, telling me I should drink tea rather than coffee, that I shouldn't smoke so much, that I should eat more and so on. Yet when I'd been there a couple of years earlier, working to a deadline on another project, spending day after day in the house, struggling to write on my beat-up manual typewriter, he'd visit my room at regular intervals, asking if I wanted another cup of coffee! When I ran out of cigarettes, he'd offer me a *bidi* – which he cadged off the cook, Sadhanand, another old-timer who had grown into a graceful, loving old man and liked to keep to himself. One of the family dogs, Choti (Little One) had adopted Sadhanand, and hung around the kitchen nibbling at the butts of his discarded *bidis*. It had become a family joke, and even Choti was regularly reprimanded over her tobacco-chewing habits, the fur around her mouth perpetually stained a yellowish-brown. I caught her at it one day in the ironing room, and she quickly put her paw over the butt as if to hide the evidence. Rupa's family's house was a lovely, reassuring place to be in.

The altercation with the two aggressive taxi-drivers the night before had unsettled me more than I had realized. Their manner had been threatening – or at any rate intimidating – from the very start of the journey. I had felt fear and paranoia, panic and suppressed anger, none of which I had expressed in any way, keeping my gaze on the back of their heads, aware that I was in their hands in a car speeding through deserted streets and alleyways. I had wondered if they were testing my nerve; weighing me up as a possible victim; discussing their plans in a Punjabi dialect I didn't understand. It had all ended all right except for the extortionate fare but the fear of potential violence had dominated my dreams nevertheless. Waking up to the sound of Panditji in the next room was the antidote I needed, and a feeling of calm descended as I watched dust particles dance in the beam of sunlight that came through a crack in the curtains.

Later that morning, I made my way to Vithalbhai Patel House in Rafi Marg to see Brinda as planned. She was not in the CPI(M) office on the ground floor. I was told she had been asked to address a rally somewhere in the city, in support of striking milkmen; she had been gone over an hour so should be back soon; there was no one upstairs in the one-room apartment she and her husband lived in; she had left no message. Having decided to wait, thinking we could possibly have lunch together, I surveyed the office. A framed picture of Stalin dominated one wall, looking incongruous, as women much younger than myself and Brinda went about their work, answering phones and banging away on old manual typewriters. I was tempted to ask the women what Stalin meant to them, but refrained, saving the question for Brinda, or Binnie, as I called her. She was one of my closest friends, and had been for years.

When Binnie arrived, enthused by the energy of the public rally of unionized workers in the old part of the city, I asked her, 'So, what's this business with Stalin?'

She gave me a bright smile and replied, 'This is a Party office. I don't choose the pictures!'

'But do you still agree with the cult around Stalin?' I persisted.

She thought for a brief second and replied, 'Without him, at the time, fascism would not have been defeated. Anyway, forget about all that, when are we going to Brindavan?'

A couple of days later Binnie and I met at New Delhi station soon after dawn to board the train to Mathura, the closest stop to the 'town of widows' – Vrindavan as it is now known. Rupa had given me the address of an ashram she had once stayed at, saying, 'It's a beautifully simple and tranquil place. Very clean and very cheap.' We took an auto-rickshaw from the station and were surprised at how short the journey turned out to be. Rupa had been right. It was a lovely place. Beyond the bright blue iron gate were vegetable gardens and spotless paths leading to the main building, where 'pilgrims' stayed.

We made our way up the stairs, following the signs pointing to the office, where we met the manager, a soft-spoken man in a *lungi* and vest who asked us to register, enquiring if we were pilgrims. We said we were journalists. He nodded and said, 'That will be fifty rupees a night,' handing us a key. On the first-floor landing, we found our room. It was sparse and spotless, containing a king-size bed with two pillows, covered with a clean white sheet, and a cupboard. There was nothing else. The adjoining bathroom, equally spotless, had a barred window looking out at the boundary wall behind the compound.

Having dumped our stuff in the cupboard, we left the room and walked back out into the sunlight to catch a cycle-rickshaw, the main form of transport in the town. Binnie suggested we look at the temples first. Squashed together on a slippery plastic-covered seat that sloped downwards, we hung on to each other for balance as we were whizzed through tiny alleys, with temples on every second corner. The place seemed to have been overtaken by monkeys. The rickshaw driver warned me to be careful about my sunglasses. Apparently, the monkeys were prone to snatch them off people's faces.

The first thing that struck me as we pulled up at one of the main temples was the line of old women who sat in a neat row along the path leading to the steps. Before them sat a man at a desk with piles of coins, neatly arranged before him according to denomination. He informed us that if we wished to contribute anything to the widows of Brindavan, we would have to give each one an equal amount. He was there to change notes into coins in order to facilitate this code of conduct. We changed ten rupees and went down the line, putting an equal amount, about twenty-five paise, into each bowl. Some of the women looked up and smiled. Others looked numb, accepting what was given as a matter of routine. Many had shaven heads. Nobody asked for anything, nobody begged in the way of street beggars. An austere order prevailed. I couldn't concentrate on the architecture of the temple, shaken by the image of these silent women sitting patiently in line, waiting for a handout. On the other hand, both Binnie and I agreed it was a fair and dignified system.

Later, at other temples, we saw grain merchants, who had shop-like spaces within, handing out a mere fistful of rice and *dal* to each widow. The women, many crippled by age, came to sing *bhajan*s on six-hour shifts a day at the particular temple. If they didn't turn up to participate in the singing, they didn't get their quota of raw grain. This was their way of earning a meal. They were, quite literally, singing for their supper. We sat among the women as they sang, and talked to several of them. I asked one young woman where she lived. She said, in a matter-of-fact sort of way, 'On the street. Where else?' I asked how she converted raw grain into food: where did she cook? 'I clean the floors in someone's house – a *thakur* [landlord] connected with this place. In return, I can use the gas in his house to make my own food.' Unlike the other women surrounding her, she was in her early thirties, good-looking, with eyes that expressed the energy of youth.

After we had finished speaking, she got up and left the room, saying she had to help with the distribution of food in the kitchen. One of the patrons of the temple, apparently a rich businessman from Delhi, had arrived and contributed what was to be their lunch. I was about to follow her when an old woman, wrinkled and bent with age, who had been listening to us talk, held my wrist and whispered in my ear, 'Don't believe what she says. That *thakur* she told you about, she lives in his house. She is his whore.' I nodded, not knowing what to say.

Binnie, who had been talking to some of the other women, confirmed the fact that they were required to come regularly to sing in shifts in order to earn their daily ration. While she went to speak to the grain merchant, I went looking for the kitchen, in search of the young woman I had been talking to earlier. She was there, dishing out portions of *dal* and *channa* into little bowls made of dried leaves, pinned together with tiny sticks. The kitchen was vast. There was a pile of *puri*s on one side, while fresh ones were being fried. Several male cooks and a few female helpers, younger women like herself, were putting things together ready for distribution, like on an assembly line in a factory. The singing, she said, would stop in a short while and then the women would queue for their lunch break. It was a special day because the food had been donated by the patron to celebrate the birth of his son. Who was he? She wasn't sure. I told her what I had heard, that she lived in the *thakur*'s home. 'No, I don't live there. I go there every night to cook my food and sweep his floors. I know people speak against me but I do what I have to do in order to survive. What else can I do? I have no one to support me. My in-laws thought I had brought them bad luck when my husband died suddenly one night. His heart just stopped, and when I woke in the morning he was dead. They thought I was responsible in some way and told me to get out of the house the day he died, before his funeral.' There were tears in her eyes as she struggled to keep up with the assembly line.

Back in the main hall, where the women were still singing, I saw Binnie talking to the grain merchant who occupied a small alcove to one side with sacks of grain, a weighing machine and little tins to measure the daily handout. He was hired by the trustees of the temple, who paid him for what he distributed. He was telling Binnie that he was paid the same rate as government ration shops and made little profit. Much to my amusement, she examined his scales and informed him that they were not correctly balanced, the implication being that he was short-changing recipients. The man scowled back at us both and said, 'What do you people know of such things?' I told Binnie I thought it was time to leave.

Back in the sunlight, we toured the alleyways precariously perched on our cycle-rickshaw. The driver, an enthusiastic young man who liked speed, had become our guide and took us from temple to temple, each one much the same as the other, packed with women singing *bhajan*s. In one particular temple, a woman with a stick in her hand wandered through the congregation, tapping the shoulders of those who were either talking or had stopped singing. She was obviously a woman of some authority, connected to the temple management. Binnie and I were both appalled. Some of the women she reprimanded must have been close to ninety, frail and skeletal, their bodies twisted and bent with age, their eyes listless. Binnie, more forthright in her indignation than me, wove her way through the seated crowd of widows to speak to the woman with the stick, but got short shrift. We should either sit down and participate in celebrating the love of God or should leave. We left, sharing the comfort of joint anger.

In her book, *Sati: A Study of Widow Burning in India*, Sakuntala Narasimhan has this to say about the cities of widows, Brindavan and Benares:

Economic distress is the reason why hordes of widows flock to places like Varanasi (Benares) and Brindavan even today. These are considered holy places of pilgrimage and there are a number of charitable alms-houses and *dharmashalas* catering to the indigent pilgrim. According to the 1981 census of India, there were 80,000 widows under the age of twenty, out of a total of twenty-three million widows in the country. Of these, over 20,000 destitute widows are estimated to be in Benares (one estimate puts it as high as 60,000). Although, compared to the situation a generation ago, more widows are economically independent today, but the lot of a widow is still largely unenviable.

To die in Benares is believed to bring special merit; therefore widows driven out of their homes or with no means of support congregate here in their thousands, to eke out a miserable existence, poorly fed, poorly clad, unwanted, uncared for and unloved. They beg or subsist on the crumbs doled out to them as charity, live in inhuman conditions, and die unlamented. Given no choice, they consider this wretchedness as punishment for the offence of having outlived the men they were married to.

Cities like Benares and Brindavan are said to be 'not just dumping grounds for widows but recruiting grounds for brothel keepers'. Preyed on by relatives, cowed down by priests and persecuted by society, many widows have been driven to prostitution to keep body and soul together. In contrast, when one upholds the values of chastity and prefers immolation as a sati, she commands admiration for her 'courage' – small wonder, then, that some widows not only went to the pyre apparently voluntarily but even insisted on their right to burn with the bodies of their husbands.

Having bought some fruit, we went back to the ashram, feeling too hot and tired to eat a proper lunch. We decided to try and sleep for a while. There were no curtains on the window and the full glare of the afternoon heat flooded the room. Still, the fan was a relief. Binnie, skilled at adapting herself to any situation, fell fast asleep within minutes, the pillow balanced on her face to keep out the light. I gazed at the fan above, thinking of the past. Binnie and I had known each other since we were eleven or twelve. We had been inseparable at school in Dehra Dun, had shared secrets, anger, feelings of betrayal, and other emotional experiences that had held us together. We had also shared much fun and laughter. Many mistook us for sisters as we looked alike as well. Bin-Bin or Bins had been my special names for her then. Now she was a well-known feminist figure, organizer, activist, campaigner and speaker at a national level, much respected by many women I had met in various Indian cities over the years.

Rupa was right, the ashram was a simple, but clean and tranquil place to be in. On the other hand, I couldn't agree with her with her about the 'spirituality' of Brindavan. What I had observed that day had been deeply disturbing in so many ways: destitute women, singing for temples which attracted visitors, living on a pittance.

Later that evening, Binnie and I wandered out again. The market place was full of small stalls and several old women begging, grateful for any small coins. Binnie was analysing the system. The air of spirituality, she said, came from the sound of women singing – almost throughout the day – in temple after temple. It was a tough regime. They had little choice. On the way out of the ashram, we had encountered an old woman with wild, tangled hair. She was new to Brindavan, having just arrived from a village in Bengal. Binnie had spoken with her in Bengali and then told me she had advised her to attach herself to a particular temple as a 'regular' in order to get her daily quota of food, it was better than relying on handouts from visitors, who in any case preferred contributing to the temple collection box to paying 'beggars'. The woman had thanked her warmly for her advice and gone her way, barefoot, dressed in a tattered and faded cotton sari, talking to herself.

Having eaten something in the bazaar, we returned to the ashram, asking ourselves whether it was worth staying on another day. There didn't seem much point. We had seen the system operate and it would be the same the next day and the day after. Besides, it was almost impossible to talk to these women for any length of time while they were in the temple, because they were expected to sing non-stop.

Sitting up late talking that night, Binnie said, 'Sexual assaults on women have now become a political weapon. It is no longer simply an act motivated by the repressed and uncontrolled desire of men. It is a way of punishment, a form of caste retribution against those who attempt to challenge accepted patterns of oppression and exploitation.' She told me of a case which had attracted much media attention and in which she was involved, together with other women's groups: the story of Bhanwari Devi, who lived in the village of Bhateri in Rajasthan.

Born into the *kumhar* caste of potters, Bhanwari Devi was illiterate, and her family owned a meagre two *bhiga*s of dry land which yielded little. Consequently, her husband Mohan plied a cycle-rickshaw in Jaipur while she moulded earthen pots in the village to make ends meet. At the time, during the mid-1980s, the government had initiated the Women's Development Programme of Rajasthan, encouraging women to enlist as *saathin*s, or support workers. These women were put through training programmes in order to build social consciousness against various forms of discrimination against women and girl children. The women who agreed to participate would be paid a small salary and their job would be to encourage women to organize around their own needs, exposing and resisting traditional forms of exploitation. Having discussed the matter with her husband and gained his support, Bhanwari was persuaded to join the scheme and became one of several hundred *saathin*s in the region.

After a brief training session in a village near Jaipur, during which time her husband returned to the village in order to look after their young children, Bhanwari returned to organize women's meetings. One of the first issues she decided to tackle was the issue of wages for the women who worked on government relief programmes, digging ditches for irrigation channels, breaking rocks and so on. Under her leadership, the village women made headway, challenging contractors and time-keepers who had ignored official guidelines on the minimum wage and underpaid them for years.

Reluctantly, even the men of the village began to respect Bhanwari's activities, seeing that families had gained materially through them. Enthused by this success, Bhanwari moved into more dangerous waters, encouraging women to resist domestic violence and other forms of abuse they had been subjected to year after year, either by their husbands or men of a higher caste than themselves. She managed to mobilize women in the village, leading delegations to the homes of men who beat their wives in order to shame them into changing their ways, offering moral support and legal advice to abandoned wives. These activities angered the men of the village. Finding comfort in the fact that she worked for the government and had the support of women's groups in Jaipur, she was undaunted and refused to be intimidated as she continued her work as a *saathin*.

In April 1992, during the festival of *Aaakha Teej* in Rajasthan when thousands of infants and children are tied together in wedlock by their parents, Bhanwari heard of a child marriage that was being planned in the village. The infant was under a year old, the daughter of Ramkaran Gujjar, a rich and powerful member of the village council. She decided to visit his home and dissuade him from taking such a step. He refused to listen saying, '*Mooch ka sawaal hai* (It is a question of respect).' At the time, the Chief Minister had made a public appeal against this practice, instructing District Collectors to take 'firm action' to prevent child marriages. Having failed in her attempt to reason with the family, Bhanwari decided to report the matter to the District administration. As a result, the police were sent to investigate. The family denied the allegation, the police departed and the marriage took place clandestinely the next morning.

This was the turning point in Bhanwari's life. The Gujjar community, which constituted half the total population of the village and were the dominant caste within it, decided she had to be punished. The first act of retribution came in the form of a social and economic boycott. They refused to sell her any milk –

the distribution of which they controlled – and resolved not to buy her earthen pots. Both she and her husband were verbally threatened and abused. Next, a tree was chopped down in their field and the crop looted. Watching these hostilities escalate, others in the village withdrew their support of her, afraid of inviting the wrath of the Gujjars upon themselves. For the sake of security, her husband, Mohan, gave up his job in Jaipur. He stopped plying his cycle-rickshaw, and within months the family were reduced to destitution.

Worse was to come. On the evening of 22 September 1992, while Bhanwari and her husband were working in their field, they were attacked by five men, including Ramkaran Gujjar. She heard her husband scream from a thicket close by, where he had gone to relieve himself. She rushed towards the sound and found herself surrounded. The men were beating him with *lathi*s. Before she could do or say anything three men turned on her while the other two held her husband down. He was bleeding from a head wound. The men threw her to the ground. Two of them, Gyarsa and Badri Gujjar, raped her in turn while the third man, Ramsukh Gujjar, held her legs wide apart. Ramkaran Gujjar – the father of the infant bride – and Shravan Panda held on to her husband.

After the men left, Bhanwari and Mohan made their way home, injured and in a state of shock. They appealed to a neighbour for help but were refused. Having been trained as a *saathin*, Bhanwari did not change her clothes or have a wash, knowing how vital the evidence would be. The closest police *thana* was in Bassi, but the last bus had left the village. They had no option but to wait till the next morning to file a complaint.

In Bassi the next day, the only doctor at the police *thana* was a man who refused to examine her, referring her to Jaipur. In Jaipur the doctor also refused to examine her without a directive from the magistrate, who had to be contacted at his home. The magistrate in turn refused to sign any judicial order at that hour of the evening so she and her husband had to spend the night in a police cell. Finally, fifty-two hours after the incident, she was medically examined and the vaginal swab proved positive.

Having been through this nightmare, aware that their children were alone at home in the village, they asked for some form of transport for the return journey. They were sent back to Bassi in a truck, where the police refused to assist in any way. All they wanted was the *lahanga* (long shirt) she was wearing because it would now be used in evidence. With nothing else to wear, she wrapped herself in her husband's blood-stained *saafa* (scarf) as they made their way on foot back to the village through the night, arriving close to dawn after a passing truck driver gave them a lift to the outskirts of the village.

'And this is what happened to a *saathin*, to a woman who had connections with a government-sponsored programme for social reform!' concluded Binnie. 'You can imagine how much worse it is for the vast majority of women. Mind you,' she added, 'as I was saying in the beginning, sexual attacks and sexual abuse are now political weapons in the fight against women. The only reassuring thing is that several women's groups are now supporting her in her legal battle although', she admitted, 'her isolation in the village remains unchanged.'

Exhausted by now, we decided to try and catch a few hours' sleep. All I had seen and heard that day left me feeling quite numb, overwhelmed by the enormity and complexity of the problems facing women throughout the country.

The next day, as we were preparing to return to Delhi, I asked Binnie if we should leave the remaining fruit, a bunch of bananas and some grapes, at a temple on the way. 'Don't be silly,' she said. 'If we want to donate anything we'll have to buy three hundred bananas! That's the system in these places.' She had been checking blackboards in the temples we had visited which listed the number of 'devotees' present each day.

In some ways, we agreed, the system was not a bad one but the distribution of food was an exploitative business in itself. What visitors were expected to do was donate money by feeding the collection boxes in the temples, which we had absolutely no intention of doing. In contrast to the women we had seen, the temple officials – including the grain merchants – looked prosperous enough, self-assured and content with their trade.

The image of women of all ages with shaven heads stayed with me. Brindavan had been full of them. In India, the loss of a woman's hair denotes the loss of her womanhood, the end of her sexuality. And yet, others profited from the widows' hair. I remember reading an article once about how the famous Tirupatti Temple in south India had made a substantial profit, earning the government much needed foreign exchange by exporting human hair to the West. This was the hair widows left behind on the temple floor, having had their heads ceremonially shaved following the death of their husbands. Apparently, Asian hair was considered to be the best for the making of wigs, and the temple had discovered a new way of making huge profits out of the misery of those who followed the rituals they prescribed. It was reminiscent of selling the bones of the dead to make jewellery, or the skin of the dead to make lampshades. It was not the first time such things had happened in history.

CHAPTER SEVENTEEN

Funds had now reached rock bottom once more, so it was time to return to London, time to try and raise some money around this book I now wanted to write. I spent a few more days in Delhi and then a few more with my family in Bombay – all of which flew past in a daze – then I was back in my own little council flat in Clapham. Relieved to be home, I remember sleeping many hours each day in the comfort and familiarity of my own bed, feeling emotionally exhausted.

I had been back barely three weeks when I received a big brown envelope in the post from Binnie. It contained a pile of news-clippings and copies of documents issued by women's organizations in India. A brief note from her merely said: 'Isn't this sickening? We intend to appeal against this judgement – to the Supreme Court if necessary – but first we must go through the High Court. Such is the legal process. I tell you!' Bhanwari Devi's rapists had been acquitted for 'lack of evidence'. The trial judge's ruling had caused consternation among women's groups, and outrage in the national press right across the country. It was late November 1995.

An editorial in the Delhi-based daily, the *Pioneer*, headed 'Morally Repugnant' stated:

> The judgement delivered by the District and Sessions Judge (Jaipur) in the case of Ms Bhanwari Devi's alleged gang rape is truly shocking, not so much for the acquittal of the accused per se, but for the grounds on which they have been let off, if

these have been accurately reported in the media. The righteous indignation of women's organisations is certainly not misplaced. On the contrary, it would be surprising if the sensibilities of right-minded and responsible citizens have not been hurt by this judgement. The track record of India's judicial system in dispensing justice in rape cases has been anything but exemplary. To that extent, the acquittal of the five persons accused of having gangraped the *saathin* working with the Women's Development Programme of Rajasthan is by itself neither historic nor even remarkable. If anything, it only further underlines the fact that rape victims in this country have only a faint hope of seeing justice being done.

What is historic, however, is the view taken by the judge in this case that the accused by virtue of their age and social standing are necessarily incapable of a crime like rape. The judgement suggests that rapists are 'usually' teenagers. This may or may not be statistically true, but extending that to mean that all those who are not teenagers cannot rape is really stretching the point. If this were to be accepted, all cases of rape should be dropped the moment it is established that the accused have crossed their teens. Equally astonishing is the claim that since the alleged rapists were middle-aged, they must necessarily be 'respectable', a contention supported neither by statistics nor by elementary logic. The most astounding reason given for acquittal, however, was that the accused were fairly highly placed in the caste hierarchy, and one of them was a Brahmin, and this ruled them out as possible rapists of a lower caste woman. Such caste characterisation of crime, apart from being morally objectionable, betrays an entirely ahistorical perspective. It is no secret that down the ages, while upper caste men may have treated those at the bottom of the social ladder as untouchable for most other purposes, this has never constrained them when it comes to using the female body for their carnal pleasure. Why then should they be expected to make an exception when it comes to rape?

Such a judgement would have been reprehensible in any rape case, but the specific circumstances of this case make it even more so. What is alleged in this case is not just that Ms Devi was raped to satiate a few men's lust, but that the humiliation was inflicted upon her because of her campaign against child marriage, which went against the feudal set up. It is, therefore, of paramount importance that justice is done, and seen to be done. It remains the duty of the judiciary and the state to ensure that this does happen, if others working for social reform are not to lose heart and believe that they are not only fighting the feudal order, but also a supposedly modern state.

Among the clippings there were several such articles and editorials in all the major Indian newspapers. Binnie had also sent me an English translation of the judge's summing-up speech. There were pages and pages of legal diatribe from which I have chosen small sections in order to answer the question posed in the above editorial, '. . . if these [remarks] have been accurately reported in the media.' The document was headed: 'English Translation Of Judgement Of District And Sessions Court In The Case: State VS Ramkaran And Others (The Bhanwari Gang Rape Case) Given On 15th November 1995 in Jaipur.' The names of the judge and both prosecution and defence lawyers followed. Here are a few relevant extracts from 'The Judgement':

> . . . The respected Defence Counsel argues that the present case goes totally against Indian culture, totally against human psychology. In the present case, one of the accused is fifty-nine years of age, the second is forty years of age, the third sixty years of age, the fourth fifty years of age and Shravan, a Brahmin by caste, is seventy years of age.
>
> The kind of case brought by the Prosecution involves rural people, amongst whom is Gyasara whom Smt. Bhanwari Devi herself describes as a respectable person of the village, who some people in the village listen to. That this person should rape her in such a manner even though it was Ramkaran's daughter and not his who had been married off as a child. And it has been said that a sixty-year-old as well as forty-year-old Badri committed the rape. Smt. Bhanwari Devi has also said that Ramsukh, who

is fifty years of age, held her hands although in her statement under Sec. 161 Cr. P.C. [Criminal Penal Code] she has at points said that Ramsukh held her legs; at other points that someone held her hands; sometimes that one or the other of the accused held down her legs with their thighs; and at other times that her legs were held below her calves. There is so much contradiction in her statement under Sec. 161 Cr. P.C. regarding this fact that they cannot be believed. Shravan belongs to a different caste [from the other accused]. He is a Brahmin. It has been said that he and Ramkaran held Mohan Lal and that then Badri and Gyarsa committed rape and that Ramsukh held Bhanwari's hands. It is beyond doubt that teenagers of the same age can commit gang-rape. But it is beyond comprehension that those who live in a rural culture, including Gyarsa, who Bhanwari Devi says is a respectable person and who some in the village listen to, would in this manner commit rape. Particularly in collusion with someone who is forty years of age and another who is seventy years of age and that too during broad day-light in the jungle in the presence of other men.

The court is of the opinion that Indian culture has not fallen to such low depths: that someone who is brought up in it; an innocent, rustic man; will turn into a man of evil conduct who disregards caste and age differences and becomes animal enough to assault a woman. How can persons of forty and sixty years of age commit rape, while someone who is seventy years old watches by; particularly in the light of Bhanwari Devi's acceptance that one of the rapists is a respected man in the village.

The court believes that the assertion of the Prosecution that Gyarsa, 60 years, Badri, 40 years, committed rape in front of the 70-year-old Shravan and 59-year-old Ramkaran, is not to be believed.

However, it was accepted that Bhanwari Devi's husband, Mohan, had been assaulted by the accused and they were all sentenced to six months and three months 'simple imprisonment, to run concurrently', under two different sections of the Indian Penal

Code. The forensic evidence had not supported the prosecution case as none of the people involved were of the blood group A, except Bhanwari Devi herself. This posed the possibility of another, unknown man being involved, especially as the vaginal swab had not been taken for several hours after the incident. No mention was made of the difficulties Bhanwari had faced in attempting to be medically examined when she first reported the matter to the police.

From the press-clippings and documents I had received, it was clear that what had outraged women's groups involved in the case were Judge Jagpal Singh's remarks concerning caste and age and his assumptions about 'respectability'. As far as the forensic evidence went, many were not surprised. They pointed to the contemptuous and hostile way in which the local police had first reacted to Bhanwari's complaint; the careless way in which forensic evidence is handled at the local level and the fact that police at that level are easily bribed. Bhanwari Devi herself was quoted as having said at a press conference that she was bitter about the fact that even a woman working for the government, a *saathin*, had not been protected by the state. She was going to appeal against the decision.

I decided to call Binnie, feeling depressed by the complexity and magnitude of the problems facing women of all ages in India. The future looked grim for the vast majority of them. After speaking with her, I was reassured by the tenacity of spirit and determination in her voice. They would appeal to the High Court and then to the Supreme Court if necessary. It was a blow to the women's movement, and the political climate in the country was against them, but they would fight on.

Two years later, in 1997, by which time I'd been commissioned to write this book, it was Binnie once again who informed me that the Rajasthan Sati Case had also ended in the acquittal of all those accused. Once again, the final outcome depended on the appeal courts. Apart from that, she said, there was a case in south India involving female infanticide: for the first time since

Independence, a tribal woman had been found guilty of the murder and been sentenced to life in prison. Her name was Karrupayee. 'Check it out, Mala, if you can,' she said. 'The rich have scans to determine the sex of unborn children and then have abortions if it's a girl. As usual, the poor are being targeted. The police never turn up at the doors of the rich who make such sex selections concerning their children, but an example is being made of this woman. I know some people involved with her case, which is now in the Madras court of appeals, and can put you in touch with them.'

I felt it was time to return to India in order to understand these new developments; in order to make some progress with the book. Besides, the time spent in London had been getting me down. I'd begun to feel out of touch and isolated from the reality I was trying to understand and write about.

I decided to travel south first and then make my way up north to Rajasthan via Delhi. I wondered how Selvi was faring. Once more, I had an offer of living at Roseneath, this time in the home of Selvi's employer Navroz, an old friend whom I had known for years. He had visited Selvi the day after her 'accident', as she referred to her husband's attempt on her life. Adam would be next door and I would get to see Selvi every day since she still worked there for Navroz, looking after the place while he commuted between Kodaikanal and Auroville. I would have a room in which I had stayed before, and would have the use of the kitchen and living room too, where the fireplace became a necessity after dusk. It was a good place to start my journey. I was looking forward to Roseneath and all it represented, grateful for the opportunity to travel once more in India after the grey skies and grim faces of winter in London. It had not been a good time, and I had made little progress with the writing, despite the support of friends and publishers. A kind of lethargy had overtaken my spirit, and sapped my energy as I tried to find a structure for the book that I was now expected to deliver within months. I knew India had been through turbulent times after the final defeat of the Congress Party, the assassination of Rajiv

Gandhi, several shaky coalition governments and now the advent of the Hindu-fundamentalist Bharatiya Janata Party. From all accounts, minority groups had paid a high price, and women made up the largest minority in the country, with a ratio of 917 women to every 1000 men.

Among the papers Binnie had sent me was another report on the horrendous death of a woman, Prakash Kaur, in the village of Jaitsar in Rajasthan. That was the case Binnie was currently involved with, having visited the village with two other women. They had written to the Chief Minister of Rajasthan, asking him to intervene in the interests of justice. An extract from their summary of the case read:

> ... They accused Prakash Kaur's twelve-year-old son, Subhash of stealing money from the *mandir* [temple] donation *thali* on May 28. They said that Subhash Kaur had fallen over the *amar jyoti* [the sacred flame] in the *mandir* and it went out. On the 29th, all three men of Prakash Kaur's family, her husband and her two sons were arrested by the police at 8 a.m. in the morning while Prakash Kaur was away in the market. When she returned, she went to the police *chowki* to protest and also to the *mandir*. At 11 a.m., a group of about 17 to 18 men, led by Desraj, came to Prakash's house. They said they would teach her a lesson because her son put out the 'sacred flame' and still she was protesting. They dragged her to the *mandir* where they shaved her head and blackened her face. They forced her to walk around the *parikrama* of the *mandir*. In the *mandir* they beat her with a stick. A stick was pushed into her vagina. Her face was blackened, she was put on a donkey and paraded in the main market place. From 1 a.m. to 3 p.m. Prakash Kaur was beaten but not a single policeman came to her rescue in all this period. The dying woman asked for water. Her killers poured hot water into her mouth and then kerosene. She died at around 3 p.m. in the *mandir*. No action was taken against her killers.

This murder, a reflection of grim reality, was spinning in my head when I boarded a flight to Bombay later that year.

CHAPTER EIGHTEEN

Karrupayee, the young tribal woman Binnie had spoken about, was the first woman in India who had ever been sentenced to life in prison for the crime of infanticide. Her husband had been acquitted, having first been charged as her accomplice or the actual murderer. As things turned out, no evidence was produced in court to prove his physical proximity to the baby after her birth in a government hospital in Madurai. From what I could gather over the telephone, Karrupayee had given birth to five children. The first two had been girls; the third, a boy who died soon after his premature birth; the fourth, a girl who had suffered the same fate; the fifth, another girl – the one she was accused of killing three days after her birth.

Karrupayee had been born into dire poverty, and belonged to the low-caste, displaced tribal community of Kallars in Tamil Nadu in south India. She was being held in Madurai Central Jail, pending her appeal. Two NGO groups were involved. One had helped convict her, another was appealing against the conviction, 'or at any rate, the severity of the sentence', as Binnie said, trying to be brief on the phone, aware of the expense of long-distance calls. 'Just come here,' she said, 'and I'll give you the names of people you can speak to in the south, people who are involved with her appeal – or call me when you get to Bombay. I'm not involved myself but I know some of the women who are supporting the appeal. It's all too complicated to explain on the phone. You'll have to go south, to Madurai, to find out more for yourself.'

I decided to travel south first, using Kodaikanal once more as a base. Madurai was easily accessible from there. Besides, I also wanted to see Selvi. Two years had passed since we'd last met and I had often wondered how she was coping with life in general. I had received the occasional formal letter from her, stilted and dry, obviously dictated to someone who thought letters in English ought to be written in a certain way. They always began: 'Most Respected Madam ...' and then went on to say things like: 'I am well. I hope you are well too. Ramya is attending school every day ...' I could picture the old man who sometimes sat outside the post office in Kodaikanal, earning his living by writing in English: filling in forms, drafting telegrams of congratulations or bereavement, gathering his few rupees for the day from those who could not handle the language. He translated what they told him as he thought appropriate. It was his skill. He knew 'proper English'. I had spoken to him once, curious about the small queue of people waiting for his attention as he scribbled away on the steps of the post office. Perhaps he was the one who had written those letters.

It was early April in 1997 by the time I was back on the winding hill road that links Kodai to the plains below. The bus was trundling along through a constant drizzle that grey day, blasting its horn around every second bend in the road that hugs the mountainside. I had a seat that overlooked the valley below and the familiar feeling of elation returned as I watched the landscape recede, engulfed by the swirling mist that often sweeps these hills.

The journey from Bangalore had been chaotic from the start. The engine of the 'Luxury Bus' had caught fire soon after we'd reached the outskirts of the city. Everyone had stumbled out on to the edge of the highway, waiting for a solution. The driver and conductor had fiddled around with the engine, but every time the ignition was turned on, black smoked filled the air. The male passengers had held a roadside conference and come to the conclusion that the vehicle was unsafe. We would not re-board that bus. They demanded a replacement. The conductor wandered off into the night looking for a phone box. After what seemed like ages, a tow-truck arrived to pull the bus to the closest depot where, we were told, we would be transferred to another bus. At 2 a.m., having been shaken awake by another passenger, I realized we'd reached the depot. Wanting a single seat again, the only one in the bus, next to the door, I rushed ahead while the other passengers were sorting and identifying baggage. The replacement bus, all its windows closed, was reversing out of a shed. When it stopped, I opened the door and climbed up the metal steps. The bus was swarming with mosquitoes. Within the seconds it took to leave my shawl on the seat to lay claim to it, I was bitten several times. Making a hasty exit, I went to speak to the man who had organized the roadside conference. He agreed with me. This was intolerable. It was well known that 'mosquitoes in this region carried the brain-malaria virus'. He would not allow us to board the bus. Eventually, the matter was sorted. All the windows were opened and, once again, it was the unfortunate conductor who had to solve the problem. He faced the swarm alone, waving a duster in the air to scatter the mosquitoes. By now, it was 3 a.m., and everyone was wide awake. The crisis had united us: flasks of tea and coffee and different kinds of food circulated among the passengers, who shared their packed meals with one another. Everyone was talking to everyone else on topics that ranged from cerebral malaria to the inefficiency of the government.

As a consequence of all this, the bus was running five hours late. When we entered the town centre, a hazy sun had begun to emerge through drifting rain clouds. I was looking forward to my short spell in the hills, looking forward to seeing Selvi again. The heat in Delhi and Rajasthan would be intense at this time of year, getting worse until the monsoon broke some time in July. That was where I was headed after this spell in the south.

As the taxi pulled up outside Adam's bungalow at the highest point of the sloping driveway, he emerged almost immediately having heard the crunch of tyres on gravel and the sound of the running engine as the driver helped unload my baggage. 'What on earth happened? We've been expecting you for hours!' he said, greeting me with a big smile and a hug. 'Selvi is here too. I've sorted out your room at Navroz's.' I suddenly felt the exhaustion that comes from relief after a mental and physical ordeal – the journey from Bangalore had certainly been that. My back and legs felt stiff, my eyes tired from the lack of sleep.

Revived by a coffee at Adam's, we made our way down the wide terraced steps that led to the back of Navroz's bungalow. Selvi was in the kitchen, cooking lunch. Looking as good as ever, she rushed to embrace me as I entered the door, full of her usual warmth. I felt quite overwhelmed by the joy of being back, by the hospitality and generosity of friends. Navroz was leaving for Auroville after lunch, with a young student to whom he was giving a lift. We chatted a while, had lunch and then I finally got to lie down and sleep for a few hours. He had left me some wood for the fire that would become essential after dusk, and a contact for his regular supplier, should I need to top up the pile during my stay.

When I woke later, the place was silent. Selvi had left. In the kitchen, the leftovers of lunch were neatly arranged in various containers, so dinner was taken care of. In the living room, Selvi had laid the fire for the night. In my room, she had arranged flowers gathered from the compound, using a glass tumbler as a vase. All this must have been done while I was asleep. She had left a message with Adam to say that she would come at around ten the next morning.

That evening, I walked into town with Adam, to wander through the market, renew acquaintances with shopkeepers and taxi-drivers, and to stock up on some food for the days ahead while Adam went down the steep slope to the meat market, where he bought offal and the stomach lining of sheep to feed the dogs. That was their daily diet on which they appeared to thrive despite the awful look of the stuff. Apparently it was full of 'goodness', he said, 'according to Miss Roberts', who had since moved further down the hill on to her own small patch of land. The bungalow she had lived in had been rented out to a computer institute, and local students came and went from it through the day. Some lived there but the place had lost its charm and looked more and more like a run-down office. The room I had overlooked what had once been Miss Roberts's vegetable garden, now overgrown with weeds. The gardener, Susai, had moved with her and was now tending her vegetable field and garden in another place. The missionaries had sold Roseneath to the South Indian Council of Churches, who planned to develop the area. Looking out of that window, I often thought of Miss Roberts and Susai, thinking it was the end of an era, a way of living. Now each bungalow had its own fencing and only the dogs roamed free, ducking and diving through the partitions. Adam, Navroz and Neelam now had a new landlord.

Back at the house, Adam helped me light the fire. The wood was damp so he added some kerosene from his place; then it took seconds. I watched as he placed damp logs around the fire to dry them out, advising me to place the whole basket in the sun the next morning. 'And don't forget to bring it in when it starts raining!' he said, emphasizing the fact that I was disorganized in such matters as we sat down to share the leftovers from lunch, to which he added a vegetable soup he had cooked for himself.

By the time Selvi arrived the next morning, I was drinking my first cup of coffee on the rough-cut steps leading down to the driveway, where the welcome heat of the sun had warmed the stone. She made herself some tea and joined me on the steps. 'Give me news of yourself,' I said. 'How have things been? Have the scars healed?'

'No,' she said, 'the backs of the knees are still bad.' On the whole though, Selvi looked well. She'd put on a little weight and had a radiant smile. She went on to speak about things in general. She just had this one part-time job. Navroz had been very good to her. He had given her a two-ring gas cooker so that she didn't have to face the smell or danger of kerosene in her home. He was rarely there, so her job was a luxury. Ramya was attending a

Tamil-medium school but she wanted her to learn English. 'It is necessary to know English these days, I'm thinking, Ma.' I had to agree that it helped. She had finally told Pradeep that he was her son and not her brother. He still lived with her parents but their relationship had become much closer. He not only understood but liked the idea of having two mothers. She had not heard from her husband, and was unlikely to see him again. She had heard that he had 'taken another wife', but said she couldn't care less. The easy way in which she spoke and smiled indicated a much happier state of mind than the last time I had seen her, when she had struggled to appear cheerful despite the pain that had shadowed her life.

Then suddenly, looking shy, tentative and nervous, Selvi said, 'I have met a very good man, Ma.'

'Great!' I replied. She became silent and started fiddling with the edge of her sari. 'What's wrong with that?' I asked. 'Is he married?' She shook her head. 'What's the problem then?' I asked.

'His youngest sister, Shanti, is not yet married...'

'So what?' I asked, trying to prompt her out of her silence.

'So ... we can't get married.'

'Why?'

'Because he will have to pay more dowry if he marries me. People have spoken badly about me. His mother is a widow and it is his duty to see that all his sisters are married, before he thinks about himself.'

'How old is he?' I enquired.

'Older than me, about forty-five I think.'

I sat and thought for a while. This problem with his sister was either an excuse on his part, or a genuine problem. We talked for a while, then she said, 'I've asked him to come here at two. I want to know what you think of him. Speak with him privately and ask if he wants to marry me or not. I want to know.'

Somewhat taken aback, I said, 'How can I do that the first time I meet him?'

'It is not the first time, Ma, it is Gandhi, the electrician who comes here often, since Miss Roberts's time. This is where I met him, although I have known his family for many years. I want to know if he is sincere.' I couldn't remember him.

Selvi got up and left to tidy and dust the house, asking me what I wanted her to cook for lunch. She'd unpacked the shopping bags that I had dumped on the table the night before. 'Cook for all of us,' I replied, 'Gandhi as well – and perhaps Adam will come too.'

'*Sambar* and rice, with drumsticks and carrots?' she asked.

'Great!' I said, 'I'll come and make some salad later.' I watched her as I wandered around the house settling into my room, unpacking and pulling water for my bath.

There was an acute water shortage that year. The lake was turning to sludge. Large tin drums surrounded the bungalows at Roseneath, positioned to collect rainwater from the roof at points where the guttering released its flow. This water was used for baths and washing dishes, and was boiled for a minimum of twenty minutes as drinking water. The water drums had to be checked regularly. Once full, they had to be covered with their metal lids in order to minimize pollution from falling leaves and birds' droppings. At night, the lids had to be removed, as that was when it usually rained. Both Adam and Selvi had explained all this to me in detail. Occasionally, there was running water from the taps, but Adam had advised me not to use it, so that it remained in the storage tanks for the times when it didn't rain. Water shortages had been a problem in Kodaikanal for years, with the town dependent solely on the lake, which in the past had been fed by underground sources from the surrounding marshes and forests. Now, timber merchants and hoteliers raked in their profits stripping ancient forests, clearing land-sites, and building ugly concrete structures to accommodate tourists who showed little regard for their surroundings: tuned into their radios at full volume, scattering litter wherever they went. The crisis had reached extreme proportions. For those who could afford it, the municipality sold water that arrived in tankers. Those who could not afford it had to do the best they could with rainwater. Fortunately for Kodai, it rains quite frequently there, almost throughout the year. Dealing with such practical matters gave each day the rhythm of regularity. Some things just had to be done. Remembering what Adam had said about the wood, I carried the basket out into the sun. I could smell the *sambar* on the boil in the kitchen.

As soon as I was introduced to Gandhi, known to all by his surname, I recognized him. I had met him some years earlier at another place Navroz had been living in at the time, Amarville, the base from which the organization he worked for operated. Gandhi was a soft-spoken, neatly dressed, confident sort of man. We had lunch together on the veranda. There had been no sign of Adam all day. As it began to drizzle, Selvi rushed out to retrieve the basket of wood. We all laughed as I had forgotten all about it, and I knew I could talk to this man. While Selvi was clearing up, amidst the clatter of pans in the kitchen, I asked Gandhi, 'So what are your plans for the future? With Selvi, I mean.' He didn't look at all fazed. He explained the situation with his sister. He had made a vow on his father's deathbed some years earlier that he would see her settled before he moved on with his own life. He owed it to his father's memory. His intentions towards Selvi were completely honourable and he did all he could to support her and Ramya, but marriage was out of the question at the moment. He'd have to double his sister's dowry if he married Selvi now because Selvi had been married before, and that was frowned upon in his community.

After he left, I told Selvi what he had said. She merely said, 'You see, I told you. It is what he says to me.' After a pause she asked, 'But do you like him? Do you think he is a good man?' I said I liked him but was not a good judge of men. She laughed. In the days that followed, Gandhi was a regular visitor. I could hear them talking in the kitchen and, judging from the tone of voices, they seemed to have a close and intimate friendship. Since they spoke in Tamil, I had no idea what they were talking about, but there were often outbursts of laughter, which I took to be a good sign.

I wondered if Selvi was hostile to his sister, Shanti, because she stood in the way of her marriage. When I asked her this one morning, she said, 'No, no, Ma. Shanti is a very good person. I will bring her to meet you.' The next morning Selvi brought me a small bundle of cards – dried wild flowers painstakingly pasted on white card – some blank, some with printed greetings within: 'Happy Birthday', 'Greetings' and 'Good Luck'. Shanti had made these cards and sold them for six rupees each, in order to raise money towards her dowry, and ease her brother's burden. Selvi wanted to know if the printed greetings were a good idea or not, as a printer had to be paid for these. I said I preferred the blank ones and asked if I could buy some. She said she'd ask Shanti to come over the next day with a wider selection.

Shanti, doe-eyed and soft-spoken like her brother, was a shy young woman in her mid-twenties. We looked through the cards together. They were decorated with ferns and flowers, some with touches of poster paint, some sprinkled with glitter. I said I thought they were all lovely, but gave my opinion on which I thought were the best. It was a moving experience; I was aware of Shanti's enquiring, anxious look as I examined her work. Wanting to help, I said I'd buy fifty and try to sell them to friends in London, where I could ask for a pound each. Her eyes widened as I told her that that was around fifty-five rupees a card at the time. She could expect no more than six rupees per card in Kodai. Not being very business-minded myself, I made no further marketing suggestions.

Later, in London, I did manage to sell a few cards to friends who were touched by the story. I kept the rest and sent some money to Selvi for Shanti, saying I had managed to sell them all, but that there wasn't much future in the market. I wanted Shanti to know that her efforts had been appreciated and that I had not forgotten our brief encounter that day.

CHAPTER NINETEEN

After about a week in Kodai, I decided I had to do something about my trip to Madurai. I had made several phonecalls to Madras in an attempt to speak to Binnie's contact there, but she was never in the office. Finally, over a very bad line from a public phone booth, I managed to get the name and telephone number of the NGO group in Madurai who were in touch with the situation: SIRD. The woman I spoke to didn't know what the initials stood for. 'That's all I know,' she said. The person I needed to speak to was in Delhi because of a sudden emergency, some family crisis. There was no telling when she would be back.

I decided to take a chance with SIRD after a visit to Madurai Central Jail. I'd contact them once I got to Madurai. Making telephone calls from Kodai was becoming a nightmare. Lines were 'down', numbers turned out to be wrong, and there was so much crackle and interference when one did get through that it was hard to hear the person at the other end. Pure frustration drove me to abandon the attempt to gather information over the phone. It was easier – and probably cheaper – to just catch a bus to Madurai. Selvi said she knew a travel agent in the market who ran minibuses. That afternoon we walked into town together and she introduced me to the agent before rushing off to collect Ramya from school.

From a cupboard-like office on the pavement, which contained a desk, a narrow bench and a phone, the travel agent organized trips to Madurai, and could also recommend a 'good hotel' next to the famous Meenakshi Temple. The minibus left at 'ten sharp' every morning, and he could arrange for me to be picked up at the gates of Roseneath. He suggested the Hotel Padmam. The minibus would drop me off there and I could book my return journey through the reception desk. I paid for an open-ended return ticket, having decided to leave the next morning. 'Ten o'clock sharp,' he emphasized as I left.

Needless to say, I waited by the Roseneath gates for well over an hour the next morning before I saw the white Maruti minibus puffing its way up the hill. 'Just as well we're going downhill,' I thought to myself, as I looked at the condition the vehicle was in. There were just two other passengers, both irate, annoyed by the delay. They were businessmen who were about to miss important meetings. Apparently, the owner had decided to delay the time of departure in the hope of enticing more passengers. It was not economical to run the bus with just three passengers. The driver and the two businessmen kept up a heated argument as we hurtled down the mountain road. After a while, their voices were drowned out by the rattling of the bus as it gathered speed.

The Hotel Padmam was a concrete block in a narrow lane. I was given an 'AC Room' on the third floor but since there was a power cut, the lift didn't work. Neither did the fan or the air-conditioner in the room. Candles had been placed on the bedside table for the night. It was stiflingly hot and humid in the spacious but airless room, with its curtains drawn to keep out the heat of the sun. However, a door at the far end of the room opened on to a tiny balcony that overlooked the street below, a small market lane buzzing with activity. I could see scooter-rickshaws parked at the end of it. The day had been a disaster so far. To top it all, I was informed by one of the waiters who had brought me a cold drink that it was the Tamil New Year, a public holiday. All offices and institutions would be closed. Why hadn't Adam or Selvi warned me? Perhaps they hadn't thought it was relevant. I resigned myself to a cold shower. At least that was working. The luxury of running water, which came out in sharp jets, made me feel a lot better.

By the evening, power had been restored and I began to appreciate the room I'd hated at first sight. With the fan and the apology for an air-conditioner working together, it was actually quite comfortable, and the staff were helpful and polite. The food was good too and the activity in the street below interesting to watch, unobserved from a height. The Meenakshi Temple, floodlit at night, was visible from the balcony, ornate and grand.

The next morning, I took a scooter-rickshaw to Madurai Central Jail in the hope of being able to find out more about Karrupayee, perhaps even meet her, in order to understand her situation better. I had seen a few press reports about the case but they were more analytical than informative. She was not quoted as having said anything throughout the whole process of her trial and conviction.

Apart from uniformed guards, the jail compound was deserted. It was still quite early. I was let in through a small opening in the main gate when I asked to see the Jail Superintendent. In a tiny office just past the gate, I was asked to write my name, address and the purpose of my visit in a register. I wrote 'Journalist' next to 'Occupation', giving my sister's address in Bombay. Against 'Purpose of Visit', I simply wrote 'Interview with Jail Super-intendent'. I was told to wait while the man at the desk spoke in Tamil on the phone. Much to my surprise, in a very short time, he called out to one of the guards and told me to follow him. We walked across the vast empty compound that resembled a parade ground, then he asked me to wait in a long, narrow shed marked 'Visitors' before disappearing into the prison building through heavy metal gates.

The shed I was waiting in was obviously where prisoners met their relatives. Metal bars divided the room lengthwise. Apart from this, it was completely bare. It had whitewashed walls, a tin roof and a doorway behind the bars at one end of the narrow corridor, from where the prisoners probably entered. After about half an hour, having paced up and down and smoked a cigarette, I began to wonder if I had made the wrong move. Perhaps I should have telephoned first, explained myself better, asked for a proper appointment. Just as I was beginning to feel despondent, the guard returned and said, 'Swamy Sahib will see you now. He has been busy with the daily inspection.'

Balan Alagiri Swamy, the Jail Superintendent, turned out to be an extremely intelligent man, with a calm and thoughtful manner, unhurried in his responses. I explained what I was trying to write about and asked if it was possible to meet Karrupayee. He said that the family had not taken kindly to the press. 'They feel the case has been sensationalized.' He would have to get her permission, and her husband's. I asked if he could tell me anything about her. 'My job is as a custodian of the prisoners. Their mental and emotional state is a matter of their own privacy. It would not be correct for me to express any opinion. The press and politicians seem to be interested in these aspects. As far as I am concerned, she is in our care and we must look after her as best we can. She is over eight months pregnant and we are doing our best to make sure that she gets the support she needs in the female wing of the prison.' He went on to say that she spoke no English, only a rural dialect. If I did meet her, it would have to be with a female warden who could translate whatever she said. I said I understood completely and asked if he could perhaps persuade her to see me. I told him I intended to meet with the people organizing her appeal. He said he was busy that day but would speak with the female wardens who knew her and let me know what she had to say. He personally had no objection to my meeting her but it had to be her decision. 'You can come back and see me around the same time tomorrow. I will give you her answer.' It was more than I had expected. I thanked him for making the time to see me and left, saying I would return the following day.

From the hotel room, I managed to get through to the SIRD office – the initials stood for the Society for Integrated Rural Development – and was given directions as to how to get there. It was not easy to locate but eventually, with the help of people in the immediate neighbourhood, I found the place. The office, on the ground floor, had a quiet efficiency about it. Men and women were working silently at different tables. I had spoken with a young woman called Pavalam, and was directed towards her. Somewhere in her twenties, she was so soft-spoken that she was barely audible at times. The whirring of the office fan, which shook and rattled alarmingly, was enough to drown her voice out. I hadn't had a problem understanding her on the phone. Perhaps it was the library-like atmosphere in the office that made her speak so softly. After a brief conversation, she introduced me to a young man at another desk, Vasudevan, and asked if I would like some coffee or tea. I said I was fine. 'We are all having,' she added gently. I thanked her and asked for coffee.

Vasudevan pointed me towards some chairs around an empty table saying, 'We'll be with you in a few minutes. There is some urgent work that has to be completed today.' They all seemed to be working on the same thing, from the remarks and questions being exchanged. Half an hour later, their task complete, we were all sitting around the table – two men, two women and me – chatting and drinking coffee. I explained my interest in the Karrupayee case. Vasudevan did most of the talking. Yes, they were working with lawyers in Madras – the capital of Tamil Nadu – putting together an appeal which was to be presented to the High Court there. Were they appealing against sentence or conviction? 'Both – for the time being,' Vasudevan replied. He seemed to be more involved with the case than the others. 'But finally,' he continued, 'our focus is on the sentence, and although she denied the charges in court, she does not deny them now.'

'You mean, she admits to killing her baby?' He nodded, going on to explain the chain of events that had led to her arrest.

It had been her fifth child. Two had died soon after their birth – malnutrition had been a major factor – and the other two girls were now thirteen and ten years old. An organization sponsored by the government – the Indian Council for Child Welfare (ICCW) – had been working in Karrupayee's village, trying to combat the practice of female infanticide which was rife among the Kallars, the caste to which she belonged. Social workers had kept an eye on her while she was pregnant. Because two of her previous children – a boy and a girl – had died soon after birth, they had arranged to have her admitted to a government hospital for the fifth delivery, assuring her that if the baby was a girl, they would ensure some form of help in terms of education for the children. When she gave birth to her daughter in hospital, they visited her and found her in a distressed state because the baby was not a boy. On their return visit two days later, they discovered that she had discharged herself from the hospital and returned to the village. When they visited her on the third day, she told them the baby had died after falling ill. They didn't believe her story and reported the matter to the police who, in turn, arrested both her and her husband, Karutha Kannan.

The contradiction, here, Vasudevan went on to explain, was that as a result of her conviction, her eldest daughter had had to quit school in order to look after her father and younger sister. The bid to educate her had failed. SIRD felt the case should have been examined more closely and more consideration should have been given to her social background. Female infanticide was rife in the country, but the rich could afford legal abortions. This was the same thing Binnie had said to me on the phone when she had first told me about Karrupayee. As a consequence of all that had happened, the family had been reduced to destitution.

We spoke for a long time. Vasudevan described the most common methods used to kill female babies. 'One popular method is to feed the female infant with poisonous milk of the wild plant *calotropic gigantea* or the oleander berries known for their lethal effect.' He said many Kallar households grew this plant, specifically for this purpose. 'Another method of killing is by stuffing a few grains of coarse paddy into the mouth. The infant breaths the grain into the windpipe and chokes to death. Sometimes the child is simply starved to death. There are rituals within this community. For instance, sometimes a flower is placed on the throat of the child, after which it is suffocated to death.' I said a priest had described the same methods to me on a previous visit. 'It is common knowledge in these parts,' he replied, 'and a very difficult situation to combat, without fundamental changes in the society itself. Poverty drives people to many things.'

While Vasudevan and I were talking, the others had gone back to their work, and I began to notice some were getting ready to leave. It was getting late. I apologized for taking up so much of his time and told him of my meeting with the Jail Superintendent. 'There shouldn't be a problem,' he said. 'You can say that you have been in touch with us. Her husband knows us well.' I asked if he could accompany me to the jail; perhaps it would help. He couldn't. He had a very busy day ahead, but I could call him between six and seven the next evening. He would be out of the office all day. Thanking him once again for his time, I walked out into the street in search of a scooter-rickshaw. It was well past seven and getting dark. Feeling much more optimistic, I returned to the hotel, where once again there was a power cut. Power cuts were a regular occurrence, and the candles were a permanent fixture in the room. I didn't find it as oppressive as I had the day before. With the door to the balcony and the windows along the same wall open, something of an evening breeze came through. I lit a couple of candles in the room and spent a while out on the balcony looking down at the crowded street below. It wasn't too long before the power came back and the room cooled down once more.

Recalling my time at the SIRD office, I looked through my notebook. There were some shocking statistics that came from the records of a government hospital in Usilampatti, the area from which Karrupayee came, the region in which the Kallar community had settled. Based on an average of the 1,200 babies born each year to women of the Kallar caste, nearly 600 were girls. Out of these, an estimated 570 died within days of their birth. Some deaths were reported after the event, and registered as deaths 'by natural causes' or due to 'under-nourishment'. Other babies simply disappeared, and doctors at the hospital estimated that eighty per cent of these babies were victims of female infanticide.

Earlier in Bombay, before leaving for Kodai, I had visited the Documentation Centre, a well-known media library in Colaba, to gather some material on the subject of female infanticide. I had carried the file around with me but had not spent any time on it so far. Unable to sleep after dinner in my room that night, I started reading. An article in the *Pioneer* dated 23 October 1996, written by Shivi Prasad, was headed: 'Female Infanticide among Kallars' and gave an insight into this tradition:

Although there is not much written evidence of female infanticide in India prior to the coming of the British, by the time of their arrival this practice was common almost throughout India. During that period, female infanticide was suspected among several communities belonging to the upper and middle classes. However, there were mainly three tribal groups where this practice was widely prevalent, namely, the Nagas of the north-east, the Khonds of Orissa and the Todas of the Nilgiri hills. Today, almost 200 years after it was first reported, this gruesome and heinous custom is still prevalent among the Kallars of Tamil Nadu and many other communities all over India.

The maximum concentration of the Kallar community is in the Usilampatti *taluka* of the Madurai district and its 300 villages. In the other districts of Tamil Nadu, they form a minority group. The role of women in this community is confined solely to looking after children and the household activities. The level of education amongst the Kallars is also very low.

... The custom of infanticide among the Kallars seems to be motivated by the relative economic backwardness of the community and the social importance of the males. Perhaps, in no other community of modern India, the economic value of male children is as pronounced as among the Kallars. The practice of dowry further lowers the economic value of the female child and is one of the major factors contributing to female infanticide.

The dowry system among the Kallars can be traced to some 25 years ago when a dam was being constructed on the Vaiga river, as part of the Green Revolution. With its completion, one side of Usilampatti district got the river water. During the 1960s and 70s, with the electrification of Usilampatti came wells with motors and pumpsets. All this helped in bringing water to the other side of the district also. With irrigation in these areas, came the introduction of new ways of cultivation: new seeds, new pesticides and new crops. Cultivation for self consumption gave way to cultivation for the market economy. Cash crops, that brought in higher returns, became more important. But the new pattern of cultivation also brought with itself, folds of changes in the lives and attitudes of the people.

Money became central to their lives. Now, men wanted to marry women whose families could offer more money and land. The menace of dowry was not confined to the rich sections of the population. Even the daily wage labourers with uncertain incomes or poor agricultural workers who did not own even a square inch of land, demanded dowry worth thousands of rupees. With all this, the value of a woman decreased and she became more of a liability.

I thought of Shanti and the cards she was making to save money for her own dowry; Selvi, and the fact that this stood in the way of her relationship with her brother; and finally Gandhi, whose responsibility it was to raise his sister's dowry without compromising himself. Although he had not said so, Selvi knew that her 'reputation' would lower the standing of the family she married into. I marvelled at the tenacity of those who kept struggling on through these difficulties, like wading through quicksand.

CHAPTER TWENTY

The next morning, I arrived at Madurai Central Jail soon after ten. The scene was completely transformed. The guard at the gate informed me that it was a day for court hearings. Large police vans were parked on one side of the compound. On the other, manacled prisoners wearing leg-irons were chained together in groups. All men, they squatted on the ground talking and smoking, watching me cross the parade ground. Super-intendent Swamy had left word at the gate to send me in. I passed the visitors' shed on the left as I headed for the main gate. That too was completely transformed. It was packed with people, male prisoners behind the iron bars; their relatives, mostly women in rural clothes, of all ages, in the area that I had been pacing the day before; outside in the dust, young children played among themselves, chasing each other round in circles. Some shouted to me in chorus, 'Hello Auntie! Hello Auntie!' I waved back.

As I entered Swamy's office, he was signing white slips attached individually to files stacked in a huge pile on his desk. He asked me to sit down, saying he wouldn't be long, as he concentrated on what he was doing. Next to him stood a peon, barefoot, wearing a freshly laundered pair of cotton shorts and a bush shirt, which had obviously been dyed pink in the wash. His white Gandhi cap had also suffered the same fate. He didn't look in the least uncomfortable or self-conscious, adding to the relaxed, calm atmosphere of the partially shaded room.

Turning his attention to me as the peon left with the pile, Swamy said, 'Just routine. I have to authorize the release of certain prisoners for court appearances. It's one of those days!'

'Yes, I saw,' I said, returning his smile. He went on to explain that he had not found the time to speak to any of the wardens in the female wing, but would send for the supervisor now. He rang the brass bell on his desk and the man in the pink shorts reappeared through the curtain. He instructed him in Tamil and then said, 'Wait!' as the man was turning to leave, asking me if I wanted a cup of tea. I said I'd just had some coffee. 'Coffee, then?' he asked. I accepted, appreciative of his helpful, gracious manner.

Swamy started telling me a bit about the prison. It was a 'Top Security' jail and the female wing was to the left as one stepped out into the courtyard. 'At the present time, there are 157 women and eleven children. Women are allowed to keep children up to the age of six.' There were 1,760 male prisoners. He was beginning to speak about the Kallars, saying, 'Traditionally, they are a criminal tribe. The word means "robber" or "thief".'

'I have heard that said by others,' I replied.

He went on, 'Also Karrupayee gets her name from the word "black" – Karrupa means *kala*, which means "black".'

'Does that have a bad connotation?' I asked.

'No, not in their culture. In other communities it does.'

The female warden entered the room as he was talking to me in English. He switched to Tamil, explaining, I suppose, who I was and what I wanted, because she glanced at me from time to time, nodding her head. She was an exceptionally attractive young woman, in a soft-flowing cotton, khaki-coloured sari uniform, green glass bangles on her wrists and a gold stud in her left nostril. She too, like the peon, was barefoot and wore silver toe rings. She stood formally before his desk, but there was nothing authoritative about his tone, just as there hadn't been with the peon. Swamy obviously had a close and relaxed relationship with the prison staff.

They seemed to be involved in a lengthy discussion, a question and answer session I could not follow, waiting for the conversation to be translated. It seemed to go on a long time, with the warden throwing the odd glance at me, although her expression was hard to read. Before I could exchange any words with her, Swamy concluded his conversation and gestured that she could leave. I wondered if it meant she was going to get Karrupayee. She wasn't. Swamy explained that she had deep reservations about me visiting Karrupayee; that Karrupayee's baby was due shortly and that raking up painful memories would upset her; she had nothing to gain by meeting me and, in any case, didn't trust journalists. He went on to say that he could see I was sympathetic to her situation and that he would try and have a word with Karrupayee himself, in the presence of the warden who had just left the room.

'It is against prison policy for any male member of staff to speak to a female prisoner without a female warden being present – and that applies to me too,' he added with a smile. His suggestion seemed more than fair enough and I thanked him, pointing out that time was short, that I could only stay a few more days. I had to return to Kodai before leaving for Rajasthan. He understood, and said he'd do the best he could. I told him of my meeting with SIRD, with Vasudevan, asking him to mention that to Karrupayee. He said he would do so. He knew they were involved with her appeal. I asked if I could call him later. He gave me his residential number and said, 'Call me after 9 p.m. This is going to be a busy day.' I left his office still feeling optimistic about meeting Karrupayee eventually, thinking of what a considerate sort of man he was. I had been lucky in that respect.

Outside, all the police vans and prisoners had gone. The grounds were empty and a handful of prisoners were now speaking to their lawyers in the visitors' shed. All the relatives had gone too. Outside, I noticed groups of village women waiting for buses that would take them back to their villages. It was baking hot in the sun, and I was looking forward to a quiet afternoon in my hotel room. Vasudevan would not be available until after six.

That evening, I called the SIRD office soon after six. Pavalam told me that Vasudevan had not returned from the village he had gone to visit that day. Perhaps he would go straight home. She could leave a message on his desk in case he came in but, in any case, I could find him in the morning after nine-thirty because they had a meeting in the office which would probably go on all morning.

Restless in my room, I wandered through a few market streets, looking at the shops and stalls, wondering if I should visit the famous temple. I walked past it, but the number of people queuing put me off and I made my way back to the hotel. The receptionist who had checked me in was on duty and greeted me warmly. Was I satisfied with the room? I said the air-conditioner didn't seem to work too well. 'Low current,' he replied, shaking his head to indicate that nothing could be done about it. I said that, on the whole, everything was fine. He asked how long I was staying and I said I didn't know, but enquired about bus timings, showing him the card the Kodai travel agent had given me. 'No problem,' he said. 'You just tell me the day before and I will inform them to bring the bus here. It leaves at seven-thirty every morning.' Not a bad system, I thought. I'd have to tell Selvi about it when I returned.

At around nine, I called the number Swamy had given me. He was not there, and I was told to call again in half an hour. He was probably on his way back from the prison. It amazed me how accessible some officials could be in India. Could I have expected anything like this from the Governor of Holloway prison, for instance, in England? I asked myself. The answer was of course 'No'. Half an hour later, I called again and this time Swamy came to the phone, but what followed was something I had not anticipated at all.

He asked me if I was the same person who had been involved with the making of Shekar Kapur's film, *Bandit Queen*. I said it was based on my book and that I had written the script. 'That changes the whole picture,' he said. I couldn't understand why. 'Because the Indian government has currently banned the film, as you probably know.' I said I did but still didn't understand what that had to do with meeting Karrupayee. He explained that he couldn't take the risk of any 'political controversy'. I would have to get the permission of the Inspector General (IG) of Police based in Madras. Swamy would have to get it in writing. A fax from the IG's office would do. My heart sank. I couldn't possibly go to Madras and besides, I'd followed this trail of seeking official permission before, and knew, in all probability, that the attempt would prove futile. I explained my difficulties in terms of time and budget. 'There is only one other suggestion I can make,' he said. 'You could either telephone or fax the IG in Madras – I'll give you the numbers – and if he has no objection, ask him to send a fax to the prison, authorizing a visit.' It didn't sound very hopeful, but I took the numbers anyway. To help further, Swamy advised me on the wording for the fax. Lengthy explanations would not be necessary. I took notes as he spoke, thanked him and said I'd get back to him if I got anywhere. 'Any time,' he said as he put the phone down.

The man at the reception desk directed me to a public fax booth in the same street. Following Swamy's advice, I sent a brief, formal request which read: 'Dear Sir, I request permission to briefly visit Prisoner Karrupayee in the Women's Wing of Madurai Central Jail. If your rules permit, I would be very grateful for your permission to do so. Kindly inform the Jail Superintendent accordingly by fax. He is anticipating your response.' Disappointed by the turn of events, I wondered what to do next, and decided to give it at least a day. I could visit the SIRD office again and discuss the matter with Vasudevan. Besides, he had said he would show me the legal documents and the judge's ruling on the case. I'd go there in the morning.

Later that night, it suddenly came to mind that Vasudevan had said he knew the family well. Perhaps I could meet Karrupayee's husband? When I spoke to Vasudevan on the phone the next day, he said that wouldn't be difficult to arrange. He would send a message to Karutha Kannan through one of their field workers, asking him to come to the office the next day. Couldn't I go to the village with a translator? 'That wouldn't be a good idea,' he replied at once. 'The villagers are very hostile to outsiders, social workers and journalists alike, after the ICCW had Karrupayee and her husband arrested. They have stopped operating in the area as a consequence. Even their literacy and childcare programmes have had to be abandoned. It is much better that you meet him here. When you come, I'll give you the information you require from the court file – that gives a good idea of the facts of this case.' I had to be content with that but it meant staying on another two days with nothing much to do that day. I asked if I could come over anyway to look at the file. He explained that everyone in the office was busy and that many documents were in Tamil. They would need translation. Pavalam would help me with that. I could go any time after nine the next morning and meanwhile he would send a message to Karrupayee's husband in the village of Kattakaruppanpatti in the district of Usilampatti. He would ask him to try and get to the SIRD office by noon. After that, I could catch an evening bus to Kodai if I wished. I was truly grateful for all his help, and told him so. 'No problem,' he said as he put the phone down.

I arrived at the SIRD office soon after nine the next morning. Pavalam was the only one there, but she had the file, so we sat down at the coffee table as she translated from various documents, while I took notes. Everything was in Tamil. She couldn't possibly translate the whole lot but would summarize the facts:

Karrupayee and Karutha Kannan had both been charged under section 302 of the Indian Penal Code, which dealt with premeditated murder. Hospital and post-mortem reports stated that the child was born healthy, weighing three kilograms. She died within two days of her birth, by which time she weighed 3.6 kilograms. Although there were no signs of any external injury, the post-mortem report revealed that the bones around the neck had been dislocated. There had been no internal bleeding and no toxic substances had been found. The report was written on 24 January 1994, seven to ten days after the child died.

Karrupayee herself had said in court: 'I had a normal delivery. I reported my discharge to the concerned doctor and I came to my place and by 1 p.m. I gave the child castor oil because the stomach was bulging. The condition of the child remained the same so I gave her a little milk. Soon after this, the child had fits and died.' Her advocate suggested that the dislocation of the bones was probably due to the process of burial, especially as a heavy grinding stone had been placed on the shallow grave.

The judge, S. Soundara Rajan, had said in his ruling: 'There is no supporting evidence against the second respondent to prove his guilt ...' and then went on to dismiss the case against her husband: 'The evidence shows that the child was only with the mother for the first two days. There is no evidence that the father had been with the child in the first two days and there was no mention about the fact that the father had motivated the wife to kill the child.' He went on to list the evidence in the case, which included a map of the place where the child had been buried, inside the house. He acknowledged that it was the custom within the community to do this if a baby died within thirty days of its birth. He dismissed the evidence of two prosecution witnesses as 'circumstantial'. One was a staff member of the ICCW who had claimed that Karrupayee had tried to bribe her to keep quiet after the baby's death. The sum involved was two hundred and fifty rupees. The second witness, a neighbour, had claimed the same. In summing up, the judge had made the point that if the death had been natural, it should have been reported, whereas it wasn't. He also said he sympathized with the social and economic pressures on women like Karrupayee, but had a duty to uphold the law.

Pavalam added, 'There is a myth amongst these people that if the third daughter is killed, the fourth child will be a boy.' She went on to say that SIRD, together with about fourteen other NGO groups, were financing the appeal in Madras.

At around noon, Vasudevan arrived to say that Karrupayee's husband and her two daughters were on their way. He had passed them on the road on his scooter. They would be here any minute. I asked him if I should offer to cover Karutha Kannan's expenses, for taking the trouble to come from the village. Vasudevan said that was not a good idea – the expenses had been covered by

SIRD. If I wanted to contribute, I could contribute to Karrupayee's defence fund.

As Karrupayee's family walked through the door, I was very touched to notice that they had all dressed up for the occasion. We were introduced, and exchanged *namaste*s. They all had handsome features. Both girls were extremely pretty and equally shy. The younger daughter, Annalakshmi, who was eight at the time, clung to her father throughout. The older one, Radhi, seemed to want to keep a distance, and perched on the edge of a desk a few feet away, looking at me warily. She was fifteen, and had studied up to the seventh standard. Now she had been forced to abandon school and had taken over her mother's old job, weeding fields for fifteen rupees a day. Annalakshmi was still in school, in the second standard. The father told me this in Tamil, translated by Vasudevan.

Karutha Kannan was a good-looking man in his mid-thirties. He worked as a loader on a building site, he said, carrying stones, sand and cement. He used to be able to earn up to a hundred rupees a day by working not only in his own village but in the surrounding area. His wife had worked as an agricultural labourer for about twenty rupees a day. He only worked in his own village now as he could not leave the girls alone in the house overnight. As a result, he earned far less.

Talking about the murder charges, he said that when the police had first started investigating, he hadn't taken it seriously. Both he and his wife had spent seven days in police custody at the time of their arrest. Neighbours had helped look after the children, who had been younger then, in 1994. After their release on bail, he had appealed to the village *panchayat* for help to fight the case. The elders of the village council had put him in touch with a lawyer. In all, he had spent sixty thousand rupees on their defence. Forty thousand had been from his life's savings in the bank, and he had borrowed the rest from a moneylender in the village. That money was all gone now and he was still in debt to the moneylender, to the tune of nine thousand rupees. He was so detailed in his account that one could not doubt the veracity of his financial situation. Basically, this business with the law courts had crippled them financially, and he could see no way out. This is why Radhi had had to give up school. Hopefully, Annalakshmi would somehow complete her education.

As he spoke, I watched the children. They were obviously a close family and the younger girl climbed on to her father's lap every now and then, to touch his face and wrap her arms around his neck. She leaned against him the rest of the time, restless and bored with the conversation, wanting his attention. His acceptance of her love and the way he shifted her weight around his body when she climbed on to his lap reflected the kind of patience and affection he obviously had for his children. She wore a bright pink ribbon in her hair and was wearing a freshly washed cotton frock with a pink floral print. Her sister must have dressed her up, I thought, looking at Radhi, who, being in her mid-teens, was far more reserved in her manner. She too was immaculately dressed in a *salwar kameez*, her hair neatly oiled and plaited.

Karutha Kannan was speaking of the injustice of the situation. Why had they singled out his family? He said that since their trial, five other babies had been killed in the village. No one had come to arrest them. What had happened to him was his fate. It was the only way to try and understand it. People in the village still offered emotional support to his family. For that he was grateful. Vasudevan added, 'It's true what he's saying, but on the other hand, since the judgement in this case, seven more cases have been filed by the police in the Theni Vaigai district, fifty kilometres away, all from the same caste.'

I asked Karutha Kannan if he agreed with the practice of killing female babies. I watched the faces of the children as he spoke in Tamil. The little one seemed disinterested, caught up in her own activities, whispering a sort of rhyme in Tamil under her breath as she fiddled with her father's shirt collar. The older one looked away from my gaze and started staring at the floor. This was a painful and uncomfortable question, and I almost wished I hadn't asked it. The answer would be a reflection of how he viewed *her* existence.

Karutha Kannan replied that it was naturally preferable to have sons, but he hadn't wanted his daughter killed. His wife had been in tears the day she was born in the hospital. He hadn't been able to console her. He had tried to reassure her that things would work out. There had been no dowry involved when he had married his wife. He had told her that men like him would come along one day for their daughters. After a long pause, he said that both he and his wife accepted their guilt. In short, he had accepted the fact that his wife had killed the child. A great silence followed as I made notes, not daring to look up at Radhi. When I did look at her, she had a faraway, sad look in her eyes I find hard to describe. That look haunts me still, every time I think of that day in Madurai.

Before leaving for Kodai, I rang Swamy once more. No message had been left at the hotel, as he had promised to do if there were any new developments. No, he had not heard from the IG. If I wanted to chase it, why didn't I call the IG at his residence in Madras and speak to him? Was there any point? 'You never know,' he replied cheerfully. 'It's worth a try since you are leaving tomorrow.' Despite his fear of 'political controversy' I felt Swamy had almost become an ally. I felt the same way towards Pavalam and Vasudevan and was grateful for all the support they had offered in just a few short days.

When I called Madras that night, the IG was out of town, so that was that. I called Swamy back to tell him this, and he said, in a genuinely warm voice, 'I wish you a lot of luck! Write about it in any case. These things need to be discussed in our society. I will try and see *Bandit Queen*!' His words lifted my spirits, and I left for Kodai early the next morning in a better frame of mind than when I had arrived. Small towns in India have always held a special charm and fascination for me, and Madurai was most certainly a place to remember with love and affection.

CHAPTER TWENTY-ONE

It was mid-May by the time I got to Jaipur via Bombay and Delhi, making my way to the Atithi Guest House once more. The dry, oven-like heat of the north was relentless and exhausting, though preferable to the humidity of Bombay, where one got drenched in sweat minutes after a cold shower. I had taken the late-night slow train from Delhi in order to arrive soon after dawn, wanting to use the day to make contact with various people.

The monsoon would not arrive in these parts – if it did at all that year – until late July or early August. Meanwhile, dust storms raged, getting grit in the mouth and up the nose, putting teeth on edge, making the eyes smart. Weatherwise, it was the very worst time of the year to be undertaking this journey. On the other hand, it had the compensation of being the only mosquito-free time of the year, being far too hot for the insects to survive or breed. They would arrive with the eagerly awaited monsoon.

On the approach to the narrow lane leading to the guest house, I noticed that the taxi rank under the tree was still there. All the drivers were fast asleep, some sprawled under the tree on the raised platform, others in their cars. I wondered if Swapan was among them. I would check later, for the trip to Deorala. Before that, there were people I had to try and meet in the city. The familiarity of the area was reassuring, and I was glad to be back. The pigs that roamed the streets seemed to be the only ones awake.

Miraculously, I got my old room back at the guest house, room number five, which led off the front veranda. Nothing had changed. The curtains, bedspreads and the spotless bathroom were exactly as I remembered them. It was like coming home to a place that had lived in the memory. In a strange way, I felt I had come full circle. This was the room from which the project had begun after Prakash had introduced me to the place. I had a feeling it would be my last visit as I had a shower and decided to order some breakfast – a meal I normally never eat.

In Delhi, through Binnie and Kamini Jaiswal – a lawyer friend who fights for women's rights in the Supreme Court, and had helped to free Phoolan Devi from prison – I had got hold of a few telephone numbers of women activists and lawyers in Jaipur. Looking through my notebook, I decided to call Kamini's friend, Ajay Tyagi, an advocate of the Jaipur High Court to ask him what he knew about the Roop Kanwar case. She had told me to call him either late in the evening or before eight in the morning – lawyers usually worked to those times as the courts opened at nine.

When I rang at around seven-thirty that morning, Ajay answered the phone. I explained who I was and he said, 'Yes, I know. Kamini called me yesterday. As it happens, you are in luck! It's some kind of religious festival and the courts are closed today, so I am free. Although I am not personally involved in this case, I know Kalpana Khera well. She is one of my "Juniors". She was also one of the first activists who got involved with the anti-sati movement at the time, when she was a law student. I will call her and bring her over to meet you, if you want, later today.' This was wonderful news, and gave me the feeling of having made a good start after all.

On the train from Delhi, I had felt somewhat despondent and apprehensive. I was chasing an old story, which had been overshadowed by other events. India had gone through much change and one crisis had followed another. Was it a lost cause? Was I writing about something that people had heard so much about that their senses had become numbed by now? I knew the feeling. In Britain, watching news programmes and TV documentaries on Northern Ireland, for instance, or documentaries on African droughts and floods, one tended to become immune to human suffering. Was this what was happening here? Many of the middle-class people I knew well reflected this attitude with aplomb, impatient with conversations about poverty and deprivation, urging me to look at what was 'good and positive' about India. It was only Americans and 'foreigners' who complained about the dirt, filth and poverty; they didn't understand the resilience of the Indian people, nor the progress the country was making. Why didn't I focus on these aspects, instead of raking up the events of the past? Members of my own family had said this to me many a time – in one context or another. On the other hand, I consoled myself with the thought that many friends, including my sister, had been extremely supportive, and felt the book was worth writing. They had kept me informed of developments while I was in London, through letters, phonecalls and press-clippings.

Kalpana Khera and Ajay Tyagi arrived soon after eleven. It was so hot that we all ordered iced *lassi*s, following Ajay's comment that it was the only sensible thing to drink at this time of the year. Tea was said to cool the system but he didn't agree with the theory. Kalpana was a quiet, attentive young woman, who allowed Ajay to speak of his opinions on this and that. I asked her what she felt about the outcome of the Deorala sati case. After a thoughtful pause, she replied, 'Perhaps we went for the wrong charge. Perhaps "abetment to suicide" might have been better, easier to prove, I mean.' She spoke both English and Hindi but seemed more comfortable with Hindi. At the time, she said, women activists in Jaipur had been so incensed and outraged by the event that they had wanted the harshest possible punishment for Roop Kanwar's in-laws, whom they held solely responsible for her death. She said she had attended the first meetings on the issue in 1987. She had demonstrated and picketed with other women, and helped mobilize public opinion against the practice of sati. But now she was no longer really in touch with the case, and suggested I contact the women and lawyers directly involved, giving me some names and telephone numbers of people in Jaipur. Today was a good day to call, she added, as it was a public holiday and the telephone numbers she had listed were all residential lines.

Soon after they left, I rang Kavita Srivastava, whose name also appeared on Binnie's list in my notebook. She said she was at home all day and invited me over, giving me detailed directions on how to get to her parents' home in the suburbs. I left almost immediately, having picked up my Walkman and notebook, refreshed by the iced *lassi* and my first meeting of the day with Ajay and Kalpana, thinking once more how open and accessible people in India were compared to the West, where making appointments to see strangers took days if not weeks – a different pace of life altogether, I thought, feeling a familiar burst of energy despite the heat.

Following Kavita's instructions, I found her family's house without too much difficulty. It was a large, low bungalow surrounded by a small, well-kept garden, with a driveway shaded by large trees. Kavita was a young woman, probably in her late twenties, with dark, energetic eyes and short cropped black hair. She led me to a small room, a sort of annexe to the main house, which she said was her 'private space during the day'. She invited me into the cool, shaded room, carpeted with rush matting, a mattress and several cushions on the floor. The walls were lined with bookshelves, and files and papers were stacked here and there, giving the room the look of an informal office. 'We work from here,' she said with a bright smile, referring to the organization she and other women had helped create – *Mahila Atya-char Virodhi Jan Andolan* (Rajasthan Peoples' Movement Against Atrocities on Women).

Kavita said she had not eaten lunch yet, and asked if I wanted to join her. She was going to get some food on a tray from the kitchen in the main house, where she lived with her parents and other members of her family. I said I wasn't hungry but she said, 'Never mind, I'll bring an extra plate anyway,' and went off, leaving me to read a leaflet her organization had published in October 1996, soon after the court's verdict on the Deorala sati case. Headed: 'A Call To Citizens To Oppose the Judgement and ensure Justice in the Roop Kanwar Case', it began:

> We are shocked at the acquittal of the thirty-two accused in the Roop Kanwar widow murder case by the Neem-ka-Thana Additional District and Sessions Court. We are dismayed that the eyes of the court could not see a crime that was witnessed by thousands. The judgement is a setback to the march towards a just human order guaranteeing life and dignity to women.
>
> The efforts of the anti 'sati' movement that spontaneously erupted in the wake of the dastardly crime committed against all womanhood came to *nought* on Friday, October 11, 1996, when the judgement delivered stated that the acquittal was due to the lack of an eyewitness. After going through some of the case papers and discussions with lawyers, it is clear that it wasn't for the lack of witnesses and evidence that the acquittal happened but the lack of dynamic commitment of the court and the Rajasthan Government to the cause of justice which has been responsible for such a judgement...

The leaflet called for a public meeting on 24 October 1996 in Jaipur, when they planned to 'publicly launch our protest against the Neem-ka-Thana verdict and begin the journey afresh to ensure justice in the Deorala widow burning case'. Though rhetorical, as such leaflets tend to be, it highlighted certain points of contention:

> We are surprised that the Rajasthan Government did not pay heed to the demands made by the prosecution in 1989 to shift the trial court to some other area due to the possible pressurisation of vulnerable witnesses as well as the accused belonging to a community which has had a feudal stronghold over the social structure of that region for hundreds of years. Even though the Sati Prevention Act 1988 was not applicable to this case and as such it could not be tried in the Special Sati Court but a des-

ignated court could have been set up under other existing provisions to try a case of such importance.

As I was still studying the leaflet, Kavita returned with a tray
of food: some *rotis*, *dal* and vegetables, as well as two glasses of
iced water. We chatted as we ate. I asked her how many people
had attended the meeting advertised in the leaflet. 'About four
hundred,' she said.

'All women?' I asked.

'Mostly,' she replied. 'But there were some men too – probably
from the press.' And what was the situation now? 'The case is in
the Appeals Court – in the Jaipur High Court – and we will
continue to campaign around the issue.' I told her of my meeting
with Kalpana Khera earlier that day, and asked if she agreed that
opting for charges of first-degree murder had perhaps been a
tactical error. 'Not at all,' she said. 'They murdered her and we
will prove it.' I opened my notebook and read out some names
to her, asking her to suggest whom I should meet. She knew
many of the women, and said, 'If you have spoken with one of us,
you have spoken to us all.' When I mentioned Raghu Chauhan, an
advocate of the High Court whom Kalpana had urged me to
meet, she said, 'Sure, meet him. He's a great guy!' She offered to
let me use her phone in order to make an appointment for that
evening, adding, as Kalpana had, that since it was a public
holiday, I was likely to catch him at home. I dialled the number
and Raghu answered the phone. With the same open hospitality
which is the hallmark of Rajasthan, he invited me over at seven
that evening.

Having spent the afternoon with Kavita, I left in search of
another suburban district of the city. She sent someone from the
main house to find me a scooter-rickshaw, by far the cheapest
way to travel the outskirts of the city. Taxis were necessary for
trips out of town, she said, and cycle-rickshaws were best in the
city centre, otherwise everyone relied on the 'auto-rickshaws'.
There was a stand not far from the house. Before I left, she
rummaged through her files and gave me another document

headed 'Facts Of The Legal Case' saying, 'Read that too after you have met Raghu Chauhan. He's working with us and is a very easygoing sort of person. He has all the relevant court documents, although they are probably all in Hindi. We've translated some of the relevant points into English. For instance, the trial judge remarked that there was no evidence to prove that Roop Kanwar was burnt alive! Can you believe that?' she asked, her eyes flashing with indignation. 'We have a good legal team,' she added, 'but the government is the problem, and judges tend to make political rather than legal decisions.'

Raghu Chauhan turned out to be much younger than I had expected, somewhere in his early forties at most. He invited me into the living room where he was watching TV with his daughter, a shy, slim child of primary school age. He told her it was almost time for bed, then turned to ask if I wanted something to drink, adding, 'I can't offer you tea or coffee as my wife is away visiting her relatives, and I am useless in the kitchen!' He had a boyish smile and a gentle charm. 'I was just about to pour myself a whisky. There are some cold drinks too, and ice in the fridge, which I am about to get.' I said I'd have the same. 'Water or soda?' he asked as he left the room, switching off the TV, reminding his daughter to brush her teeth before coming down to say goodnight to 'auntie' – a term all Indian children are encouraged to use to address adult women. As they both left the room, I could hear him talking to her in Hindi. He had a soft-spoken, affectionate way with her and she, in turn, responded with quiet obedience.

I had already explained the purpose of my visit on the telephone, saying that I had heard the Deorala sati case had collapsed because of a lack of evidence. As he re-entered the room with an ice bucket and a couple of bottles of soda, he said, as if continuing the conversation, 'No, it is not a case of complete lack of evidence, although it may appear to be so, as a large number of witnesses have turned hostile. Most of them say they were not an eyewitness to the crime, but came when the pyre had almost burned itself out.'

'So where does that leave you in terms of an appeal?' I asked.

'In our view,' he said, 'there are three main witnesses. First, there is the priest. Number two is the *nai* [the barber] and number three is the man who supplied the wood for the pyre. Now, these three people in their testimony have *categorically* [his emphasis] stated a few facts which unfortunately the judge tends to overlook. Number one, they state that when this news of the husband's death reached the village, Roop Kanwar was there; that she decided to commit sati and came out of her room dressed in the finery of her bridal clothes. The priest says that when the procession started, she followed the dead body of Maal Singh. No one in the family – or in the village – tried to dissuade her from taking this step. That is abetment to suicide. So, that's the first piece of evidence. Then we have the evidence of the woodcutter. He says, "She ordered me to place the wood on her and on the body." This brings the case to what we call culpable homicide – under section 300 there's an exception – murder. The exception states that if a person who is above eighteen years of age asks someone to perform an act that the other person knows will cause the death of that person, it is culpable homicide. And this is the second crux of the argument that we have taken, that the charges have not been framed properly because she ordered someone to place the logs and light the pyre. It is not murder, but it is pretty close to murder. Section 304, part I of the Indian Penal Code does not recognize euthanasia, and culpable homicide is punishable by a sentence of ten years, so it is not as if it could be reduced to a petty crime.'

I had been watching Raghu as he spoke, pacing the floor much as he probably did in court I thought, feeling quite relaxed as I sipped my ice-cold whisky and soda, glancing occasionally at my Walkman to make sure the tape was spinning. 'So, do you think the demand of the women's movement, which insisted that the family be tried for murder, was a legal error?'

'Not at all,' he replied immediately. 'Initially, the police decide the charge, but that can be changed by the judge after he hears the evidence from both sides. He examines the statements taken during the process of investigation. The actual charges are framed by the courts.' I asked what he felt the future held, legally speaking. 'It's a problematic situation,' he replied. 'You see, once a defendant is acquitted on a serious charge, he cannot be tried for the same offence on a lesser charge. We have to push for re-trial on the same charges.'

'How will that get you anywhere, given the circumstances and the political climate in the village?' I asked.

'The attempt is worth it because it keeps the protest against such practices alive in the public conscience,' he replied with a shrug.

'Are you paid for your services?' I asked.

'No. There is a team of lawyers who have volunteered to help these women's groups, in the public interest. To tell you the truth, I earn my living doing quite the opposite!'

'Such as?' I asked.

'You will be surprised – perhaps shocked – if I tell you!' I said I wanted to know anyway, having warmed to his precise and thoughtful manner. 'The thing is,' he continued, 'in criminal law, when you are practising, you really can't have moral compunctions because it comes in the way of your practice.' I must have looked puzzled, given his 'moral' stand on the sati issue. He continued, 'There's a client of mine who is alleged to have murdered his wife and when he came we talked about it. I said, "Why did you kill your wife?" He said to me – of course he would never say this in court – that there was much dispute in the household because she had brought, as part of her dowry, not only a black and white TV – instead of a colour TV – but had also not brought the antenna! As a result, no one in the family could watch the TV. This caused a major dispute in the household, so she was killed. So I asked him, "Do you think the worth of a woman is only an aerial?" He said, "No, not really," but in his view, that is the sort of thing that should have been provided by her parents. It's that sort of attitude at this level which is certainly bothersome. It raises questions about human life and how much we value it – how we treat it. Can it be turned into a commodity? And, yes, I think in the Indian mind the woman can be equated with a commodity – or a number of commodities – she is not seen as a human being. She is chattel.'

He went on to tell me that when he had initially started his practice, most of the cases he handled were from urban areas. 'You could pinpoint the areas of Jaipur,' he said. 'For instance, take Johri Bazaar, which is the hub of the jewellery trade and provides the backbone to the city's economy. Most families who live there are in that particular trade. Dowry deaths are very prevalent in this community despite their wealth, and that is the ironic thing. Similarly, there is Shastri Nagar, which is a professional, middle-class community and one finds that most cases of this kind come from such neighbourhoods.' He paused for a while, still pacing the floor, as I tried to absorb all he was saying. He continued, 'The change I have seen over the last fifteen years is that we are getting many more cases from the rural areas. The reasons are the same. Consumerism is now spreading to the rural areas. The demands that they are making on their wives are the same. They would either like a motorbike, or a fridge, or a colour TV, or even a sewing machine, and women are being tortured on similar grounds so that is a frightening aspect. Instead of trying to contain the crime within urban centres, nothing has been done, and the spread to rural areas is alarming. It indicates that the moral fabric of even rural society has gone – or is beginning to break down. Where there was a certain sense of freedom between the sexes and where there was respect for the opposite sex, apparently, that is no longer there.'

He paused for a long time, then continued, trying to summarize a complex situation for my benefit, 'But, you see, another interesting social aspect is that you do not find this sort of thing among the lower castes, the Minas, the Gujjars or the semi-tribal communities. Most of these cases come from the upper castes, because among the Minas and Gujjars for instance, it is not the girl's side which pays dowry but the boy's side which pays a bride price. Then there are other communities, where it has been agreed upon by the caste *panchayat* that no dowries will be exchanged, so in these communities, you don't have incidents of dowry, consequently, you don't have dowry deaths. Within the upper castes where dowry is prevalent, you do have an increasing number of dowry deaths.' He concluded by saying that, in his view, education and literacy lay at the root of the problem; if women were educated and given the opportunity to be economically independent at the time of their marriage, such situations would not arise. Rajasthan, he said, had one of the lowest literacy rates among women, 'Barely twenty-two per cent or something like that.' This was a major problem that had not been addressed by any government since Independence.

As I was leaving, I asked Raghu what he thought should happen in the meantime. He replied, 'The government should give the education of women top priority. Also we need a social movement – as we had around this sati case after Roop Kanwar's death – we need social revolutionaries, social reformers who will come out and say, "Listen, this thing can't go on." We can't live in feudal times. We have to turn ourselves into a modern society, and in modern societies these things do not happen. I also think the caste barriers have to be broken and marriages have to be based on the concept of love rather than arrangement. It should be seen as a contract rather than a sacrament. We'll get there slowly but it will probably take generations. We are all merely passing through this life, and have a duty to do what we can to improve the world in which we live.'

It was close to midnight by then, and there was no transport in sight. Raghu said he would willingly have taken me to the hotel on his scooter, but could not leave his daughter alone in the house. Instead, we walked together through dusty lanes towards the main road, keeping an eye out for an empty scooter-rickshaw. All was quiet and still, and there was barely any traffic on the roads. He kept talking as we strolled through the night. 'Finally, I would say the psychological nature of our people will have to change over a period of time.' How long would that take? I wondered. 'It's happening,' he replied reassuringly. 'There are two excellent trends that have emerged recently, as a result of the kind of social activity I've already told you about, which I think we need. Firstly, there is a presumption that has been inserted into the Evidence Act, which says that if a woman dies in suspicious circumstances within the first seven years of her marriage, then the presumption would be that she had been killed either by her husband or by his relatives. Now, this is very significant because it puts the burden of proof on the accused. They have to prove that she died of natural causes and that they had nothing to do with it. Number two is the judicial trend, which has got more and more strict. For instance, it is almost impossible to get bail in alleged dowry death cases. Most judges would say that a husband or a mother-in-law should never be granted bail. I had a case recently, here in Jaipur, where the mother-in-law was seventy-six years old and quite seriously ill, yet the judge said, "Even if you come before me repeatedly on this matter, I will not grant you bail." '

'How did you feel?' I asked.

'On the whole, I felt we were making progress. I defend such people because it is my job but I do not support their behaviour. Did you know,' he asked, 'that nearly sixty per cent of women in Indian jails are over sixty years old? They are the mothers-in-law of the alleged victims of dowry deaths.' I said I had read an article in *India Today* that had referred to similar statistics. The photograph that had accompanied the article came to mind as I said this. It showed three old women in a prison cell who had created a puja corner and were seen praying before the *murthi*, heads covered. The caption said that they were all being held on charges of murder.

Looking back at Raghu Chauhan, I thought about what an extraordinarily honest man he was, as he spotted a cycle-rickshaw parked under a tree and quickened his pace. The old man asleep on the seat agreed to take me for three times the normal fare, which I offered with relief and gratitude. In parting, as we waited for the old man to regain his senses from a deep sleep, Raghu said, 'Remember, there are loopholes in the law which we all tend to exploit. For instance, I have dealt with cases where the police have failed to gather evidence, for whatever reason. Traces of kerosene are found at the scene of the crime, yet the family cook on gas. A matchbox, left at the scene of the crime, has not been fingerprinted. There is no evidence of murder and the client gets off. Another loophole: The law says that demands of dowry have to be proven to "immediately precede" the death of the woman. If the demand was made six months earlier, the husband and in-laws can say that the matter was resolved and there was harmony in the household. Often the woman is illiterate, so there's no written record, no letter to the parents or even a friend. We exploit these loopholes in order to get our clients off.'

'Does it give you an unsettled conscience?' I asked.

'At times,' he replied. 'But history takes its own course and, in the end, I believe in the need for change. Meanwhile, I do what I am trained to do in order to make a living. If I lose a case in court, all that my clients need to know is that I have done my best for them, within the framework of the law. What I think about them personally does not enter the frame.'

As I travelled through the silent city late that night, watching the old man pedalling away on his bicycle, I too felt pangs of conscience. The man was frail and obviously very poor. When we reached the Atithi Guest House, I gave him a hundred-rupee note out of a sense of guilt, though I had only agreed to pay thirty. He looked surprised, and said he had no change. I said I didn't want any. He bent down and touched my feet saying, 'May God bless you. May your sons have long lives.' I didn't have the heart to tell him I had no sons. I merely thanked him, tears coming to my eyes. It was probably the whisky getting to me, I thought, as I climbed into bed and turned on the fan. It was well past midnight, and even the hotel receptionist had gone to sleep, stretched out on the bare floor behind the counter. I'd stepped over him, barefoot, to take my key off the hook marked 5.

CHAPTER TWENTY-TWO

I must have slept like the dead because when I woke the sun was streaming through the gingham curtains, casting the room in a blue-green light. It was almost lunchtime, and I suddenly felt hungry. It was too late to make the trip to Deorala that day, which had been my intention. I decided instead to make some arrangement for transport early the next morning. Meanwhile, I had a free day. It was far too hot to wander around town, so I decided to stay in my room and read instead, after skimming through the menu for something to eat.

The computer printout Kavita had given me the day before, headed 'Facts of the Legal Case', referred to the same three witnesses that Raghu Chauhan had spoken about the night before. The document stated:

> According to Shri Shambu Dayal Agarwal, who argued the case on the 9th and 10th of October 1996 as Special Public Prosecutor (SPP) in this case, the three prime witnesses, Babulal, the Pandit who carried out the last rites of Maal Singh and Roop Kanwar, Bodu Khati, who supplied the wood, Bansi Nai, the barber who had shaved the body of Maal Singh in the house, were sufficient to establish that it was a case of murder and the involvement of others as abettors. According to him, a look at their statements in examination and cross examination also established this.

It was a lengthy document, running to several pages, detailing the contradictions in the legal proceedings, which failed to prove the crime. Kavita Srivastava concludes:

The judge completely disregarded the aspects of circumstantial evidence which stick out glaringly in this case. For instance, the fact that the parents of Roop Kanwar were not informed about the death of Maal Singh, they heard about it and the burning of Roop Kanwar only through the newspaper the next day, secondly, it is normal practice all over the north of India that women do not accompany the funeral procession to the funeral ground, so Roop Kanwar and other women members of the family and the village could only have gone if there was the consent of the men of that family and the rest of the village. Thirdly, Roop Kanwar went dressed as a bride, with *mehndi* [henna] and other jewellery. She must definitely have been dressed up by the family. (She could not possibly have put *mehndi* on her own hands.) Lastly, the family members of Maal Singh did not inform the police about this decision. If they wanted to prevent it, they could have at least made attempts to prevent it...

... According to reliable sources, of the nine 'Sati' cases that have been tried since 1952 in Sikar district, this was the first case where the accused were charged with murder. In the past, the cases were only registered as that of abetment to suicide and in none of the cases have the accused been convicted. In the eight earlier cases there was no appeal in the High Court either. This time, although no conviction happened, the matter will not rest till taken to the High Court and justice actually happens.

Among the papers Kavita had given me copies of, I saw the First Information Report (FIR) dated 4 September 1987, recorded at Thoi Police *Thana* at 5.50 p.m. This was the report Ram Rathi, whom I had met in Sikar, had filed on the day of Roop Kanwar's death. It stated that the police station was eighteen miles from the 'Cremation grounds in Village Deorala', listing the names of five of the accused whom he had spoken to that day. Under a sub-heading which read: 'Nature of the crime, section and goods lost', it said, 'The accused provoked Roop Kanwar to cremate herself along with her husband Maal Singh's body and to commit sati. Crime Section 306 of the Indian Penal Code.' The statement itself was brief and excluded all the village gossip he had told me about.

I decided to step out and organize a taxi for the next day, having decided to set out at about 6 a.m., in order not to miss Sumer Singh on a Sunday morning. With luck, I'd find the whole family in. Sumer Singh's sons had yet to be tried by the Juvenile Court in Jaipur, but it was almost a foregone conclusion that they would be acquitted like the rest. It was a mere formality that would take its own time.

At the taxi rank, only the owner was there. All the drivers and cars were out on other jobs. I asked if Swapan still worked for him and he said, 'Oh, yes!' looking up at me with the look of recognition. 'Are you staying at Atithi?' he asked, as if I'd been there the day before yesterday. I nodded and gave him the room number. He looked through his ledger and said, 'He'll be back at around 7 p.m. I'll send him to you and then you can work out your own arrangements with him.' He asked how long I would require the taxi and when I told him for the day, for the return trip to Deorala, he put a line through one column of the open page, obviously the duty roster which listed the activities of different drivers. It was all done casually, without much discussion, in a style that was unique to India and Rajasthan in particular, I thought as I returned to the relative cool of my room. Having slept for many hours, I felt restless and turned to a book I had bought in Delhi, *From the Seams of History*, a collection of essays on Indian women edited by Bharati Ray. It was a study of Bengal and the role of women within that state at the turn of the nineteenth century, when the British had outlawed the practice of sati. Komal Kothari had always emphasized the difference between widow burning in Bengal and sati in Rajasthan. I was still grappling with the distinction and had bought the book in an attempt to understand the difference. Leafing through it, I found much of interest. The first essay, 'Caste, Widow-remarriage and the Reform of Popular Culture in Colonial Bengal' written by Sekhar Bandyopadhyay, began:

Social reforms in Bengal in the nineteenth century affected many aspects of human relations and existential realities, the most important of them being gender relations and the condition of women. Yet, towards the close of the century a large section among the latter who were widows by civil status were still being 'forced' to live celibate and austere lives, despite the reform endeavours of men like Rammohun Roy, Iswar Chandra Vidyasagar and others. As the realities stand, while the former had succeeded in achieving his goal, the latter's mission ended in what has been described as an 'unavoidable defeat'. *Sati*, the eradication of which was on Rammohun's reform agenda, was abolished by Regulation XVII of 1829. Widow burning was made a penal offence, any violation of which would immediately invite the regulating hand of the state. Rammohun could thus save widows from being immolated with the help of the constant presence of state power and the law-enforcing apparatus. But Vidyasagar failed to see many widows remarried, as in this case the Act of 1856 only legalized their marriage, but could not make it socially acceptable; nor was it possible to enforce it with the help of the police force . . .

. . . In Bengal, widow-remarriage was strictly forbidden among the upper castes and most of the middle ranking castes in the nineteenth century. The 1891 list of castes that forbade widow-remarriage included, apart from the Brahmans, Kayasthas and Vaidyas of the upper stratum, the various trading castes as well as the Sadgops, Sundis, Mahishyas, Telis, Mayras and Napits. It was allowed among the lower castes, but they too appear to have shared the values of their social superiors. Widow-remarriage even when permitted, was looked down upon and was disparagingly referred to as a *sanga* marriage, a practice prevalent in many other parts of India as well. Among the Namasudras of Bengal, for example, the married couples of a widow-remarriage occupied a lower place in the estimation of their caste fellows and were referred to as *Krishna-Paksha* (dark fortnight after full moon), while those married in a regular way were described as *Sukla-Paksha* (bright fortnight after new moon). The very use of the terms 'dark' or 'bright' indicates the respective values attached by the community to the two forms of marriage. And by the beginning of the twentieth century, they too, like many other *antyaja jati*s [non-conformists] around them had almost completely discontinued the practice and begun to conform to the traditional upper-caste behavioural norms of widowhood. At the turn of the century, therefore, it was perhaps only the lowest menial groups, like the 'Doms, Boonas, Bagdis and "low people" of various kinds' and the so-called 'aborigines' who practised widow-remarriage without any stigma attached to it, while the rest of the Bengali Hindu society strictly forbade this custom. Nothing can be a better indicator of the failure or 'defeat' of the reform movement to introduce widow-remarriage.

Another essay in the same book, 'Attired in Virtue: The Discourse on Shame (*lajja*) and Clothing of the *Bhadramahila* in Colonial Bengal', by Himani Bannerji, starts with a striking quotation from a woman of the time:

> In those days there were particular rules for women. Whoever became a *bou* [bride/daughter-in-law] was to veil herself for an arm's length or so, and not to speak to anybody. That's what made a good *bou*. Clothes then, unlike now, were not made of such fine fabric, but were rather coarse and heavy. I used to wear that piece of heavy cloth, and veil myself down to my chest, and do all those chores. And I never talked to anyone. My eyes never looked out from within that cloth enclosure, as though I were blindfolded like the bullocks of the oilpresser. Sight did not travel further than my feet.
>
> Rashasundari Dasi, *Amar Jiban* (My Life), 1987.

This custom of the heavy veil was still widely prevalent throughout Rajasthan. I had felt its oppression, having tried on a village woman's veil once as an experiment. Within a few minutes I had felt the suffocation of claustrophobia and thrown it off my head, in need of air, amidst much laughter from the women of the family.

As far as the tradition of sati went, I could see that there was indeed a cultural difference between Bengal and Rajasthan. Whereas in Rajasthan sati had traditionally been the practice of royalty – the queens and concubines of departed kings – in Bengal widow burning was encouraged in order to prevent the widow from inheriting any part of the family's land or wealth. In the end, the results were the same. Women burned alive on their husbands' pyres because the society did not offer them a life worth living as widows, as single women. They were pushed to the bottom of the social heap, denied independent lives and shunned by society for the rest of their lives, regardless of their age. In Rajasthan, where child marriages still took place in their thousands each year, a young girl could easily become a widow long before the age of puberty, before any sexual interaction at all with her husband or anyone else. It was a grim and ghastly reality that was to persist into the next century.

A knock on the door distracted me from the book. It was Swapan, with the same bright, enthusiastic smile. We spoke for a while. He had had a bad year, he said. His wife had died of tuberculosis, leaving behind two young sons who now lived with his parents. They were trying to find him another bride, being of an advanced age themselves, fretful for the future, unable to cope with the energy of young children. He sent money home on a monthly basis, and was open to the idea of a second marriage. What struck me was his lack of emotion when he spoke of his dead wife. That too had been an arranged marriage, when she had been about sixteen and he just over twenty. They hadn't lived together for any length of time, given his job in the city. He saw no option but to remarry. There were no jobs in his village in Uttar Pradesh. History would repeat itself. When he did eventually remarry, he would not be able to afford to bring his family to Jaipur. 'This is the way things are, Didi, what can I do?' I didn't have any easy answers.

Readily agreeing to pick me up early the next morning for the trip to Deorala, Swapan left, saying, 'My friend who owns the *paan* shop, the Pandit's son I told you about last time, has expanded his business after his father's acquittal on the sati case. I think Sumer Singh paid them quite a lot of money after it was all over.'

'Has he told you that?' I asked.

'Not in so many words but I know it is what happened. Now he even plays cards for such high stakes that I hardly see him any more!' he said with a laugh as he left.

CHAPTER TWENTY-THREE

Punctual and enthusiastic as ever, Swapan turned up at six the next morning. He was driving the same bright blue Ambassador. Almost two years on, one of the rear windows was still jammed, and could not be lowered more than a few inches from the top. That was the first thing I noticed, and it gave me a comfortable feeling of familiarity once again. We were on the road to Deorala once more.

In this, the hottest and driest season of the year, vast tracts of cracked, scarred earth and barren fields lined both sides of the highway all the way. It was manic-speed-time too, as the potholes had not yet appeared. They too would come with the by now desperately awaited monsoon. As we turned off the highway on to the dust track through which a narrow strip of Tarmac ran, barely wide enough for a car or jeep, I noticed scores of women gathered at scattered wells on the way. Many were on the road between villages carrying brass, clay or plastic pots of water on their heads, trudging through the dust, their faces hidden by heavy cotton *ordni*s. For them, collecting water or firewood for the household was the start of their day's work.

Parking the taxi in the same spot under the neem tree on the outskirts of the village, Swapan asked how long I expected to be. There was someone he wanted to visit himself, but a blast of the horn would be his signal to return in case I got back to the car before him. He left the back door unlocked as we walked off in different directions.

I saw Sumer Singh from a distance. He was sitting cross-legged on the bare wooden bed, having his face shaved and his moustache trimmed by the village barber, the same man, as it turned out, who had attended to his son's body and been arrested as a result. It was the barber who saw me first, muttering what looked like a warning. Sumer Singh turned his head and, recognizing me, called out in a welcoming manner. The barber glared with open hostility, razor suspended in his hand. 'Come in, come in,' said Sumer Singh, ignoring the barber, shaving soap still on one side of his face. As I walked up the steps, he shouted to Usha in the kitchen, 'Make some fresh tea, Malaji has come from London!' Asking me to sit down, he resumed his shave in silence. Feeling a little uncomfortable, as the barber continued to throw me the odd hostile look, I said I had heard the news of his acquittal in London, adding lamely that it must have been a relief for his family.

'The whole village is relieved,' he replied, head tilted upwards as the barber shaved his chin. 'I will talk to you in a minute,' he said in Hindi, muttering something in Rajasthani to the barber, probably telling him to hurry up. After the shave, his face was wiped and his moustache carefully trimmed. Next, his toenails were trimmed with another blade. A woman in a faded yellow *ghaghra*, stained with dirt, and a matching veil, emerged from the house sweeping the floor. I watched as she crouched to sweep under the bed, moving the debris towards the steps and into the dusty lane below. I wondered who she was, but realized as she took her leave, head bowed, broom in hand, that she was a hired hand, a low-caste woman who cleaned for others. I watched her disappear down the lane, picking up rubbish from the drain on the way. The barber too was dismissed with a wave of the hand once he had completed his task. He hadn't said a word, and was clearly not expected to participate in any conversation. After he left, I enquired if he was Bansi Nai, one of the co-defendants, and Sumer Singh looked surprised but nodded. I told him I had seen some of the court papers. He nodded again and said, 'He thought you were one of those women from Jaipur but I told him you were not!'

As Usha arrived with the tea, still shy and withdrawn, Sumer Singh suggested I sit indoors under the fan while he went to have a bath. We could talk after that. I picked up my bag as he instructed his daughter to take the tray back in, pointing to the room that had been Roop Kanwar's shrine. It had been converted into a living room. Switching on the ceiling fan, which had not been there before, he asked me to make myself comfortable, saying he would be back in ten minutes. I looked around at the transformation. The family had acquired a three-piece suite, carved in heavy wood and upholstered in maroon velvet. I could only guess what it must have cost; several thousand rupees certainly. The framed photograph of Roop Kanwar and Maal Singh on their wedding day was still on the wall gathering dust, no longer draped in fresh flowers. Instead, a link-chain made of gold-coloured foil, much like those children make in nursery schools, hung over the portrait. Next to it hung a large poster of Kalyan Singh Kalvi, the Rajput politician who had supported them at the time of her death and who had died himself from a heart attack since then, I was informed later. The adjoining wall was covered with framed religious posters; pictures of legendary Rajput heros dressed in saffron, portrayed wielding swords on horseback. Framed among these pictures was one of the postcards of Roop Kanwar and Maal Singh on the pyre amidst hand-painted flames that had sold for twenty rupees each in 1987. The wall was a gallery of Rajput pride.

Over the door I suddenly noticed what looked like the metal licence plate of a car, black on yellow. On closer examination, I read 'Sumer Singh Shekhwat MA, BA' painted in Hindi, like a name-plate on an office door, I thought, although this was in the room, facing inwards. I noticed a row of books on a concrete shelf, all of them in Hindi except for one in English, entitled *Sati: Widow Burning in India,* by V. N. Datta. Taking it to the sofa, I began reading the front flap:

The practice of Sati is not extinct in India as evident from the gruesome incident at Deorala in Rajasthan when a young bride was burnt to death on her husband's funeral pyre...

Just then, Sumer Singh returned, wearing a starched white *kurta* and pyjama trousers. 'Have you read this?' I asked, closing the book and returning it to the bookshelf.

'Yes,' he said, 'I read some English books from time to time.' I asked him what he thought of the book. He shrugged and I decided to drop the subject, asking him instead what he felt about the fact that a group of women and their lawyers were appealing against the court's verdict. 'Oh, they are nothing! Let them keep themselves occupied. What do they understand anyway, given their lifestyles?'

Out of some instinctive reaction, I suddenly said, 'Do you mind if I smoke a cigarette?'

He looked surprised but said, 'Not at all, please go ahead.' I asked for an ashtray and he said, 'Just use that empty cup – you see, I don't smoke myself – and none of my sons do either.' His manner was casual, surprisingly unjudgemental. 'Have you written your book?' he asked with a polite smile.

'No,' I said, 'I haven't even started it yet.'

'So, what have you been doing then?' he asked, smiling in a paternal sort of way.

'Oh, just this and that,' I said, 'trying to survive, talking to other women whose stories I wish to include in the book.' He nodded, not particularly interested, giving me the impression he didn't think much of anything that was written in English. It was another world, and no threat to his existence.

Because our interaction had been so cordial, he assumed I was sympathetic to his cause and glad of his acquittal. He treated me like an honoured guest. Usha was summoned and told to make breakfast. I protested, saying I was not at all hungry. He ignored my reaction, reassuring me that it was no trouble at all, and that I could smoke as many cigarettes as I liked in his house. He had no prejudice against other people's habits, he said with a flourish of his hand.

I asked if there had been any changes at the *Sati Sthal* in the village. Did they still plan to erect a temple? 'Let's see,' he replied. 'We have no immediate plans.' I said I would like to visit the site again. He offered to walk with me and we strolled down the lane towards it. During that short walk, I realized just what a political victory the acquittal had been for Sumer Singh. People greeted him with reverence. He granted some of them arrogant nods and stopped to exchange a few words with others. It was clear that his status in the village had been enhanced since the last time I had accompanied him down these paths. I felt as if I was in the company of the Godfather of the village.

At the *sthal*, the police tent had gone. The desolate image of the diminished female figure that hung from the *trishul* was almost unchanged. A few fresh flowers and two coconuts lay at the *trishul*'s base – the symbol of some recent visit. Sumer Singh said, 'Now you can place anything you want here,' which reminded me of the time I had first met him with Prakash, armed with a fresh green coconut.

Getting his meaning, I replied, 'This time I have come unprepared.'

'That's all right,' he said as he took me for a casual stroll through the market.

On the way back to the house, we came across a group of young men talking under the shade of a tree. One of them was Pushpinder, Sumer Singh's son, who had been accused of lighting the pyre, of sending Roop Kanwar to her death. Sumer Singh introduced us, and I said we had met before. He had taken me to meet Roop's aunt at the ashram. Pushpinder too greeted me with exaggerated warmth, and I noticed once again that he had the same handsome features as his dead brother. As we walked away, his father said, 'He is engaged to be married but first, I have to find a suitable husband for my daughter.'

'For Usha?' I asked. 'But she is still a child!'

'No,' he said. 'For Manju, my other daughter who is studying in Jaipur. She is sixteen now.' It was the first time I had heard him speak of her.

Back in the newly decorated living room, Sumer Singh insisted that I eat something Usha had cooked especially for me. There was no way of refusing, despite my growing discomfort with the situation. There seemed to be nothing left to say, or ask. The political victory had certainly been his and I didn't see any point in a moral debate. 'Come upstairs,' he said. 'I will show you something.' He took me up to what had been Roop Kanwar's room. That too had been newly decorated, but the same red velvet bedspread covered the same vast double bed that took up half the room. The TV, now also wrapped in plastic, like the refrigerator, had been moved to sit on top of the refrigerator in the far corner. 'This will be Pushpinder's room when he gets married,' Sumer Singh announced with pride and another flourish of the hand. I felt the same chill I had first felt when I had entered this room two years earlier, coconut in hand, although now it was hot and sunny and freshly painted. Not quite knowing how to react, I sat down on the small black Rexine sofa and looked around, trying to think of a way to leave without having to eat anything. I suddenly felt overwhelmed by a sense of sadness and defeat. Another woman would pass through this room, more sons would probably be conceived here and the lot of Rajput women would remain unchanged. Roop Kanwar's death had been meaningless. Nothing had really changed.

Meanwhile, Sumer Singh was giving instructions from the top of the stairs to someone in the open courtyard below. He reappeared briefly in the doorway saying, 'I have an urgent appointment in Ajitgarh today, can you give me a lift? We can talk on the way, in the meantime I must meet someone for a few minutes, but Usha is bringing you something to eat before we leave.' I nodded, still in a daze.

Minutes later, Usha appeared with a *thali* of food and a pile of *puri*s. I said, 'I can't possibly eat that much!' but she left without a word, flashing a shy smile in my direction from the doorway. As I started toying with the food, drained of any appetite, Bhu-pinder the younger son arrived. Polite and good-looking like his brother, he said, 'My father is just talking to someone, he has asked me to keep you company and make sure you get anything you want.' I asked for a glass of water, saying I would like to talk with him too. When he returned, I asked what he felt about the outcome of the court case. He gave me a deep, intense look and then, staring at the ground he said, 'She was very good to me. I miss her very much. I didn't like going to prison but it wasn't that bad.' He had been in primary school at the time of his arrest.

Much to my surprise, I felt a surge of sympathy for him, and said reassuringly, 'Anyway, it's all over now.'

He sat down in the armchair next to me and said, 'Tell me, *Masi*, what is it like to live in London?'

While we were talking, Sumer Singh returned, and his son rose to his feet. It was an autocratic household, and Sumer Singh was in complete control. Looking at the refrigerator and TV set wrapped in plastic, I asked, 'Why do you not use those things?' I knew they were part of the dowry that Roop Kanwar had brought to the family.

His instant reply was, 'That will go to Manju when she gets married – it was her will.'

'Whose will?' I asked.

'*Unki*,' he replied, referring to the *Sati Mata* of the family in a reverent tone.

'How do you know? You said you were not there that day, that you fainted and were taken to hospital.'

He ignored the aggression in my voice and merely said, very calmly, his voice full of confidence, 'You asked me once "Did she leave an *ok*", well this was her *ok*. She wanted Manju to inherit everything she had brought to this house, so we are following her wishes.' I remembered immediately that when I had first raised the question of the *ok* – traditionally a death wish involving some form of material denial rather than gain – he had been puzzled by the question. Now, Roop Kanwar's death had provided him with his daughter's dowry. I assumed that all the money collected at the time of Roop Kanwar's death, in the name of religion, for the purpose of building a temple to her memory, had gone towards home improvements; the expensive furniture below, the redecorated room above and the ceiling fan with brass fittings. The new furniture and fittings had probably all come from Jaipur by truck. Perhaps Roop Kanwar's brother's trucking company had provided the service, just as they had supported her in-laws at the time of her death.

On the way to Ajitgarh, I asked Sumer Singh whether the village had serious problems with water. 'It's always bad at this time of year,' he replied casually, looking out at the parched landscape that surrounded us. 'But I invested in a tube well some years ago. It's two hundred metres deep, and ...'

'When?' I interrupted, remembering my previous encounter with him, when he had claimed to be a small landowner, with only rainwater to rely upon.

'Oh, I can't remember, several years ago at any rate.' I didn't think it was worth challenging the veracity of his statement. He had already lied his way through serious criminal charges, and was indifferent to my opinion in any case. I felt quite powerless, weakened by reality. In these parts, men ruled supreme and women were in for a bitter war that would probably have to rage for generations, with many falling by the wayside, both the born and the unborn. The female child faced a long and twisted road. I was glad that I was no longer a child.

AFTERWORD

Two years later, on the brink of a new millennium, history was
to repeat itself in the remote village of Satpurva, an obscure
hamlet with a population of around 250 people in the Bun-
delkhand region of Uttar Pradesh, north of Delhi. On 11 November 1999, another widow was reported to have 'leapt into' her
husband's funeral pyre and burned to death. As had happened
before, in 1987, the news spread rapidly, by word of mouth, and
once again 'pilgrims' from the surrounding area were reported
to have started heading for the village in their thousands, pro-
claiming the birth of a new *Sati Mata*.

Initially, sections of the media too reacted with shameful specu-
lation. Early reports in the national press spoke of a 'young
widow' dressed in her 'bridal finery' dying heroically out of
devotion to her husband. Later, under closer scrutiny, the story
changed. I was in London, still working on this book, when I
started receiving press-clippings from Bombay, from my sister
and other friends who knew of my interest in the situation.

A lengthy, half-page article in one of the Delhi dailies headed
'The Sati That Never Was' revealed another reality. The journalist, Vishal Thapar, had visited the village and discovered that
the 'young widow', Charan Shah, had been a woman of fifty-five,
who had nursed her husband, Manshah, through tuberculosis for
over twenty years. He had finally succumbed to the disease at
the age of sixty that day. She had had three sons, one of whom
had died four years earlier, and her husband's death added to
that grief. Her son's widow, Phoolan, had been remarried to

266

Madanshah, the younger of her two surviving sons. This is a custom commonplace in Hindu culture, geared to keep property rights within the family. The third son, Shishpal, had lit his father's funeral pyre on the day he died. He was interviewed by the reporter, who commented that he spoke of the incident 'stoically':

> Immediately after I lit the pyre, we all went to the nearby *nullah* to bathe as we feared contracting TB germs from the body. We were still there when Jageshwar, the shepherd, ran to inform us that my mother had jumped into the pyre, which had become a raging fireball because of the kerosene we had poured to make it burn faster. We rushed there. I saw my mother burning. I fainted.

His version of events was supported by Manshah's sister-in-law, Prakash Rani, who had been with the widow at the time. She said:

> When the men left for the cremation, the women gathered in Manshah's house to console Charan and, according to custom, clean and smear cowdung in the room in which he had died. Charan looked restrained. I saw her place her hand on her grandson's head. Then, we suddenly realised she was missing. I stepped out to look for her. She was walking towards the cremation ground. But she bolted when I asked her to return.

The journalist goes on to say:

> The incident occurred around noon on 11 November, and within two hours, the news about 'sati' had spread to the neighbouring villages. About a hundred people gathered at the spot, broke coconuts, burnt incense and offered coins. For, one thing is obvious: even if it was not a ritualistic sati, there's approval and admiration for Charan Shah's suicide. That she died on her husband's funeral pyre is enough for the villagers to declare her a sati...

Also among the press-clippings was a report in the *Times of*

India (16 November 1999) which quoted my friend Binnie, who had been interviewed by the writer of the article. The journalist asked why the practice of sati found sanction among certain sections of Indians, despite the existence of legal bans and strictures:

> ... Queried, Brinda Karat of the All India Democratic Forum for Women, 'Where have the social reform movements of the nineteenth century disappeared at the end of the 20th century? Why have these reform movements been turned on their heads by political agendas and regressive social mindsets?' According to her, obscurantist mindsets are currently finding sanction not only among a section of those who are illiterate, but also within the educated middle class. This, she said, was due to the 'complete vulnerability' of the average Indian who 'fails to find any support system in society and is forced to fall back on supernatural beliefs'.
>
> Women, she said, were particularly vulnerable and continued to remain victims of a patriarchal legacy even today. This was due to the 'continued glorification of the feminine role model where a woman is supposed to be a self-sacrificing *prati-vrata* woman,' she pointed out. 'The concept of the woman as appendage happens to be the cornerstone of everything, be it preached religion or even contemporary mainstream cinema where the heroine may dance to modern music, but her reason for living lies in her complete identification with the hero.' The glorification of sati was just an extension of this stereotype, she said.

Reading this, I felt so proud of Binnie – of women like her who continue to campaign relentlessly for a change in the social order despite all the odds and the balance of political power which is most certainly still against them in modern India.

Another article (*Mid-Day*, Bombay: 13 December 1999) written by B. K. Karanjia, headed 'Murder By Sati' and subtitled 'More crimes have been committed in the name of religion than for any other cause', includes the following statements:

Opinion continues to be divided on this issue. Justice Krishna
Iyer, formerly of the Supreme Court, calls sati 'murder most
foul and part of a continuum of issues from female foeticide,
infanticide, dowry death to widow immolation'. Vijayaraje
Scindia of the royal family of Gwalior, now a member of the BJP
maintains: 'A voluntary act of self immolation by a widow in
dedication of her husband does not constitute an offence.' But is
Sati really voluntary? Not so, claims Sakuntala Narasimhan in
her deeply researched study *Sati: A Study of Widow Burning in
India* which makes compelling reading...

I too found her study of sati compelling reading and have often
referred to her work in the course of writing this book. The
article goes on:

What then is the solution? Female activists cry out for stricter
laws against sati, but as Sakuntala Narasimhan points out, laws
only prohibit the deed, the social background that provokes the
deed needs to be tackled. Sati is the logical progression of social
aberrations like dowry, widow denigration, women's inequality
(The Shankaracharya of Puri believes 'a woman compared to a
man is quite degraded'), obsession with male progeny, mar-
ginalisation of women from the mainstream of life. People's
social perceptions need to be changed radically by proper education. The collective conscience needs to be roused against such
ritualistic murders.

No one in their right mind could argue against that perspective
but change comes painfully slowly, particularly in India, where
the present government refuses to protect or empower the powerless in society, whether they be women, Muslims or Christian
clerics. At the turn of the twentieth century, it stood by while
nuns were raped in Gujerat and priests were burned alive in
Orissa; it has allowed the atrocities against women to continue;
it has deprived common people of onions – the cheapest of all
vegetables – water and even *salt*. In November 1998, the *Asian
Age* reported 'panic' in Delhi over the shortage of onions the

price of which had risen ten-fold. It also reproduced a photograph showing people queuing for fistfuls of salt. This was an ironic reminder of Gandhi's Salt Marches during our fight for independence from British rule.

The present government, hanging together with the support of a fragile coalition – made up of various political parties with ambitions of their own – has introduced dangerous levels of religious and regional fundamentalism into a culture that had other dreams of freedom.